1st

Accounting
and
Reporting

— For the US CPA Exam —

Volume
1

목 차

서문 · Preface

Accounting and Reporting for the US CPA Exam 의 특징입니다.

● WHO?

미국 공인회계사 시험을 응시하는 수험생을 대상으로 한 교재이다. 미국 공인회계사 시험 4과목 중 하나
인 'Business Analysis and Reporting(BAR)' 과목에서 중요한 부분을 차지하고 있는 'Technical Accounting
and Reporting' 영역과 'State and Local Governments' 영역을 대비하기 위한 교재이다.

● WHAT?

미국공인회계사 시험의 추세 및 난이도에 맞게 구성된 내용으로 장마다 미국 공인회계사 시험에 출제되
는 'Task-Based Simulation' 유형의 문제를 대비하기 위한 다양한 문제를 수록하였다.

● HOW?

미국공인회계사 오랜 강의 경력의 경험과 노하우를 압축한 교재이다. 'Business Analysis and Reporting
(BAR)' 과목은 Discipline exam의 과목이므로 Core exam보다 난이도가 높다. 따라서 Accounting and
Reporting에서 높은 점수를 획득하여야 하므로 이 교재와 강의로 스마트한 합격을 기원한다.

● CHAPTER

본서의 구성은 다음과 같다. 1장~9장은 기업회계의 난이도가 높은 주제에 대한 내용이며, 10장은 미국 주정부와 지방정부의 재무제표 및 회계처리에 대한 내용이다. 특히 10장은 깊이 있는 이해보다 정부의 재무제표를 빨리 익숙하게 만드는 것이 높은 점수를 획득하는 지름길이다.

공인회계사 / 미국공인회계사 / 미국재무분석사(CFA)

김용석.

I. CBT 과목구성

    미국 공인회계사 시험은 2004년도에 PBT에서 CBT로 변경이 되었으며, 2017년에는 TBS(Task-Based Simulation)의 비중을 높인 새로운 방식으로 변경되었다. 2023년에 시험제도는 새롭게 변경이 되어 2024년 1월 1일 이후의 시험은 아래의 표와 같다.

Section	Section time	MCQ	TBS
AUD-Core	4 hours	50%(78)	50%(7)
FAR-Core	4 hours	50%(50)	50%(7)
REG-Core	4 hours	50%(72)	50%(8)
BAR-Discipline	4 hours	50%(50)	50%(7)
ISC-Discipline	4 hours	60%(82)	40%(6)
TCP-Discipline	4 hours	50%(68)	50%(7)

MCQ : Multiple Choices Questions
TBS: Task-Based Simulation

The CPA licensure model requires all candidates to pass three Core exam sections and one Discipline exam section of a candidate's choosing.

The Core exam sections assess the knowledge and skills that all newly licensed CPAs (nlCPAs) need in their role to protect the public interest. The three Core exam sections, each four hours long, are: Auditing and Attestation(AUD), Financial Accounting and Reporting (FAR) and Taxation and Regulation(REG).

The Discipline exam sections assess the knowledge and skills in the respective Discipline domain applicable to nlCPAs in their role to protect the public interest.The three Discipline exam sections, each four hours long, are: Business Analysis and Reporting (BAR), Information Systems and Controls (ISC) and Tax Compliance and Planning (TCP).

II. Business Analysis and Reporting (BAR)

The Business Analysis and Reporting section of the Uniform CPA Examination assesses the knowledge and skills nlCPAs must demonstrate with respect to:

- Financial statement and financial information analysis with a focus on an nlCPA's role in comparing historical results to budgets and forecasts, deriving the impact of transactions, events (actual and proposed) and market conditions on financial and nonfinancial performance measures and comparing investment alternatives.

- Select technical accounting and reporting requirements under the Financial Accounting Standards Board (FASB) Accounting Standards Codification and the U.S. Securities and Exchange Commission (SEC) that are applicable to for-profit business entities and employee benefit plans.

- Financial accounting and reporting requirements under the Governmental Accounting Standards Board (GASB) that are applicable to state and local government entities.

The following table summarizes the content areas and the allocation of content tested in the BAR section of the Exam:

	Content area	Allocation
Area I	Business Analysis	40~50%
Area II	Technical Accounting and Reporting	35~45%
Area III	State and Local Governments	10~20%

(1) Area I : Business Analysis

- Financial statement analysis, including comparison of current period financial statements to prior period or budget and interpretation of financial statement fluctuations and ratios.

- Non-financial and non-GAAP measures of performance, including use of the balanced scorecard approach and interpretation of non-financial and non-GAAP measures to assess an entity's performance and risk profile.

- Managerial and cost accounting concepts and the use of variance analysis techniques.

- Budgeting, forecasting and projection techniques.

- Factors that influence an entity's capital structure, such as leverage, cost of capital, liquidity and loan covenants.

- Financial valuation decision models used to compare investment alternatives.

- The Committee of Sponsoring Organizations of the Treadway Commission (COSO) Enterprise Risk Management framework, including how it applies to environmental, social and governance (ESG) related risks.

- The effect of changes in economic conditions and market influences on an entity's business.

(2) Area II : Technical Accounting and Reporting

- Indefinite-lived intangible assets, including goodwill.

- Internally developed software.

- Revenue recognition, specifically focusing on the analysis and interpretation of agreements, contracts and other supporting documentation to determine whether revenue was appropriately recognized.

- Stock compensation.

- Research and development costs.

- Business combinations.

- Consolidated financial statements, specifically focusing on topics including variable interest entities, noncontrolling interests, functional currency and foreign currency translation adjustments.

- Derivatives and hedge accounting.

- Leases, specifically focusing on recalling and applying lessor accounting requirements and analyzing the provisions of a lease agreement to determine

- whether a lessee appropriately accounted for the lease.

- Public company reporting topics, specifically focusing on Regulation S-X, Regulation S-K and segment reporting.

- Financial statements of employee benefit plans.

(3) Area III : State and Local Governments

- Basic concepts and principles of the government-wide, governmental funds, proprietary funds and fiduciary funds financial statements.

- Preparing government-wide, governmental funds, proprietary funds and fiduciary funds financial statements and other components of the financial section of the annual comprehensive financial report.

- Deriving the government-wide financial statements and reconciliation requirements.

- Accounting for specific types of transactions such as net position, fund balances, capital assets, long-term liabilities, interfund activity, nonexchange revenue, expenditures and expenses and budgetary accounting within the governmental entity financial statements.

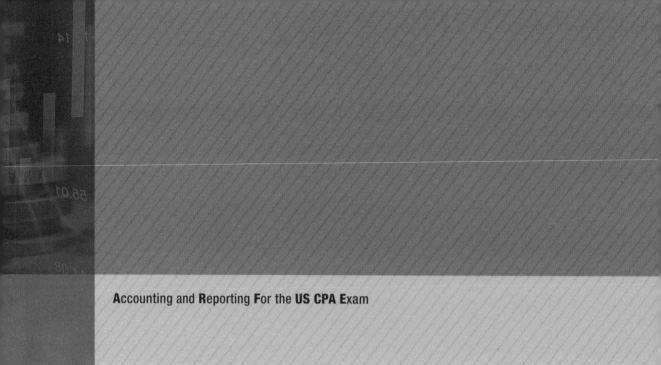

Accounting and Reporting For the **US CPA** Exam

Volume
1

Accounting and Reporting

Chapter

Business combinations

Business combinations

01 Business combination (ASC 805)

1 Introduction

(1) 의의

사업결합(business combination)은 취득자(acquirer)가 사업(business)에 대한 지배력(control)을 획득하는 거래를 말한다. 사업결합의 유형에는 합병(merger)이나 주식취득(acquisition)이 있다.

Merger (흡수합병)	A+B ⇨ A
Consolidation (신설합병)	A+B ⇨ C
Acquisition (주식인수)	A+B ⇨ A+B : 연결재무제표 작성 대상

합병은 피투자회사(B)의 법률적 실체가 소멸되는 사업결합의 형태로 흡수합병과 신설합병으로 구분되며 주식인수는 피투자회사(B)의 법률적 실체가 유지되어 재무제표의 보고실체가 되므로 투자회사(A)의 재무제표와 합산하는 연결재무제표 (consolidated financial statements)를 작성하여야 한다.

(2) 합병과 주식인수의 차이점

	Merger	Acquisition
피투자자(B)의 법률적 실체	소멸	유지
피투자자(B)의 자산 및 부채	투자자(A)의 장부에 기록된다.	피투자자(B)의 장부에 기록된다.
연결재무제표의 작성	No	Yes
취득지분율	100%	50% 초과
회계처리방법	Acquisition method 피투자자의 자산부채를 공정가치로 처리	

(3) 이전대가를 현금인 경우의 회계처리의 비교

투자자(A)는 다음과 같이 회계처리를 한다.

Merger		Acquisition	
Asset (B) xxx (FV)			
Goodwill xxx (plug)		Investment xxx	
Liability(B) xxx (FV)		Cash xxx	
Cash xxx			

2 Acquisition method (ASC 805)

(1) 사업결합은 취득법을 적용하여 다음의 절차를 따른다.

    1) 취득자의 식별

    2) 취득일의 결정

    3) 식별가능한 자산, 부채 및 피취득자에 대한 비지배지분의 인식과 측정

    4) 영업권 또는 염가매수차익의 인식과 측정

(2) Identifying the acquirer

취득자는 피취득자에 대한 지배력(control)을 획득하는 기업이다.

(3) Determining the acquisition date

취득자는 취득일을 식별하며, 취득일은 피취득자에 대한 지배력을 획득한 날이 일반적으로 취득자가 법적으로 대가를 이전하여, 피취득자의 자산을 취득하고 부채를 인수한 날인 종료일이다.

(4) Recognizing and measuring assets, liabilities and non-controlling interest (NCI) in the acquiree.

취득일 현재, 취득자는 영업권과 분리하여 식별할 수 있는 취득 자산, 인수 부채, 피취득자에 대한 비지배지분을 인식한다. 식별가능한 각 자산과 부채는 취득일의 공정가치로 측정하며, 피취득자에 대한 비지배지분은 취득일의 공정가치로 측정한다.

⇨ 피취득자의 기존의 영업권의 공정가치는 "0"이다.

(5) Consideration transferred

　사업결합에서 이전대가는 공정가치로 측정하며, 그 공정가치는 취득자가 이전하는 자산, 취득자가 부담하는 부채와 취득자가 발행한 지분의 취득일의 공정가치 합계로 산정한다. 취득일에 공정가치와 장부금액이 다른 취득자의 자산과 부채를 이전대가에 포함하는 경우, 취득자는 이전한 자산이나 부채를 취득일 현재 공정가치로 재측정하고, 그 결과 차손익이 있다면 당기손익으로 인식한다.

> 1) FV of the assets transferred by the acquirer
> 2) FV of the liabilities incurred by the acquirer
> 3) FV of the equity interests issued by the acquirer
> 4) FV of contingent consideration

(6) Contingent consideration

　Contingent consideration is initially measured at fair value and classified as asset, liability or equity. In subsequent period, the changes in the fair value of assets and liabilities are recognized in the consolidated income statement and equity are not remeasured. Instead, settlement is accounted for within equity.

　조건부대가는 특정 미래 사건이 일어나거나 특정 조건이 충족되는 경우에 피취득자(acquiree)의 이전 소유주에게 추가로 이전하여야 하는 의무를 말한다.

1) 현금 등 자산을 제공할 지급의무가 있는 경우 : 부채로 인식

2) 지분상품을 제공할 지급의무가 있는 경우 : 자본으로 인식

3) 이전대가를 돌려받는 권리를 취득자에게 부여한 경우 : 자산으로 인식

🔴 시장점유율이 20% 이상 증가하는 경우 100만주를 발행하는 조건부 대가

- 조건부대가의 후속 측정
  - 자산 또는 부채로 분류한 경우 : 공정가치 변동을 당기손익으로 인식
  - 자본으로 분류한 경우 : 공정가치 변동을 반영하지 않음

(7) Non-controlling interest (비지배지분)

　비지배지분은 종속기업에 대한 지분 중 지배기업에 직접이나 간접으로 귀속되지 않는 지분

으로 취득일 시점의 공정가치로 측정한다. 지배기업은 비지배지분을 연결재무상태표에서 자본에 포함하되 지배기업의 소유주지분과는 구분하여 별도로 표시한다.

지배기업은 당기순손익과 기타포괄손익의 각 구성요소를 지배기업의 소유주와 비지배지분에 귀속시킨다. 또 지배기업은 비지배지분이 부(−)의 잔액이 되더라도 총포괄손익을 지배기업의 소유주와 비지배지분에 귀속시킨다.

(8) Acquisition-related costs

취득관련원가는 취득자가 사업결합을 하기 위해 발생시킨 원가이다. 그러한 원가에는 중개수수료 즉 자문, 법률, 회계, 가치평가 및 그 밖의 전문가 또는 컨설팅 수수료, 내부 취득 부서의 유지 원가를 포함한 일반관리원가, 채무증권과 지분증권의 등록 · 발행 원가를 포함한다.

> 1) Stock issue costs ⇨ decrease APIC
> 2) Bond issue costs ⇨ decrease bond payable
> 3) 나머지 취득관련원가 ⇨ expense

피취득자의 토지나 건물 등의 소유권을 이전하기 위한 취득세 등 특정 자산의 취득에 따른 부대원가는 특정 자산과 직접 관련된 원가이므로 해당 자산의 취득원가로 처리한다.

(9) Intangible assets that are identifiable

취득자가 인식의 원칙과 조건을 적용하면 피취득자의 이전 재무제표에서 자산과 부채로 인식하지 않았던 자산과 부채를 일부 인식할 수 있다. 예를 들면 취득자는 피취득자가 내부에서 개발하고 관련 원가를 비용으로 처리하였기 때문에 피취득자 자신의 재무제표에 자산으로 인식하지 않았던 브랜드명, 특허권, 고객 관계와 같은 식별할 수 있는 무형자산의 취득을 인식한다.

• 다음 무형자산은 피취득자의 영업권과 구별하여 인식한다.

Marketing–related	− Trademarks − Newspaper mastheads, − Internet domain names − Noncompetition agreements
Customer–related	− Customer lists − Order or production backlog − Customer contracts and related customer relationships

Artistic-related	– Books – Magazines – Pictures
Contract-based	– Licensing – Royalty – Lease agreement – Franchise agreement
Technology-based	– Patented technology – Computer software – Unpatented technology

(10) In-Process R&D

US GAAP and IFRS recognize in-process research and development acquired in a business combination as a separate intangible asset and measure it at fair value. In subsequent period, this R&D is subject to amortization if successfully completed or to impairment if on product results.

(11) Restructuring costs

US GAAP and IFRS do not recognize restructuring costs that are associated with the business combination as part of the cost of the acquisition. Instead, they are recognized as an expense in the periods the restructuring costs are incurred.

(12) Business combination achieved in stages

취득자는 때때로 취득일 직전에 지분을 보유하고 있던 피취득자에 대한 지배력을 획득한다. 예를 들어 20X1년 12월 31일에 기업 A는 기업 B에 대한 비지배지분 35%를 보유하고 있고 있다. 동일자에 기업 B의 지분 40%를 추가로 매수하여 기업 B에 대한 지배력을 갖게 된다. 그러한 거래를 단계적 취득이라고도 한다.

단계적으로 이루어지는 사업결합에서, 취득자는 이전에 보유하고 있던 피취득자에 대한 지분을 취득일의 공정가치로 재측정하고 그 결과 차손익이 있다면 당기손익으로 인식한다.

(13) Recognizing and measuring goodwill or a gain from a bargain purchase.

다음 A와 B를 영업권 또는 염가매수차익을 인식한다.

A	① FV of consideration transferred ② FV of non−controlling interest (NCI)
B	FV of net identifiable net assets of acquiree

A > B ⇨ Goodwill = A − B

A < B ⇨ A bargain purchase gain = B − A

영업권의 측정은 영업권에 대한 비지배지분의 몫을 인식해야 하는지 full goodwill method (전부영업권)과 partial goodwill method(부분영업권)으로 구분된다. FASB는 사업결합의 영업권 측정을 full goodwill method를 강제하고 있지만 IASB는 사업결합의 영업권 측정을 full goodwill method과 partial goodwill method 중 선택할 수 있다.

full goodwill method

영업권에 대한 비지배지분의 몫을 인식하며 비지배지분의 측정을 취득시점의 피투자회사의 공정가치로 측정한다.

partial goodwill method

영업권에 대한 비지배지분의 몫을 인식하지 않으며 비지배지분의 측정을 취득시점의 피투자회사의 순자산의 공정가치로 측정한다.

In a business combination to be accounted for as a purchase, Planet Company paid $300,000 for an 75% interest in Sun on January 2, Year 1. At the time, Sun's net assets had a fair value of $280,000.

full goodwill method

NCI (비지배지분) = 300,000×25% ÷ 75% = $100,000

Goodwill = 300,000 + 100,000 − 280,000 = $120,000

partial goodwill method

NCI (비지배지분) = 280,000×25% = $70,000

Goodwill = 300,000 + 70,000 − 280,000 = $90,000

	Planet (book value)	Star (book value)	Star (fair value)	Difference
	Balance sheets **1/1/20X1 (before combination)**			
Cash	231,000	67,000	67,000	0
A/R	34,000	9,000	9,000	0
Inventories	23,000	16,000	17,000	1,000
PPE	179,000	50,000	58,000	8,000
Customer list	0	0	3,000	3,000
Total Assets	467,000	142,000	154,000	12,000
A/P	4,000	2,000	2,000	
Bond Payable	300,000	34,000	34,000	
Capital stock	100,000	50,000		
APIC	15,000	15,000		
RE	48,000	41,000		
Total	467,000	142,000		

Book value of identifiable net asset of acquiree (Star) = $106,000
Fair value of identifiable net asset of acquiree (Star) = $118,000

On January 2, 20X1, Planet controlled Star by paying cash consideration.
(case−1) 100% merger and consideration = $134,000
(case−2) 100% merger and consideration = $100,000
(case−3) 100% acquisition and consideration = $134,000
(case−4) 90% acquisition, consideration = $120,600 and FV of NCI = 13,400
(case−5) 90% acquisition, consideration = $125,600 and FV of NCI = 13,400

• Case 1 Merger (goodwill)

Working sheets (as of 1/2/20X1)				
	Planet	Adjustments		Merger
		Debit	Credit	
Cash	231,000	67,000	134,000	164,000
A/R	34,000	9,000		43,000
Inventory	23,000	17,000		40,000
Equipment	179,000	58,000		237,000
Customer list	0	3,000		3,000
Goodwill	0	16,000		16,000
Total assets	467,000			503,000
A/P	4,000		2,000	6,000
B/P	300,000		34,000	334,000
NCI	0			0
Capital stock	100,000			100,000
APIC	15,000			15,000
R/E	48,000			48,000
Total L & E	467,000			503,000

※ Goodwill = $134,000- 118,000 = $16,000

• Case 2 Merger (Bargain purchase gain)

	Planet	Adjustments		Merger
		Debit	Credit	
Cash	231,000	67,000	100,000	198,000
A/R	34,000	9,000		43,000
Inventory	23,000	17,000		40,000
Equipment	179,000	58,000		237,000
Customer list	0	3,000		3,000
Goodwill	0	0		0
Total assets	467,000			521,000
A/P	4,000		2,000	6,000
B/P	300,000		34,000	334,000
NCI	0			0
Capital stock	100,000			100,000
APIC	15,000			15,000
R/E	48,000		18,000	66,000
Total L & E	467,000			521,000

Working sheets (as of 1/2/20X1)

※ A bargain purchase gain = $118,000 - 100,000 = $18,000

• Case 3 Acquisition (100%)

Journal entry (Planet)	Dr) Investment in Star 134,000 Cr) Cash 134,000

Consolidation entry	Dr) Capital stock (S) 50,000
	     APIC (S) 15,000
	     RE (S) 41,000
	     Inventory 1,000
	     PPE 8,000
	     Customer list 3,000
	     Goodwill 16,000 (plug)
	     Cr) Investment in Star 134,000

Concepts	Dr) Equity (S) 106,000
	     Differences 12,000
	     Goodwill 16,000 (plug)
	     Cr) Investment in Star 134,000

※ 주식인수는 합병과는 달리 피취득자의 법률적 실체가 소멸되지 않았기 때문에 두 기업의 재무제표를 합산한 후 취득자의 투자주식과 피취득자의 자본을 상계제거하며 자산부채의 시가차이와 영업권을 인식하는 연결재무제표를 작성한다.

※ case-3의 연결재무제표는 case-1의 합병재무제표와 동일하다.

Working sheets (as of 1/2/20X1)			Adjustments		Con
	Planet	Star	Debit	Credit	
Cash	97,000	67,000			164,000
A/R	34,000	9,000			43,000
Inventory	23,000	16,000	1,000		40,000
Equipment	179,000	50,000	8,000		237,000
Customer list	0		3,000		3,000
Investment	134,000			134,000	0
Goodwill	0		16,000		16,000
Total assets	467,000	142,000			503,000
A/P	4,000	2,000			6,000
B/P	300,000	34,000			334,000
NCI	0	0	0		0
Capital stock	100,000	50,000	50,000		100,000
APIC	15,000	15,000	15,000		15,000
R/E	48,000	41,000	41,000		48,000
Total L & E	467,000	142,000			503,000

• Case 4 Acquisition (90%)

FV of Consideration = $134,000 \times 90\% = 120,600$

FV of NCI = $120,600 \times 1/9 = 134,000 \times 10\% = 13,400$

Journal entry (Planet)	Dr) Investment in Star 120,600
	Cr) Cash 120,600
Consolidation entry	Dr) Capital stock (S) 50,000
	APIC (S) 15,000
	RE (S) 41,000
	Inventory 1,000
	PPE 8,000
	Customer list 3,000
	Goodwill 16,000 (plug)
	Cr) Investment in Star 120,600
	Non-controlling interest 13,400
Concepts	Dr) Equity (S) 106,000
	Differences 12,000
	Goodwill 16,000 (plug)
	Cr) Investment in Star 120,600
	Non-controlling interest 13,400

※ 90%의 주식인수의 연결과정에서는 두 기업의 재무제표를 합산한 후 취득자의 투자
주식과 피취득자의 자본을 상계제거하며 자산부채의 시가차이, 영업권 및 비지배지
분을 인식하는 연결재무제표를 작성한다.

※ case-4의 연결재무제표는 case-4의 연결재무제표보다 자산과 자본이 각각 13,400 더 크
다.

Working sheets (as of 1/2/20X1)					
	Planet	Star	Adjustments		Con
			Debit	Credit	
Cash	110,400	67,000			177,400
A/R	34,000	9,000			43,000
Inventory	23,000	16,000	1,000		40,000
Equipment	179,000	50,000	8,000		237,000
Customer list	0		3,000		3,000
Investment	120,600			120,600	0
Goodwill	0		16,000		16,000
Total assets	467,000	142,000			516,400
A/P	4,000	2,000			6,000
B/P	300,000	34,000			334,000
NCI	0	0	0	13,400	13,400
Capital stock	100,000	50,000	50,000		100,000
APIC	15,000	15,000	15,000		15,000
R/E	48,000	41,000	41,000		48,000
Total L & E	467,000	142,000			516,400

• Case 5 Acquisition (90%)

FV of Consideration = 125,600 = 120,600 + 5,000 (경영권 프리미엄)

FV of NCI = 134,000 × 10% = 13,400

Journal entry (Planet)	Dr) Investment in Star	125,600
	Cr) Cash	125,600
Consolidation entry	Dr) Capital stock (S)	50,000
	APIC (S)	15,000
	RE (S)	41,000
	Inventory	1,000
	PPE	8,000
	Customer list	3,000
	Goodwill	21,000 (plug)
	Cr) Investment in Star	125,600
	Non-controlling interest	13,400
Concepts	Dr) Equity (S)	106,000
	Differences	12,000
	Goodwill	21,000 (plug)
	Cr) Investment in Star	125,600
	Non-controlling interest	13,400

※ 90%의 주식인수의 연결과정에서는 두 기업의 재무제표를 합산한 후 취득자의 투자
주식과 피취득자의 자본을 상계제거하며 자산부채의 시가차이, 영업권 및 비지배지분
을 인식하는 연결재무제표를 작성한다.

※ case-4의 연결재무제표는 case-3의 연결재무제표보다 자산과 자본이 각각 13,400 더
크다.

Working sheets (as of 1/2/20X1)					
	Planet	Star	Adjustments		Con
			Debit	Credit	
Cash	105,400	67,000			172,400
A/R	34,000	9,000			43,000
Inventory	23,000	16,000	1,000		40,000
Equipment	179,000	50,000	8,000		237,000
Customer list	0		3,000		3,000
Investment	125,600			125,600	0
Goodwill	0		21,000		21,000
Total assets	467,000	142,000			516,400
A/P	4,000	2,000			6,000
B/P	300,000	34,000			334,000
NCI	0	0		13,400	13,400
Capital stock	100,000	50,000	50,000		100,000
APIC	15,000	15,000	15,000		15,000
R/E	48,000	41,000	41,000		48,000
Total L & E	467,000	142,000			516,400

Example-1

On January 1, 20X1, Planet Corp. and Star Corp. had condensed balance sheets as follows:

Accounts	Planet Corp.	Star Corp.
Current assets	100,000	30,000
Non-current assets	120,000	50,000
Current liabilities	60,000	20,000
Non-current liabilities	80,000	10,000
Stockholders' equity	80.000	50,000

On January 2, 20X1, Planet purchased 90% of the outstanding common shares of Star. On that date, the fair value of non-controlling interest was $6,000. The carrying amount of Star's net assets at the purchase date totaled $50,000. Fair values equaled carrying amount for all items except for inventory, for which fair values exceeded carrying amount by $7,000.

Prepare Planet's consolidated balance sheet on January 2,20X1.

On January 2, 20X1, Planet controlled Star
(case-1) By paying cash consideration of $54,000
(case-2) By issuing common stock of $54,000
(case-3) By issuing bond of $54,000

Case -1

Accounts	Planet	Star	Adjustments	Consolidated
Current assets	46,000	30,000	+7,000	83,000
Non-current assets	120,000	50,000	+3,000	173,000
Investment	54,000	0	(54,000)	0
Current liabilities	60,000	20,000		80,000
Non-current liabilities	80,000	10,000		90,000
NCI			+6,000	6,000
Stockholders' equity	80.000	50,000	(50,000)	80,000

Case -2

Accounts	Planet	Star	Adjustments	Consolidated
Current assets	100,000	30,000	+7,000	137,000
Non-current assets	120,000	50,000	+3,000	173,000
Investment	54,000	0	(54,000)	0
Current liabilities	60,000	20,000		80,000
Non-current liabilities	80,000	10,000		90,000
NCI			+6,000	6,000
Stockholders' equity	134.000	50,000	(50,000)	134,000

Case -3

Accounts	Planet	Star	Adjustments	Consolidated
Current assets	100,000	30,000	+7,000	137,000
Non-current assets	120,000	50,000	+3,000	173,000
Investment	54,000	0	(54,000)	0
Current liabilities	60,000	20,000		80,000
Non-current liabilities	134,000	10,000		144,000
NCI			+6,000	6,000
Stockholders' equity	80.000	50,000	(50,000)	80,000

Example-2

On January 2, 20X1, Planet Corp. and Star Corp. had condensed balance sheets as follows:

Accounts	Planet Corp.	Star Corp.
Current assets	100,000	30,000
Non-current assets	120,000	50,000
Current liabilities	60,000	20,000
Non-current liabilities	80,000	10,000
Stockholders' equity	80.000	50,000

On January 1, 20X1, Planet purchased 90% of the outstanding common shares of Star by paying cash consideration of $54,000. On that date, the fair value of non-controlling interest was $6,000. The carrying amount of Star's net assets at the purchase date totaled $50,000. Fair values equaled carrying amount for all items except for inventory, for which fair values exceeded carrying amount by $7,000.

Prepare Planet's consolidated balance sheet on January 2,20X1.

Accounts	Planet	Star	Adjustments	Consolidated
Current assets	100,000	30,000	+7,000	137,000
Non-current assets	120,000	50,000	+3,000 (54,000)	119,000
Current liabilities	60,000	20,000		80,000
Non-current liabilities	80,000	10,000		90,000
NCI			+6,000	6,000
Stockholders' equity	80.000	50,000	(50,000)	80,000

Example-3

During 20X1, Paper Corp. acquired 80% of Sugar Corp. by issuing 200,000 shares of its common stock. The acquisition was announced on March 1, 20X1, when Paper's common stock was selling for $60 per share, and finalized on July 1, 20X1, when the market price of Paper's common stock was selling for $50 per share. Sugar's net assets had a book value of $10,300,000 on March 1, and a book value of $10,700,000 on July 1, 20X1, Book value equaled fair value for all recognized assets and liabilities, except land, which had a fair value $500,000 higher than book value. Sugar also had a non-compete agreement with a fair value of $240,000 and in-process R&D of with a fair value of $360,000.

In Planet's December 31, 20X1, balance sheet, what amount should be reported as goodwill?

· Answer ·

FV of consideration = 200,000 × $50 = $10,000,000

FV of net assets = $10,700,000 + 500,000 + 240,000 + 360,000 = $11,800,000

FV of NCI = $10,000,000 × 20% ÷ 80% = $2,500,000

Goodwill = $10,000,000 + 2,500,000 − 11,800,000 = $700,000

Example-4

During 20X1, Paper Corp. acquired 80% of Sugar Corp. by issuing 200,000 shares of its common stock. The acquisition was finalized on July 1, 20X1, when the market price of Paper's common stock was selling for $50 per share. Sugar's net assets had a book value of $10,700,000 on July 1, 20X1, Book value equaled fair value for all recognized assets and liabilities, except bond payable, which had a fair value $500,000 higher than book value. Sugar also had a non-compete agreement with a fair value of $240,000 and in-process R&D of with a fair value of $360,000.

In Planet's December 31, 20X1, balance sheet, what amount should be reported as goodwill?

• Answer •

FV of consideration $= 200,000 \times \$50 = \$10,000,000$

FV of net assets $= \$10,700,000 - 500,000 + 240,000 + 360,000 = \$10,800,000$

FV of NCI $= \$10,000,000 \times 20\% \div 80\% = \$2,500,000$

Goodwill $= \$10,000,000 + 2,500,000 - 10,800,000 = \$1,700,000$

Example-5

Pepper Corp. acquired 100% of Salt Corp. by issuing 20,000 shares of its $1 par common stock that had a market price of $10 per share and providing contingent consideration for cash that had a fair value of $50,000. Pepper also incurred $15,000 in legal and consulting fees and $11,000 in registration fees for equity securities issued. On acquisition date, Salt had assets with a book value of $200,000, a fair value of $350,000 and related liabilities with a book value of $70,000, a fair value of $120,000.

> (1) Prepare Pepper's journal entry if Salt ceased to operate as a separate business.
> (2) Prepare Pepper's journal entry and consolidation adjustment entry if Salt continued to operate as a separate business.

• Answer •

(1) Pepper's journal entry

Accounts	Debit	Credit
Assets(S)	350,000	
Goodwill(S)	20,000	
Liabilities(S)		120,000
Capital stock(P)		20,000
APIC(P)		180,000
Contingent liability(P)		50,000

Accounts	Debit	Credit
Fees expenses(P)	15,000	
APIC(P)	11,000	
Cash(P)		26,000

(2) Pepper's journal entry

Accounts	Debit	Credit
Investment(P)	250,000	
Capital stock(P)		20,000
APIC(P)		180,000
Contingent liability(P)		50,000

Accounts	Debit	Credit
Fees expenses(P)	15,000	
APIC(P)	11,000	
Cash(P)		26,000

(3) Pepper's consolidation adjustment entry

Accounts	Debit	Credit
Equity(S)	130,000	
Assets(S)	150,000	
Goodwill(S)	20,000	
Liabilities(S)		50,000
Investment(P)		250,000

Example-6

Pepper Corp. acquired 100% of Salt Corp. by issuing 31,000 shares of its $10 par common stock with a market price of $15 per share, in exchange for all the outstanding capital stock of Salt and Salt ceased to operate as a separate business. The equity account of Pepper and Salt on the date of the exchange :

Accounts	Pepper	Salt
Common stock	$100,000	$200,000
Additional paid-in capital	12,500	17,500
Retained earnings	60,000	105,000
Total	172,500	322,500

Prepare Pepper's equity section of balance sheet immediately after the business combination.

• Answer •

Common stock = $100,000 + 31,000 \times 10 = \$410,000$

Additional paid−in capital = $12,500 + 31,000 \times (15-10) = \$167,500$

Retained earnings = $\$60,000$

Total equity = $410,000 + 167,500 + 60,000 = \$637,500$

Example-7

Blue Company purchased 80% of the common stock of Red Company for $700,000 plus direct acquisition costs of $30,000. At the time of the purchase, Red Company had the following balance sheet :

Assets		Liabilities and Equity	
Cash	$120,000	Account payable	$200,000
Inventory	200,000	Bond payable	400,000
Land	100,000	Common stock	100,000
Building	450,000	APIC	150,000
Equipment	230,000	Retained earnings	250,000
Total	$1,100,000	Total	$1,100,000

The market values of assets are

Inventory	300,000
Land	200,000
Building	600,000
Equipment	200,000

Prepare the elimination entries that would be made on a consolidated worksheet prepared on the date of purchase.

• Answer •

(1) Blue's journal entry

Account	Debit	Credit
Investment	700,000	
Expenses	30,000	
Cash		730,000

(2) Blue's consolidation adjustment entry

Account	Debit	Credit
Common Stock	$100,000	
Additional Paid-In Capital	150,000	
Retained Earnings	250,000	
Inventory	100,000	
Land	100,000	
Building	150,000	
Equipment		30,000
Goodwill	55,000	
Investment		700,000
Non-Controlling Interest		175,000

Example-8

On January 1, Year 1, Planet acquired 30% of Star's outstanding common stock for $400,000. During Year 1, Star had net income of $100,000 and paid dividends of $30,000. On January 1, Year 2, Planet acquired an additional 45% interest on Star for $1,012,500. The fair value of Star on January 1, Year 2 was $2,250,000 and the fair value of Star's net assets on January 1, Year 2 was $2,000,000. What amount of gain and goodwill from this transaction will Planet record in Year 2?

• Answer •

Year 1

지분율이 30%이므로 지분법으로 회계 처리하므로 투자주식의 장부금액은 다음과 같다.

$400,000 + (100,000 - 30,000) \times 30\% = \$421,000$

Year 2

취득자는 이전에 보유하고 있던 피취득자에 대한 지분을 취득일의 공정가치로 재측정하고 그 결과는 당기손익으로 인식한다.

이전에 보유하고 있던 피취득자에 대한 지분의 취득일의 공정가치

$= 2,250,000 \times 30\% = \$675,000$

당기손익 $= 675,000 - 421,000 = \$254,000$

75%의 사업결합에 해당되므로 영업권은 다음과 같다.

goodwill $= 2,250,000 - 2,000,000 = \$250,000$

FV of NCI $= 2,250,000 \times 25\% = \$562,500$

02 Consolidations (ASC 810)

1 Introduction

연결회계는 법적으로 다른 회계 실체들이 하나의 경제적 실체를 형성하는 경우 이들을 하나의 회계실체로 간주하고 단일의 재무제표(consolidated F/S, 연결재무제표)를 작성하는 회계이다. 연결재무제표를 작성하기 위해서는 피투자기업의 형태에 따라 2가지 모형 중 하나를 적용한다.

> Is the legal entity a VIE?
> YES → Variable Interest Model
> NO → Voting Interest Model

2 Voting Interest Model

(1) General

연결재무제표를 작성하기 위해서는 한 기업이 다른 기업의 경영을 좌우할 수 있을 정도의 지배력(control)을 확보하여야 한다.

지배력은 의결권의 과반수 및 실질적 권리를 동시에 고려하여야 한다. 피투자기업의 의결권 과반수를 보유하지 못한 투자자는 지배력(control)이 없으며, 피투자기업의 의결권 과반수를 보유한 투자자는 그 권리가 실질적인가를 평가하여 지배력(control)을 판단한다.

우선주는 의결권이 없으므로 적용되지 않으며, 의결권이 50%인 경우 지배력이 없으므로 투자자는 지분법 회계를 적용한다.

A 기업이 B기업의 지분을 80% 소유하고 B기업이 C기업의 지분을 60% 소유한 경우 A는 C를 간접적으로 지배하고 있기 때문에 B와 C를 모두 연결재무제표에 포함한다.

Voting Interest Model을 적용하는 경우 아래의 순서로 연결재무제표 작성 여부를 판단한다.

(Step-1) Does the reporting entity own a majority voting interest?

> YES → Next Step
> NO → Stop consolidation

(Step-2) Do conditions exist that indicate that control does not rest with the reporting entity?

> Yes → Stop consolidation
> NO → Consolidation entity

(2) Conditions that control does not rest with the majority owner

피투자기업의 의결권 과반수를 보유한 투자자에게 지배력(control)이 없는 예는 다음과 같다.

1) The subsidiary is in legal reorganization

2) The subsidiary is in bankruptcy

3) The subsidiary operates under foreign exchange restrictions, controls, or other governmentally imposed uncertainties so severe that they cast significant doubt on the parent's ability to control the subsidiary.

4) The parent is a broker-dealer and control is likely to be temporary.

5) Some instances, the powers of a shareholder with a majority voting interest are restricted in certain respects by approval or veto rights granted to the noncontrolling shareholder. (allow the noncontrolling shareholder to effectively participate in significant decisions of the investee that are made in the ordinary course of business.)

(3) Not justify the exclusion of the subsidiary from consolidation.

1) A difference in fiscal periods of a parent and a subsidiary

2) A difference in industry of a parent and a subsidiary

3) A difference in country of a parent and a subsidiary

(4) Economic entity group

Consolidated statements are presented as if the group of legal entities were one economic entity group because the resources of two or more companies are under the control of the parent company.

(5) Consolidation procedures

The consolidation process eliminates reciprocal items that are shown on both Parent's and Subsidiary's book to avoid double-counting the same items which would misstate the financial statements of the combined entity.

(6) Limitation

Consolidated F/S are prepared from worksheets which begin with the trial balance (T/B) of Parent and Subsidiary.

⇨ 연결조정분개는 정산표에서의 수정이므로 두 기업의 장부를 수정하지 못한다.

3 Presentation

(1) Balance sheet

Non−controlling interest (NCI; 비지배지분)은 대차대조표의 자본에 단일항목으로 표시한다. 따라서 연결대차대조표의 납입자본 및 이익잉여금은 지배기업의 소유주 자본을 표시한다.

(2) Income statement

비지배주주의 귀속 손익을 손익계산서에 구분하여 표시한다.

지배회사가 종속회사를 80%소유하고 지배회사의 당기순이익 = 200, 종속회사의 당기순이익 = 100이라면 연결손익계산서의 당기순이익은 다음과 같이 표시한다.

Net income	300
NI attributable to NCI	20
NI attributable to acquirer	280

(3) Statement of changes in equity

비지배주주의 자본의 증가 또는 감소를 구분하여 표시한다.

지배회사의 배당금 = 40, 종속회사의 배당금 = 20 이라면 다음과 같이 표시한다.

	C/S	APIC	R/E	NCI	Total
NI			+280	+20	+300
Dividend			-40	-4	-44

4 Variable Interest Model

(1) SPE (유동화전문회사)

A special purpose entity (SPE) or special purpose vehicle(SPV) is a legal entity created to fulfill narrow, specific or temporary objectives. SPEs are typically used by companies to isolate the firm from financial risk. A company will transfer assets to the SPE for management or use the SPE to finance a large project thereby achieving a narrow set of goals without putting the entire firm at risk.

자산유동화란 일반적으로 SPC가 자산보유자로부터 유동화자산을 양도 또는 신탁받아 이를 기초로 유동화증권을 발행하고 해당 유동화자산의 관리·운용·처분에 의한 수익이나 차입금 등으로 유동화증권의 원리금 또는 배당금을 지급하는 일련의 행위를 말한다. 자산유동화는 자산보유자의 신용과 분리하여 유동화자산 그 자체에서 발생되는 현금흐름을 바탕으로 자금 을 조달하는 새로운 금융기법으로서 자산보유자의 재무구조 개선, 자금조달 비용 절감 및 투자자 확대 등의 이점이 있다.

자산유동화증권(ABS : asset backed securities)은 기업 및 금융기관이 보유하고 있는 각종 대출채권이나 매출채권, 부동산 기타 다양한 형태의 자산을 기초로 증권을 발행하여 자본시장 에서 자금을 조달하는 것을 말한다.

(2) Variable Interest Entities (VIE)

A legal entity should be subject to consolidation under VIE model if any of the following conditions exist.

---

(1) The total equity investment at risk is not sufficient to permit the legal entity to finance its activities without additional subordinated financial support.

(2) The equity investors lack one or more of the following characteristics
  1) The ability to make decisions through voting rights
  2) The obligation to absorb the expected losses of the entity
  3) The right to receive the expected residual returns of the entity.

(3) The some equity investors have voting rights that are not proportionate to their economic interests and substantially all of the legal entity's activities are conducted on behalf of an investor that has disproportionately few voting rights.

An equity investment at risk of less than 10 percent of the legal entity's total assets should not be considered sufficient to finance its activities without subordinated financial support. But an entity has sufficient equity investment at risk when :

a) The legal entity has demonstrated that it can finance its activities without additional subordinated financial support.

b) The legal entity has at least as much equity invested as other entities that hold only similar assets of similar quality in similar amounts and operate with no additional subordinated financial support.

c) The amount of equity invested in the legal entity exceeds the estimate of the legal entity's expected losses.

(3) Primary beneficiary

An enterprise that consolidates a variable interest entity is the primary beneficiary of the variable interest entity.

A reporting entity with a variable interest in a VIE should assess whether the reporting entity has a controlling financial interest in the VIE and, thus, is the VIE's primary beneficiary.

A reporting entity should be deemed to have a controlling financial interest in a VIE if it has both of the following characteristics:

1) The power to direct the activities of a VIE that most significantly impact the VIE's economic performance

2) The obligation to absorb losses of the VIE that could potentially be significant to the VIE or the right to receive benefits from the VIE that could potentially be significant to the VIE.

Example-9

KIMCPA, an auto manufacturer, wants to raise $55,000 in capital by borrowing against its financial receivables. To accomplish this objectives, KIMCPA can choose between two alternatives.

(Method 1)
Create a special purpose entity, invest $5,000 in the SPE, have the SPE borrow $55,000 and the use the funds to purchase $60,000 of receivables from KIMCPA.

(Method 2)
Create a special purpose entity, invest $5,000 in the SPE, have the SPE issued stock for $55,000 and the use the funds to purchase $60,000 of receivables from KIMCPA.

SPE Balance Sheet

	Method 1	Method 2
Accounts receivable	60,000	60,000
Long-term debt	55,000	0
Equity	5,000	60,000

Method 1

VIE 요건 1에 해당되므로 SPE는 연결재무제표 작성 대상이다.

Method 2

VIE 요건 2 또는 3에 해당되는지 여부를 검토한 후 요건에 해당된다면 SPE는 연결재무제표 작성 대상이다.

03 Tasked-Based Simulation

[Q 1-1] Non-controlling interest

In a business combination to be accounted for as a purchase, Planet Company paid $1,300,000 for an 80% interest in Sun on January 2, Year 1. At the time, Sun's net assets had a book value of $1,000,000, while the market value of Sun's patents was $200,000 more than book value. All other assets and liabilities had book values equal to market value. Sun depreciates its assets on a straight-line basis. Both tangible and intangible assets are amortized over 10 years. For the current year, Sun had net income of $400,000 and declared and paid dividends of $100,000.

• Instructions • ▸

(1) In its Year 1 consolidated balance sheet, what amount should Planet report as goodwill under full goodwill method ?

(2) What is the non-controlling interest that will be reported on Planet's Year 1 consolidated balance sheet?

[Q 1-2] Merger & Acquisition

On January 1, Year 1, Planet and Star had the following balance sheet.

	Planet	Star
Cash	231,000	47,000
A/R	34,000	9,000
Inventories	23,000	16,000
PPE	179,000	50,000
Intangible assets	0	0
Total Assets	467,000	122,000
A/P	4,000	2,000
Bond Payable	300,000	14,000
Capital stock ($10par)	100,000	50,000
APIC	15,000	15,000
RE	48,000	41,000
Total liabilities and equity	467,000	112,600

Fair values of Star's assets were follows:
Inventory : $15,000, PPE : 60,000, Customer list : 3,000

(Case 1)

Planet paid $150,000 for 100% of the common stock of Star and Star ceased to operate as separate business. Prepare Planet's consolidated B/S.

(Case 2)

Planet issued 3,000 shares of $10 par value common stock for 100% of the common stock of Star and Star ceased to operate as separate business. The market value of Planet's stock is $50.
Cost incurred in relationship to the purchase are as follows:
Finder's fees =$4,000, Appraisal fees=1,000, Stock registration fees = 3,000
Prepare Planet's consolidated B/S.

(Case 3)

Planet issued 2,500 shares of $10 par value common stock and provided contingent consider-
ation of $30,000 that had a fair value of $25,000 for 100% of the common stock of Star and
Star ceased to operate as separate business. The market value of Planet's stock is $50. Prepare
Planet's consolidated B/S.

(Case 4)

Planet issued 2,400 shares of $10 par value common stock for 80% of the common stock of
Star and the market value of Planet's stock is $50. Prepare Planet's consolidated B/S under
full goodwill method and under partial goodwill method. Finder's fees =$4,000, Appraisal
fees=1,000, Stock registration fees = 3,000
Prepare Planet's consolidated B/S.

[Q 1-3] Consolidated statements : date of acquisition

Kippers Steel has approached the management of Gage Company and has made an offer to acquire 90% of Gage's outstanding stock on July 1, Year 1. Kippers Steel will give 20,000 shares of its previously unissued, $1 par, $35 market value, common stock in exchange for a 90% ownership interest. Out-of-pocket costs of the acquisition incurred by Kippers Steel would be as follows:

Legal fees and finder's fees : $27,000   Stock issuance costs : 18,000

Comparative balance sheets just prior to the combination are as follows:

	Kippers Steel	Gage
Cash	$200,000	$80,000
Other current assets	650,000	180,000
Marketable securities	180,000	50,000
Property, plant, and equipment (net)	2,500,000	800,000
Patents	240,000	60,000
Total assets	$3,770,000	$1,170,000
Current liabilities	$410,000	$320,000
Bonds payable	1,000,000	300,000
Common stock($1par)	300,000	
Common stock($25par)		25,000
Paid-in capital in excess of par	1,200,000	275,000
Retained earnings	860,000	250,000
Total liabilities and equity	$3,770,000	$1,170,000

On July 1, Gage's book values approximate market values, except for the following:

Marketable securities $60,000   Bonds payable 296,000

Property, plant, and equipment 950,000   Patents 80,000

• Instructions •

Prepare a consolidated balance sheet for July1, Year 1, immediately subsequent to the acquisition.

[Q 1-4] Consolidation entry

Prepare in general journal form the work paper entries to eliminate Planet Company's investment in Star Company in the preparation of a consolidated balance sheet at the date of acquisition for each of the following independent cases:

CASE	% of stock owned	Investment cost	Star Company Equity Balances		
			C/S	APIC	RE
a	100%	$351,000	160,000	92,000	43,000
b	90%	232,000	190,000	75,000	(29,000)
c	80%	199,000	180,000	40,000	(4,000)

Any difference between book value of net assets and the value implied by the purchase price relates to subsidiary property plant and equipment except for case (c). In case (c) assume that all book values and fair values are the same.

[Q 1-5] Contingent consideration

Planet Company acquired all the net assets of Star Company on December 31, 20X1, for $2,160,000 cash. The balance sheet of Star Company immediately prior to the acquisition showed:

	Book value	Fair value
Current assets	$960,000	$960,000
Plant and equipment	1,080,000	1,440,000
Liabilities	180,000	216,000
Common stock	480,000	
APIC	600,000	
R/E	780,000	

As part of the negotiations, Planet agreed to pay the stockholders of Star $360,000 cash if the post-combination earnings of Planet averaged $2,160,000 or more per year over the next two years. The estimated fair value of the contingent consideration was $144,000 on the date of the acquisition.

Required

A. Prepare the journal entries on the books of Planet to record the acquisition on December 31, 20X1.
B. At the end of 20X2, the estimated fair value of the contingent consideration increased to $200,000. Prepare the journal entry to record the change in the fair value of the contingent consideration, if needed.
C. In 20X3, the earnings did not meet the earn out target and the estimated fair value of the contingent consideration was zero. Prepare the journal entry to record the change in the fair value of the contingent consideration.

[Q 1-6] Contingent consideration

Assume the same information as in [Q 1-5] except that instead of paying a cash earn out, Planet Company agreed to issue 10,000 additional shares of its $10 par value common stock to the stockholders of Star if the average postcombination earnings over the next three years equaled or exceeded $2,500,000. The fair value of the contingent consideration on the date of acquisition was estimated to be $200,000. The contingent consideration (earn out) was classified as equity rather than as a liability.

Required

A. Prepare the journal entries on the books of Planet to record the acquisition on December 31, 20X1.

B. On January 1, 20X5, the additional 10,000 shares of Planet's stock were issued because the earn out targets were met. On this date, Planet's stock price was $50 per share. Prepare the journal entry to record the issuance of the shares of stock.

[Q 1-7] Contingent consideration

Planet Company acquired the assets (except for cash) and assumed the liabilities of Star Company on January 1, 20X1, paying $720,000 cash. Star Company's December 31, 20X0, balance sheet, reflecting both book values and fair values, showed:

	Book value	Fair value
A/R	$72,000	$65,000
Inventory	86,000	99,000
Land	110,000	162,000
Buildings (net)	369,000	450,000
Equipments (net)	237,000	288,000
Liabilities	263,000	263,000
Common stock ($2 par value)	153,000	
APIC	229,000	
R/E	229,000	

As part of the negotiations, Planet Company agreed to pay the former stockholders of Star Company $200,000 cash if the postcombination earnings of the combined company reached certain levels during 20X1 and 20X2. The fair value of contingent consideration was estimated to be $100,000 on the date of acquisition.

Required

A. Record the journal entry on the books of Planet Company to record the acquisition on January 1, 20X1.

B. During 20X1, the likelihood of meeting the post combination earnings goal increased. As a result, at the end of 20X1, the estimated fair value of the contingent consideration increased to $120,000. Prepare any journal entry needed to account for the change in the fair value of contingent consideration.

C. During 20X2, the likelihood of meeting the post combination earnings goal significantly decreased and the contingent consideration target was not met. Prepare any journal entry needed to account for the change in the fair value of contingent consideration

[Q 1-8] MCQ

01. Which one of the following statements is incorrect?

    a. In an asset acquisition, the books of the acquired company are closed out, and its assets and liabilities are transferred to the books of the acquirer.

    b. In many cases, stock acquisitions entail lower total cost than asset acquisitions.

    c. Regulations pertaining to one of the firms do not automatically extend to the entire merged entity in a stock acquisition.

    d. A stock acquisition occurs when one corporation pays cash, issues stock, or issues debt for all or part of the voting stock of another company; and the acquired company dissolves and ceases to exist as a separate legal entity.

02. Which of the following can be used as consideration in a stock acquisition?

    a. Cash

    b. Debt

    c. Stock

    d. Any of the above may be used

03. Which of the following is incorrect?

    a. Under acquisition accounting, direct acquisition costs are recorded by decreasing goodwill as a contra account.

    b. Under acquisition method accounting, indirect acquisition costs (such as expenses incurred by a firm's permanent M&A department) are expensed.

    c. Security issue costs, such as brokerage fees, reduce the Excess Paid In Capital account.

    d. Accounting and consulting fees incurred in a business combination are expenses under the current standards for acquisitions.

04. Which of the following statements best describes the current authoritative position with regard to the accounting for contingent consideration?

a. If contingent consideration depends on both future earnings and future security prices, an additional cost of the acquired company should be recorded only for the portion of consideration dependent on future earnings.

b. The measurement period for adjusting provisional amounts always ends at the year-end of the period in which the acquisition occurred.

c. A contingency based on security prices has no effect on the determination of cost to the acquiring company.

d. The purpose of the measurement period is to provide a reasonable time to obtain the information necessary to identify and measure the fair value of the acquiree's assets and liabilities, as well as the fair value of the consideration transferred.

05. Which of the following statements concerning bargain purchases (purchase price below fair value of identifiable assets) is correct?

a. Any previously recorded goodwill on the seller's books is eliminated and no new goodwill is recorded.

b. Long-lived assets, including in-process R&D and excluding marketable securities, are recorded at fair market value minus an adjustment for the bargain, under current GAAP.

c. An extraordinary gain is recorded in the event that all long-lived assets other than marketable securities are reduced to the original purchase price, under current GAAP.

d. Current assets, long-term investments in marketable securities (other than those accounted for by the equity method), assets to be disposed by sale, deferred tax assets, prepaid assets relating to pension or other post-retirement benefit plans, and assumed liabilities are the only accounts that are always recorded at fair market value, under current GAAP.

06. Which of the following adjustments do not occur in the consolidating process?

    a. Elimination of parent's retained earnings

    b. Elimination of intra-company balances

    c. Allocations of difference between implied and book values

    d. Elimination of the investment account

07. Assuming an acquisition is not a bargain, the impact of reflecting a net deferred tax liability account is that the firm will also reflect an increased amount of:

    a. Land

    b. Difference between Implied and Book Value

    c. Common Stock

    d. Goodwill

08. True or False

    (1) In computing the difference between the implied and book values, the implied value of the acquired entity will always equal the purchase price to the parent.

    (2) In the Computation and Allocation of Difference (between Implied Value and Book Value) schedule for a stock acquisition, the implied value of subsidiary equity is computed as: (purchase price) divided by (percentage acquired by parent).

    (3) Once the eliminating/adjusting entry columns of the worksheet are completed, the entries are posted to the books of the company's general ledger and therefore need not be repeated in the following year in the consolidating process.

    (4) In allocating the difference between implied and book values, if the difference is more than needed to adjust all net assets to market values, then the excess is goodwill.

Accounting and Reporting For the **US CPA** Exam

Volume
1

Accounting and Reporting

Chapter

02

Intangibles
With Indefinite Lives

Chapter 02 Intangibles With Indefinite Lives

1 Introduction

The accounting for a recognized intangible asset is based on its useful life to the reporting entity. An intangible asset with a finite useful life should be amortized; an intangible asset with an indefinite useful life should not be amortized.

무형자산은 내용연수가 유한하다면 내용연수 동안 체계적인 방법으로 상각을 하지만, 내용연수가 비한정인 무형자산은 상각하지 않는다. 무형자산의 회계처리에 대한 개요는 다음과 같다.

Types	Purchased	Internally created	Amortization	Impairment test
Limited-life intangibles	Capitalize	Expense	Yes	Two-step approach
Indefinite-life intangibles	Capitalize	Expense	No	One-step approach

내용연수가 유한한 무형자산의 회계처리는 FAR-Core Exam에서 출제되며, 내용연수가 비한정인 무형자산은 BAR Exam에 출제되므로 이 책에서는 내용연수가 비한정인 무형자산에 대해서만 설명한다.

2 Determining the useful life of an intangible asset

If no legal, regulatory, contractual, competitive, economic, or other factors limit the useful life of an intangible asset, the useful life of the asset should be considered to be indefinite.

The term indefinite does not mean the same as infinite or indeterminate.
(무형자산의 내용연수가 비한정이라는 것은 무한을 의미하지는 않는다.)

The useful life of an intangible asset is indefinite if that life extends beyond the foreseeable horizon—that is, there is no foreseeable limit on the period of time over which it is expected to contribute to the cash flows of the reporting entity.

Example-1

An acquired trademark that is used to identify and distinguish a leading consumer product has been a market-share leader for the past eight years. The trademark has a remaining legal life of 5 years but is renewable every 10 years at little cost. The acquiring entity intends to continuously renew the trademark, and evidence supports its ability to do so. An analysis of product life cycle studies; market, competitive, and environmental trends; and brand extension opportunities provides evidence that the trademarked product will generate cash flows for the acquiring entity for an indefinite period of time.

• Answer •

The trademark would be deemed to have an indefinite useful life because it is expected to contribute to cash flows indefinitely. Therefore, the trademark would not be amortized until its useful life is no longer indefinite.

Example-2

An acquired airline route authority from the United States to the United Kingdom expires in three years. The route authority may be renewed every five years, and the acquiring entity intends to comply with the applicable rules and regulations surrounding renewal. Route authority renewals are routinely granted at a minimal cost and have historically been renewed when the airline has complied with the applicable rules and regulations. The acquiring entity expects to provide service to the United Kingdom from its hub airports indefinitely and expects that the related supporting infrastructure (airport gates, slots, and terminal facility leases) will remain in place at those airports for as long as it has the route authority. An analysis of demand and cash flows supports those assumptions.

• Answer •

Because the facts and circumstances support the acquiring entity's ability to continue providing air service to the United Kingdom from its U.S. hub airports indefinitely, the intangible asset related to the route authority is considered to have an indefinite useful life. Therefore, the route authority would not be amortized

Costs of internally developing, maintaining, or restoring intangible assets that are not specifically identifiable, that have indeterminate lives, should be recognized as an expense when incurred. (내부적으로 창출한 무형자산은 자산으로 인식하지 않고, 발생 즉시 비용으로 인식한다.)

3 Impairment of indefinite-life intangibles

(1) General

An intangible asset that is not subject to amortization should be tested for impairment annually and more frequently if events or changes in circumstances indicate that it is more likely than not that the asset is impaired.

(내용연수가 비한정인 무형자산은 상각하지 아니하고 매년 그리고 손상징후가 있을 때 손상검사를 하여야 한다.)

An entity may first perform a qualitative assessment to determine whether it is necessary to perform the quantitative impairment test. An entity has an option to bypass the qualitative assessment for any indefinite-lived intangible asset in any period and proceed directly to performing the quantitative impairment test.

(자산손상 징후가 있는지를 검토하고 손상검사를 하지만, 기업의 선택에 따라 자산손상 징후의 검토를 생략하고 직접 손상검사를 할 수도 있다.)

(2) Qualitative assessment (손상징후의 검토)

Factors considered in this assessment include the following:

1) Macroeconomic conditions such as deterioration in general economic conditions.

2) Industry and market considerations such as a deterioration in the environment in which an entity operates, an increased competitive environment or a change in the market for an entity's products or services.

3) Legal, regulatory, contractual, political factors.

4) Financial performance such as negative or declining cash flows.

5) Changes in management, key personnel, strategy, or customers; contemplation of bankruptcy; or litigation.

(3) Quantitative impairment test (손상검사)

무형자산의 공정가치가 장부금액에 미달하는 경우 당해 자산은 손상된 것이며, 공정가치로 감액하고 손상차손(impairment loss)을 당기손익으로 인식한다.

Carrying amount of a intangible asset $<$ Fair value of the intangible asset
$\rightarrow$ No impairment loss
Carrying amount of a intangible asset $>$ Fair value of the intangible asset
$\rightarrow$ Impairment loss = carrying amount $-$ fair value

After an impairment loss is recognized, the adjusted carrying amount of the intangible asset should be its new accounting basis.
(손상차손을 인식한 후 공정가치는 새로운 취득원가로 본다.)

Subsequent reversal of a previously recognized impairment loss is prohibited.
(손상차손 인식 이후에 공정가치가 장부금액을 초과하여도 장부금액을 공정가치로 증액하지는 않는다.)

The amortization expense and impairment losses for intangible assets should be presented in income statement line items within continuing operations.

Example-3

ABC purchased a broadcast license for $280,000. The license every 10 years if the company does not violate Federal Communication Commission (FCC) rules. ABC has renewed the license twice at a minimal cost.

Recently, the FCC decided to action significantly more of these licenses. As a result, ABC expect reduced cash flows for the remaining life of its existing license.

ABC estimate expected undiscounted cash flows on the license to be $290,000 and the fair value of the license is estimated to be $250,000.

Is the license impaired? If so on, what is the amount of the impairment and related journal entry?

· Answer ·

무형자산의 공정가치가 장부금액에 미달하므로 당해 자산은 손상된 것이다.

Impairment loss = carrying amount − fair value

= 280,000 − 250,000 = 30,000

Dr) Impairment loss   30,000

    Cr) License   30,000

※ 만일 무형자산의 내용연수가 유한하였다면 recoverability test에 따라 해당 자산은 손상되지 않았다.

⟨recoverability test⟩

undiscounted cash flow ⟩ carrying amount → No impairment

Example-4

A trademark for a line of automobiles was acquired several years ago in an acquisition of an automobile entity. The line of automobiles had been produced by the acquired entity for 35 years with numerous new models developed under the trademark. At the acquisition date, the acquiring entity expected to continue to produce that line of automobiles, and an analysis of various economic factors indicated there was no limit to the period of time the trademark would contribute to cash flows. Because cash flows were expected to continue indefinitely, the trademark was not amortized. Management recently decided to phase out production of that automobile line over the next four years.

• Answer •

Because the useful life of that acquired trademark is no longer deemed to be indefinite, the trademark would be tested for impairment. The carrying amount of the trademark after adjustment, would then be amortized over its remaining four–year useful life following the pattern in which the expected benefits will be consumed or otherwise used up.

02 Goodwill

1 Recognition

Costs of internally developing, maintaining, or restoring goodwill should be recognized as an expense when incurred.

(내부적으로 창출한 영업권은 금액을 신뢰성 있게 측정할 수 없고, 기업이 통제할 수 있는 자원이 아니기 때문에 자산으로 인식하지 않고 발생 즉시 비용으로 인식한다.)

Goodwill is an asset representing the future economic benefits arising from other assets acquired in a business combination that are not individually identified and separately recognized.

(사업결합에서 자산으로 인식하는 영업권은 사업결합에서 획득하였지만 개별적으로 식별하여 별도로 인식하는 것이 불가능한 미래 경제적 효익을 나타내는 자산이다.)

2 Subsequent measurement

Goodwill should not be amortized. Instead, goodwill should be tested at least annually for impairment at a level of reporting referred to as a reporting unit.

(영업권은 상각하지 않고 매년 손상검사를 한다. 영업권은 다른 자산과 독립적으로 현금흐름을 창출하지 못하기 때문에 reporting unit 수준에서 손상검사를 한다.)

For the purpose of testing goodwill for impairment, all goodwill acquired in a business combination should be assigned to one or more reporting units as of the acquisition date.

(영업권은 사업결합 시점에 손상검사를 위하여 reporting unit에 배분하여야 한다.)

A reporting unit is an operating segment or one level below an operating segment (also known as a component).

3 Impairment of goodwill

(1) General

영업권은 매년 그리고 손상징후가 있을 때 손상검사를 하여야 한다. 자산손상 징후가 있는 지를 검토하고 손상검사를 하지만, 기업의 선택에 따라 자산손상 징후의 검토를 생략하고 직접 손상검사를 할 수도 있다.

(2) Qualitative assessment (손상징후의 검토)

내용연수가 비한정인 무형자산의 손상징후의 검토와 동일하다.

(3) Quantitative impairment test (손상검사)

Impairment of goodwill is the condition that exists when the carrying amount of a reporting unit that includes goodwill exceeds its fair value.

A goodwill impairment loss is recognized for the amount that the carrying amount of a reporting unit, including goodwill, exceeds its fair value, limited to the total amount of goodwill allocated to that reporting unit.

A = Carrying amount of a reporting unit that includes goodwill.
B = Fair value of a reporting unit that includes goodwill.

A $<$ B → No impairment loss

A $>$ B → Impairment exists
Impairment loss = MIN [A−B, Goodwll]

Subsequent reversal of a previously recognized impairment loss is prohibited.

Example-5

Microsoft has three reporting units, Office, LinkedIn and Gaming.

	Office	LinkedIn	Gaming
Allocated goodwill	100	150	200
Carrying amount of a reporting unit that includes goodwill.	5,000	3,000	2,000
Fair value of net assets of a reporting unit	5,500	3,200	1,500
Fair value of a reporting unit	5,700	2,900	1,700

Determine whether the reporting units' goodwill is impaired.

• Answer •

(1) Office reporting unit

   5,000 < 5,700 → No impairment loss

(2) LinkedIn reporting unit

   3,000 > 2,900 → Impairment exists

   Impairment loss = MIN [3000−2900, 150] = 100

(3) Gaming reporting unit

   2,000 > 1,700 → Impairment exists

   Impairment loss = MIN [2000−1700, 200] = 200

   Dr) impairment loss   300   Cr) goodwill   300

4   Accounting alternative for amortizing goodwill

A private company or not-for-profit entity may make an accounting policy election to apply the accounting alternative for amortizing goodwill.

Goodwill should be amortized on a straight-line basis over 10 years, or less than 10 years if the entity demonstrates that another useful life is more appropriate.

03 Research and Development Costs

1 Research and Development Costs

(1) General

Research is planned search or critical investigation aimed at discovery of new knowledge with the hope that such knowledge will be useful in developing a new product or a new process or in bringing about a significant improvement to an existing product or process.

Development is the translation of research findings or other knowledge into a plan or design for a new product or process or for a significant improvement to an existing product or process whether intended for sale or use

(2) Accounting for Research and Development Costs

At the time most research and development costs are incurred, the future benefits are at best uncertain. Research and development costs should be charged to expense when incurred with three exceptions.

내부 프로젝트의 연구단계와 개발단계에서 발생한 지출은 미래 경제적 효익에 대한 불확실성이 크기 때문에 발생 시점에서 비용으로 인식한다. 그러나 아래의 3가지 상황에서의 지출은 자산으로 인식한다.

1) Materials, equipment and facilities that have alternative future uses
   → should be capitalized and as tangible assets and the depreciation of such equipment or facilities are research and development costs.
   ※ Materials, equipment and facilities that have no alternative future uses should be charged to expense when incurred.

2) The costs of research and development activities conducted for others under a contractual arrangement.

3) Research and development assets acquired in a business combination (In-Process R&D)

(3) Examples of Activities Typically Included in Research and Development

1) Laboratory research aimed at discovery of new knowledge

2) Searching for applications of new research findings or other knowledge

3) Conceptual formulation and design of possible product or process alternatives

4) Testing in search for or evaluation of product or process alternatives

5) Modification of the formulation or design of a product or process

6) Design, construction, and testing of preproduction prototypes and models

7) Design of tools, jigs, molds, and dies involving new technology

8) Design, construction, and operation of a pilot plant that is not of a scale economically feasible to the entity for commercial production

9) Engineering activity required to advance the design of a product to the point that it meets specific functional and economic requirements and is ready for manufacture

10) Design and development of tools used to facilitate research and development or components of a product or process that are undergoing research and development activities.

(4) Examples of Activities Typically Excluded from Research and Development

1) Engineering follow-through in an early phase of commercial production

2) Quality control during commercial production including routine testing of products

3) Trouble-shooting in connection with break-downs during commercial production

4) Routine, ongoing efforts to refine, enrich, or otherwise improve upon the qualities of an existing product

5) Adaptation of an existing capability to a particular requirement or customer's need as part of a continuing commercial activity

6) Seasonal or other periodic design changes to existing products

7) Routine design of tools, jigs, molds, and dies

8) Legal work in connection with patent applications or litigation, and the sale or licensing of patents.

9) Market research or market testing activities.

10) The acquisition, development, or improvement of a process by an entity for use in its selling or administrative activities.

(5) Disclosure

Disclosure should be made in the financial statements of the total research and development costs charged to expense in each period for which an income statement is presented. Such disclosure should include research and development costs incurred for a computer software product to be sold or leased.

Example-6

During the current year, Tesla Motor Co. incurred the following costs related to a new solar-powered car:

1) Salaries of laboratory employees researching how to build the new car : $250,000
2) Legal fees for the patent application for the new car : $20,000
3) Engineering follow-up during the early stages of commercial production : $50,000
4) Marketing research to promote the new car : $30,000
5) Design, testing, and construction of a prototype : $400,000
6) Research and development services performed by Tesla for Apple : $150,000
7) Research and development services performed by Nvidia for Tesla : $40,000
8) Machine A that has a useful life of five years and can only be used in one research project : $250,000
9) Machine B that will be used for two years on a research and development project and then used by the production division for an additional eight years : $250,000

What amount should Tesla Motor report as research and development expense in its income statement for the current year?

• Answer •

research and development expense
  = 250,000 + 400,000 + 40,000 + 250,000 + 250,000/10 years = 965,000
legal fees for the patent ($20,000) → capitalize
engineering follow-up ($50,000) → administrative expense
marketing research ($30,000)   → selling expense
conducted for others ($150,000) → receivables

2 Computer software intended to be sold, leased or licensed.

(1) Before technological feasibility

1) All costs incurred to establish the technological feasibility should be charged to expense when incurred.

→ All planning, designing, coding, and testing activities to meet its design specifications.

2) Technological feasibility is established upon completion of a detail program design or a working model.

(2) After technological feasibility and before release product for sale

Costs of incurred subsequent to establishing technological feasibility should be capitalized as an intangible asset.

→ Costs of producing product masters, coding and testing performed subsequent to establishing technological feasibility.

(3) After release product for sale

1) Capitalized software costs amortization should start when the product is available for general release to customers.

2) Costs incurred for duplicating the computer software, documentation, and training materials from product masters and for physically packaging the product for distribution should be charged to inventory.

3) Costs of maintenance and customer support should be charged to expense when incurred.

(4) Amortization of capitalized software costs

Capitalized software costs should be amortized on a product−by−product basis.

Amortization = Max[① or ②]

① The ratio that current gross revenues for a product bear to the total of current and anticipated future gross revenues for that product (수익비례법)

② The straight−line method over the remaining estimated economic life of the product. (정액법)

(5) NRV of capitalized software costs

At each balance sheet date, the amount by which the unamortized capitalized costs of a computer software product exceed the net realizable value of that asset should be written off.

→ MIN [unamortized amount, NRV]

The net realizable value is the estimated future gross revenues from that product reduced by the estimated future costs of completing and disposing of that product.

The amount of the write−down should not be subsequently restored.

Example-7

Microsoft Corp. incurred costs to develop and produce a routine, low-risk computer software product, as follows:

Completion of detail program design : $13,000

Coding and testing cost to establish technological feasibility : $10,000

Other coding costs after establishment of technological feasibility : $24,000

Other testing costs after establishment of technological feasibility : $20,000

Costs of producing product masters for training materials : $15,000

Duplication of computer software and training materials from product masters (1,000 units) : $25,000

Packaging product (500 units) : $9,000

What amount should Microsoft report as research and development expense in its income statement for the current year? In Microsoft's balance sheet, what amount should be reported in inventory and capitalized software cost, subject to amortization?

• Answer •

(1) research and development expense = 13,000 + 10,000 = 23,000

(2) capitalized software cost = 24,000 + 20,000 + 15,000 = 59,000

(3) inventory = 25,000 + 9,000 = 34,000

Example-8

On December 31, Year 1, Adobe Co. had capitalized software costs of $600,000 with an economic life of four years.
Sales for Year 2 were 10% of expected total sales of the software. At December 31, Year 2, the software had a net realizable value of $400,000.

its December 31, Year 2 balance sheet, what amount should Adobe report as net capitalized cost of computer software?

• Answer •

(1) amortization = Max[600,000 x 10%, 600,000/4 years] = 150,000
(2) unamortized amount = 600,000 − 150,000 = 450,000
(3) balance sheet = Min[450,000, 400,000] = 400,000

Example-9

On December 31, Year 1, Adobe Co. had capitalized software costs of $600,000 with an economic life of four years.
Sales for Year 2 were 40% of expected total sales of the software. At December 31, Year 2, the software had a net realizable value of $400,000.

its December 31, Year 2 balance sheet, what amount should Adobe report as net capitalized cost of computer software?

• Answer •

(1) amortization = Max[600,000 x 40%, 600,000/4 years] = 240,000
(2) unamortized amount = 600,000 − 240,000 = 360,000
(3) balance sheet = Min[360,000, 400,000] = 360,000

3 Internal-Use Software

(1) Preliminary Project Stage

Internal and external costs incurred during the preliminary project stage should be expensed when incurred.

(2) Application Development Stage

1) Internal and external costs incurred to develop internal-use computer software during the application development stage should be capitalized.

2) Training costs are not internal-use software development costs and should be expensed when incurred.

3) Data conversion costs should be expensed when incurred.

(3) Postimplementation-Operation Stage

Internal and external training costs and maintenance costs during the postimplementation-operation stage should be expensed when incurred.

(4) Upgrades and Enhancements

1) Costs incurred for upgrades and enhancements shall be expensed or capitalized.

2) Costs incurred for maintenance shall be expensed as incurred.

04   Tasked-Based Simulation

[Q 2-1] Goodwill Impairment

Presented below is net asset information related to the Boeing Defense Division of Boeing Corporation.

Boeing Defense Division
Net Assets
As of December 31, 20X1
(in millions)

Cash	$ 50
Accounts receivable	200
Property, plant, and equipment	2,600
Goodwill	200
Less: Notes payable	(2,700)
Net assets	$ 350

The purpose of the Boeing Defense Division to develop a nuclear-powered aircraft. If successful, traveling delays associated with refueling could be substantially reduced. Many other benefits would also occur.

To date, management has not had much success and is deciding whether a write-down at this time is appropriate. Management estimated its future net cash flows from the project to be $400 million.

Management has also received an offer to purchase the division for $335 million (deemed an appropriate fair value). All identifiable assets' and liabilities' book and fair value amounts are the same.

• Instructions •

(1) Prepare the journal entry to record the impairment at December 31, 20X1.
(2) At December 31, 20X2, it is estimated that the division's fair value increased to $345 million. Prepare the journal entry to record this increase in fair value.

[Q 2-2] Goodwill Impairment

On July 31, 20X1, Planet Company paid $3,000,000 to acquire all of the common stock of Star Incorporated, which became a division (a reporting unit) of Asia. Star reported the following balance sheet at the time of the acquisition.

Current assets	$ 800,000	Current liabilities	$ 600,000
Noncurrent assets	2,700,000	Long-term liabilities	500,000
Total assets	$3,500,000	Stockholders' equity	2,400,000
		Total liabilities and equity	$3,500,000

It was determined at the date of the purchase that the fair value of the identifiable net assets of Star was $2,750,000. Over the next 6 months of operations, the newly purchased division experienced operating losses. In addition, it now appears that it will generate substantial losses for the foreseeable future. At December 31, 20X1, Star reports the following balance sheet information.

Current assets	$ 450,000
Noncurrent assets (including goodwill)	2,400,000
Current liabilities	(700,000)
Long-term liabilities	(500,000)
Net assets	$1,650,000

Finally, it is determined that the fair value of the Star Division is $1,850,000.

• Instructions •

(1) Compute the amount of goodwill recognized on July 31, 20X1.
(2) Determine the impairment loss to be recorded on December 31, 20X1.
(3) Assume that fair value of the Star Division is $1,600,000 instead of $1,850,000. Determine the impairment loss to be recorded on December 31, 20X1.
(4) Prepare the journal entry to record the impairment loss and indicate where the loss would be reported in the income statement.

[Q 2-3] Research and Development Costs

During 20X1, Apple Company purchased a building site for its proposed research and development laboratory at a cost of $60,000. Construction of the building was started in 20X1. The building was completed on December 31, 20X2, at a cost of $320,000 and was placed in service on January 2, 20X3. The estimated useful life of the building for depreciation purposes was 20 years. The straight-line method of depreciation was to be employed, and there was no estimated residual value.

Management estimates that about 50% of the projects of the research and development group will result in long-term benefits (Le., at least 10 years) to the corporation. The remaining projects either benefit the current period or are abandoned before completion. A summary of the number of projects and the direct costs incurred in conjunction with the research and development activities for 20X3 appears below.

	Number of Projects	Salaries and Employee Benefits	Other Expenses (excluding Building Depreciation Charges)
Completed projects with			
long-term benefits	15	$90,000	$50,000
Abandoned projects or projects			
that benefit the current period	10	65,000	15,000
Projects in process-results			
indeterminate	5	40,000	12,000
Total	30	$195,000	$77,000

Upon recommendation of the research and development group, Apple Company acquired a patent for manufacturing rights at a cost of $88,000. The patent was acquired on April 1, 20X2, and has an economic life of 10 years.

• Instructions •

How would the items above relating to research and development activities be reported on the following financial statements?

(1) The company's income statement for 20X3

(2) The company's balance sheet as of December 31, 20X3.

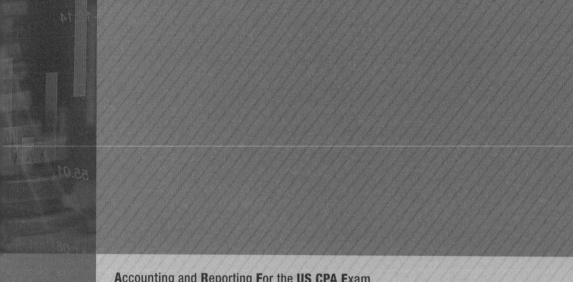

Accounting and Reporting For the US CPA Exam

Volume
1

Accounting and Reporting

Chapter

03

Foreign Currency Translation

Chapter 03 | Foreign Currency Translation

01 Introduction

1 Foreign currency accounting

(1) ASC 830

ASC 830의 외환회계는 외환거래와 외화표시재무제표의 환산으로 구분하여 환율변동으로 인한 손익을 다르게 보고한다.

1) Foreign currency transaction

Transactions whose terms are denominated in a currency other than the entity's functional currency.

※ 외화로 결제되지 않는 해외거래에서는 환율변동손익이 발생하지 않는다.

2) Foreign currency translation

The process of expressing in the reporting currency of the reporting entity those amounts that are denominated or measured in a different currency.

(2) Objectives of foreign currency translation

1) Provide information that is generally compatible with the expected economic effects of a rate change on a reporting entity's cash flows and equity

2) Reflect in consolidated statements the financial results and relationships of the individual consolidated entities as measured in their functional currencies in conformity with U.S. GAAP.

(3) 환율의 기초

1) 환율표시방법

Direct method	1 foreign currency = 0.50 USD
Indirect method	1 USD = 2 foreign currency

2) 거래시점에 의한 환율의 분류

Spot rate (현물환율)	현재시점에서 거래되는 환율
Forward rate (선도환율)	미래시점에서 거래되는 약정환율

3) 환율의 변동

Appreciation (평가절상)	외화의 가치가 상승 ⇒ 외화 자산 환차익, 외화 부채 환차손
Depreciation (평가절하)	외화의 가치가 하락 ⇒ 외화 자산 환차손, 외화 부채 환차익

2 Terminology

(1) Functional Currency (기능통화)

An entity's functional currency is the currency of the primary economic environment in which the entity operates; normally, that is the currency of the environment in which an entity primarily generates and expends cash.

기능통화는 영업활동이 이루어지는 주된 경제 환경의 통화로서 다음의 지표들을 고려하여 결정한다.

- Cash flow indicators
- Sales price indicators
- Sales market indicators
- Expense indicators
- Financing indicators
- Intra—entity transactions and arrangements indicators

The assets, liabilities, and operations of a foreign entity shall be measured using the functional currency of that entity.

(2) Reporting Currency

The currency in which a reporting entity prepares its financial statements.

(3) Local Currency

The currency of a particular country being referred to.

3 Functional currency

Functional currency = Local currency	Translation into US $ 해외종속회사의 재무제표는 기능통화로 표시되어있기 때문에 재측정 없이 환산을 한다.
Functional currency = Reporting currency	Remeasurement into US $ 해외종속회사의 재무제표를 기능통화로 재측정하며 환산을 하지 않는다.
Functional currency = Another currency	Step1〉 Remeasurement into another currency 해외종속회사의 재무제표를 기능통화로 재측정한다. Step2〉 Translation into US $ 기능통화를 보고통화로 환산을 한다.

○ Translation gain/loss

: 환율변동손익을 기타포괄손익(OCI)으로 보고한다.

○ Remeasurement gain/loss

: 환율변동손익을 당기순이익(NI)으로 보고한다.

02 ⟩ Foreign currency translation

1 Translation of foreign currency statements

(1) Translation

functional currency ⇨ reporting currency

기능통화로 표시된 외화재무제표를 보고통화로 표시하는 것

(2) Translation adjustments

Translation adjustments ⇨ reported in other comprehensive income (OCI)
Cumulative translation adjustments ⇨ reported in accumulated other comprehensive income (AOCI)

　　보고통화로의 환산손익은 기타포괄손익(OCI)에 보고하며 해외사업장을 처분하는 경우에는 기타포괄손익과 별도의 자본항목으로 인식한 해외사업장관련 외환차이의 누계액(AOCI)은 해외사업장의 처분손익을 인식하는 시점에 (재분류조정으로) 자본에서 당기손익으로 재분류한다.

(3) Current Rate Method (exchange rate)

Assets & Liabilities	Current rate (보고기간말의 환율)
Revenues & Expenses	해당 거래일의 환율 ⇨ Average rate (평균 환율)
Contributed capital	Historical rate (거래시점의 환율)
Retained earnings	당기순이익 ⇨ Average rate (평균 환율) 배당금　　 ⇨ 배당선언시점의 환율

Example-1

Planet Corporation, based in San Francisco, purchased 100% of Star Company's out-standing capital stock on January 1, 20X1, for $58,000. Star is a German company, and the exchange rate for EUR was $1.20 when Planet acquired its interest. Star's stockholders' equity on January 1, 20X1, consisted of 40,000 EUR capital stock. Star's functional currency is the EUR and its adjusted trial balance in pounds at December 31, 20X1 is as follows :

Star Company Adjusted Trial Balances in EUR at December 31, 20X1

Debits	Cash	3,000
	Account receivables	6,000
	Inventory	8,000
	Equipment	90,000
	Cost of goods sold	30,000
	Depreciation expense	10,000
	Other expenses	8,000
	Totals	155,000
Credits	Accumulated depreciation	30,000
	Account payable	10,000
	Notes payable	12,000
	Capital stock	40,000
	Retained earnings	0
	Sales	63,000
	Totals	155,000

Exchange rate for EUR for 20X1

January 1, 20X1	1.20
December 31, 20X1	1.32
Average for 20X1	1.25

Translation은 손익계산서를 먼저 확정하고 대차대조표에서 환산손익을 계산한다.

Step-1 : Income statement

	EUR	Rate	U$
Sales	63,000	1.25	78,750
Cost of goods sold	30,000	1.25	37,500
Depreciation expense	10,000	1.25	12,500
Other expenses	8,000	1.25	10,000
Net income	15,000		18,750

Step-2 : Balance sheet

	EUR	Rate	U$
Cash	3,000	1.32	3,960
Account receivables	6,000	1.32	7,920
Inventory	8,000	1.32	10,560
Equipment	90,000	1.32	118,800
Accumulated depreciation	(30,000)	1.32	(39,600)
Total assets	77,000		101,640
Account payable	10,000	1.32	13,200
Notes payable	12,000	1.32	15,840
Capital stock	40,000	1.20	48,000
Retained earnings	15,000	N/A	18,750
AOCI	0	plug	5,850
Total liabilities and equity	77,000		101,640

※ 20X1년 EUR 평가절상으로 인하여 환산이익이 발생하였고 $5,850의 환율변동이익은 지배회사의 기타 포괄손익에 보고한다.

2 Remeasurement of foreign currency statements

(1) Remeasurement

local currency ⇨ functional currency

기능통화가 아닌 다른 통화로 표시된 외화재무제표를 기능통화로 표시하는 것

(2) Remeasurement gain or loss

> Remeasurement gain or loss
> ⇨ reported in income from continuing operation

(3) Temporal Method (exchange rate)

Assets & Liabilities	화폐성 항목	Current rate (보고기간말의 환율)
	역사적원가로 측정하는 비화폐성 항목	Historical rate (거래시점의 환율)
	공정가치로 측정하는 비화폐성 항목	Current rate (보고기간말의 환율)
Revenues & Expenses	매출원가 및 감가상각비	Historical rate (거래시점의 환율)
	기타 항목	Average rate (평균 환율)
Contributed capital		Historical rate (거래시점의 환율)
Retained earnings	당기순이익 ⇨ 대차대조표에서 Plug 배당금 ⇨ 배당선언시점의 환율	

Example-2

Planet Corporation, based in San Francisco, purchased 100% of Star Company's outstanding capital stock on January 1, 20X1, for $58,000. Star is a German company, and the exchange rate for EUR was $1.20 when Planet acquired its interest. Star's stockholders' equity on January 1, 20X1, consisted of 40,000 EUR capital stock. Star's functional currency is the U$ and its adjusted trial balance in pounds at December 31, 20X1 is as follows :

Star Company Adjusted Trial Balances in EUR at December 31, 20X1

Debits	Cash	3,000
	Account receivables	6,000
	Inventory	8,000
	Equipment	90,000
	Cost of goods sold	30,000
	Depreciation expense	10,000
	Other expenses	8,000
	Totals	155,000
Credits	Accumulated depreciation	30,000
	Account payable	10,000
	Notes payable	12,000
	Capital stock	40,000
	Retained earnings	0
	Sales	63,000
	Totals	155,000

Exchange rate for EUR for 20X1

January 1, 20X1	1.20
December 31, 20X1	1.32
Average for 20X1	1.25
Historical rate for inventory	1.23
Historical rate for cost of goods sold	1.24
Historical rate for equipment	1.26

Historical rate for accumulated depreciation	1.28
Historical rate for depreciation expense	1.27

Remeasurement는 대차대조표를 먼저 확정하고 손익계산서에서 환산손익을 계산한다.

Step-1 : Balance sheet

	EUR	Rate	U$
Cash	3,000	1.32	3,960
Account receivables	6,000	1.32	7,920
Inventory	8,000	1.23	9,840
Equipment	90,000	1.26	113,400
Accumulated depreciation	(30,000)	1.28	(38,400)
Total assets	77,000		96,720
Account payable	10,000	1.32	13,200
Notes payable	12,000	1.32	15,840
Capital stock	40,000	1.20	48,000
Retained earnings	15,000	plug	19,680
AOCI	0	N/A	0
Total liabilities and equity	77,000		96,720

Step-2 : Income statement

	EUR	Rate	U$
Sales	63,000	1.25	78,750
Cost of goods sold	30,000	1.24	37,200
Depreciation expense	10,000	1.27	12,700
Other expenses	8,000	1.25	10,000
Net income before adjustment	15,000		18,850
Remeasurement gain or loss		plug	+830
Net income after adjustment	15,000		19,680

※ 환산손익 조정 전 당기순이익 $18,850과 대차대조표에서 잔액 조정된 당기순이익 $19,680의 차이금액 $830을 재측정손익으로 지배회사의 당기손익에 보고한다.

3 Highly inflationary economies

(1) Highly inflationary economy

A highly inflationary economy is one that has cumulative inflation of approximately 100 percent or more over a 3-year period.

(2) The functional currency in highly inflationary economies

The financial statements of a foreign entity in a highly inflationary economy shall be remeasured as if the functional currency were the reporting currency.

4 Statement of cash flows

The statement of cash flows should report the effect of exchange rate changes on cash & cash equivalents as a separate part of the reconciliation of the change in the total of cash & cash equivalents during the period.

	Local Currency	US Dollars
Cash flows from operating activities	37	16
Cash flows from investing activities	(325)	(142)
Cash flows from financing activities	275	113
Effect on exchange rate on cash		9
Net increase(decrease) in cash	(13)	(4)
Cash at beginning of year	38	15
Cash at end of year	25	11

5 Monetary or Non-Monetary

(1) Monetary and non-monetary items

중요한 화폐성 및 비화폐성 항목의 분류는 다음과 같다.

	Monetary	Non-monetary
Assets	Cash Receivables Debt investments Advances to suppliers—no fixed	Inventories PPE Intangible assets Equity investments Advances to suppliers—fixed
Liabilities	Almost	Warranty obligations Advances from customer—fixed
Equity	No	Yes

(2) Purchasing power gain or loss

물가상승시에 구매력 손익은 다음과 같다.

	Monetary	Non-monetary
Assets	purchasing power loss	해당사항 없음
Liabilities	purchasing power gain	

따라서 화폐성 자산과 부채의 크기에 따라 구매력손익은 결정된다.

monetary assets $>$ monetary liabilities $\Rightarrow$ purchasing power loss
monetary assets $<$ monetary liabilities $\Rightarrow$ purchasing power gain

03   Tasked-Based Simulation

[Q 3-1]

Pence Corporation, based in San Francisco, purchased 90% of Sevin Company's outstanding capital stock on January 1, 20X1, for $768,000. Sevin is a British company, and the exchange rate for British pounds was $1.60 when Pence acquired its interest. Sevin's stockholders' equity on January 1, 20X1, consisted of £400,000 capital stock and £100,000 retained earnings. Sevin's functional currency is the British pound, and its comparative adjusted trial balance in pounds at December 31, 20X1 and 20X2, are as follows :

Sevin Company Adjusted Trial Balances in British Pounds at December 31.

Debits	20X1	20X2
Cash	30,000	50,000
Account receivables	60,000	90,000
Inventory	80,000	150,000
Equipment	900,000	1,000,000
Cost of goods sold	300,000	360,000
Depreciation expense	100,000	110,000
Other expenses	80,000	90,000
Dividends	50,000	50,000
Totals	1,600,000	1,900,000

Credits	20X1	20X2
Accumulated depreciation	200,000	310,000
Account payable	200,000	220,000
Notes payable	20,000	20,000
Capital stock	400,000	400,000
Retained earnings	100,000	250,000
Sales	680,000	700,000
Totals	1,600,000	1,900,000

Exchange rates for British pounds for 20X1 and 20X2 are as follows:

	20X1	20X2
Current exchange rate January 1	$1.60	$1.70
Average exchange rate	1.65	1.75
Exchange rate for dividends	1.68	1.78
Current exchange rate December 31	1.70	1.80

[Instruction]

Prepare a translation worksheet to restate Sevin's adjusted trial balance at December 31, 20X1 and December 31, 20X2, in U.S. dollars.

Par of Chicago acquired all the outstanding capital stock of Sar of London on January 1, 20X1, for $1,200,000. The exchange rate for British pounds was $1.60 and Sar's stockholders' equity was £800,000, consisting of £500,000 capital stock and £300,000 retained earnings. The functional currency of Sar is the U.S. dollar. Exchange rates for British pounds for 20X1 are as follows:

Current rate December 31, 20X0	$1.60
Current rate December 31, 20X1	1.70
Average exchange rate for 20X1	1.65
Exchange rate for dividends	1.64

Sar's cost of goods sold consists of £200,000 inventory on hand at January 1, 20X1, and purchases of £600,000 less £150,000 inventory on hand at December 31, 20X1, that was acquired at an exchange rate of $1.68.

All of Sar's plant assets were on hand when Par acquired Sar, and Sar's other expenses were paid in cash or relate to accounts payable. Sar's adjusted trial balance at December 31, 20X1, in British pounds is as follows:

Debits	
Cash	£50,000
Accounts receivable	200,000
Short-term note receivable	50,000
Inventories	150,000
Land	300,000
Buildings—net	400,000
Equipment—net	500,000
Cost of sales	650,000
Depreciation expense	200,000
Other expenses	400,000
Dividends	100,000
	£3,000,000

Credits

Accounts payable	£ 180,000
Bonds payable—10%	500,000
Bond interest payable	20,000
Capital stock	500,000
Retained earnings	300,000
Sales	1,500,000
	£ 3,000,000

[Instruction]

Prepare a remeasurement worksheet to restate Sar's adjusted trial balance at December 31, 20X1, in U.S. dollars.

[Multiple Choice Questions]

01. When consolidated financial statements for a U.S. parent and its foreign subsidiary are prepared, the account balances expressed in foreign currency must be converted into the currency of the reporting entity. One objective of the translation process is to provide information that:

a. Reflects current exchange rates

b. Reflects current monetary equivalents

c. Is compatible with the economic effects of rate changes on the firm's cash flows

d. Reflects each translated account at its unexpired historical cost

02. A company is translating account balances from another currency into dollars for its December 31, 20X1, statement of financial position and its calendar year 20X1 earnings statement and statement of cash flows. The average exchange rate for 20X1 should be used to translate:

a. Cash at December 31, 20X1

b. Land purchased in 20X1

c. Retained earnings at January 1, 20X1

d. Sales for 20X1

03. A subsidiary's functional currency is the local currency, which has not experienced significant inflation. The appropriate exchange rate for translating the depreciation on plant assets in the income statement of the foreign subsidiary is the:

a. Exit rate

b. Historical exchange rate

c. Weighted average exchange rate over the economic life of each plant asset

d. Weighted average exchange rate for the current year

04. The year-end balance of accounts receivable on the books of a foreign subsidiary should be translated by the parent company for consolidation purposes at the:

a. Historical rate

b. Current rate

c. Negotiated rate

d. Average rate

05. A German subsidiary of a U.S. firm has the British pound as its functional currency. Under the provisions of ASC Topic 830, the U.S. dollar from the subsidiary's viewpoint would be:

a. Its local currency

b. Its recording currency

c. A foreign currency

d. None of the above

06. Which of the following foreign subsidiary accounts will be converted into the same number of U.S. dollars, regardless of whether translation or remeasurement is used?

a. Accounts receivable

b. Inventories

c. Machinery

d. Prepaid insurance

07. Which one of the following items from the financial statements of a foreign subsidiary would be translated into dollars using the historical exchange rate?

a. Accounts payable

b. Amortization of bond premium

c. Common stock

d. Inventories

08. Average exchange rates are used to translate certain items from foreign income statements into U.S. dollars. Such averages are used to:

a. Approximate the effects of using the current exchange rates in effect on the transaction dates

b. Avoid using different exchange rates for some revenue and expense accounts

c. Eliminate large and temporary fluctuations in exchange rates that may reverse in the near future

d. Smooth out large exchange gains and losses

09. Pal, a U.S. Corporation, made a long-term, dollar-denominated loan of $600,000 to its British subsidiary on January 1, 20X1, when the exchange rate for British pounds was $1.73. If the subsidiary's functional currency is its local currency, this transaction is a foreign currency transaction of:

a. The parent company but not the subsidiary

b. The subsidiary company but not the parent

c. Both the subsidiary and the parent

d. Neither the subsidiary nor the parent

Accounting and Reporting For the **US CPA E**xam

Volume
1

Accounting and Reporting

Chapter

Lessor Accounting

Lessor Accounting

01 Lease Classification

1 Introduction

리스(lease)는 대가와 교환하여 기초자산(underlying asset)의 사용권을 일정 기간 이전하는 계약이나 계약의 일부를 말한다. 이때 대가와 교환하여 기초자산 사용권을 일정 기간 제공하는 기업을 리스제공자(lessor), 대가와 교환하여 기초자산의 사용권을 일정 기간 얻게 되는 기업을 리스이용자(lessee)라고 한다.

리스는 기초자산의 소유에 따른 위험과 보상을 이전하는 정도에 따라 다음과 같이 분류한다.

Lessor	Lessee
Sales-type lease (판매형리스) Direct financing lease (직접금융리스) Operating lease (운용리스)	Finance lease (금융리스) Operating lease (운용리스)

리스는 리스약정일(commencement date)에 분류하며 리스변경(modification)이 있는 경우에만 분류를 다시 판단한다. 추정치의 변경(예: 기초자산의 내용연수 또는 잔존가치 추정치의 변경)이나 상황의 변화(예: 리스이용자의 채무불이행)는 회계 목적상 리스를 새로 분류하는 원인이 되지 않는다.

BAR시험에서는 리스제공자(lessor)의 회계처리만 출제되므로 리스제공자(lessor)의 회계처리에 대해서만 살펴본다.

2 Terminology

(1) Commencement date (리스개시일)

The date on which a lessor makes an underlying asset available for use by a lessee.
(리스제공자가 리스이용자에게 리스자산을 사용할 수 있게 하는 날)

(2) Initial direct costs (리스개설직접원가)

Incremental costs of a lease that would not have been incurred if the lease had not been obtained.
(리스를 체결하지 않았다면 부담하지 않았을 리스체결의 증분원가)

(3) Lease term (리스기간)

The noncancellable period for which a lessee has the right to use an underlying asset, together with all of the following:
(리스이용자가 기초자산 사용권을 갖는 해지불능기간과 다음 기간을 포함하는 기간)

1) Periods covered by an option to extend the lease if the lessee is reasonably certain to exercise that option

2) Periods covered by an option to terminate the lease if the lessee is reasonably certain not to exercise that option

(4) Variable lease payments (변동리스료)

Payments made by a lessee to a lessor for the right to use an underlying asset that vary because of changes in facts or circumstances occurring after the commencement date, other than the passage of time.
(리스료의 일부로서 시간의 경과가 아닌 리스개시일 후 사실이나 상황의 변화 때문에 달라지는 부분으로 리스순투자에는 포함하지 않는다)

(5) Residual value guarantee (잔존가치보증 : GRV)

A guaranteed by the lessee or any other third party unrelated to the lessor made to a lessor that the value of an underlying asset returned to the lessor at the end of a lease will be at least a specified amount .

(리스이용자나 제3자가 리스제공자에게 제공한 보증으로 리스종료일의 기초자산 가치가 적어도 특정 금액이 될 것이라는 보증을 말한다.)

(6) Unguaranteed residual value (무보증잔존가치 : URV)

The amount that a lessor expects to derive from the underlying asset following the end of the lease term that is not guaranteed by the lessee or any other third party unrelated to the lessor

(리스제공자가 실현할 수 있을지 확실하지 않은 기초자산의 잔존가치 부분)

→ residual value = GRV + URV

(7) Rate implicit in the lease (리스의 내재이자율)

아래의 금액을 동일하게 하는 할인율

FV of the underlying asset + deferred initial direct costs
= PV of lease payments + PV of RV

→ 재무관리에서 말하는 리스제공자의 IRR(내부수익률)이다.

(8) Executory costs

The normal expenses associated with owning a leased asset, including insurance, maintenance, and taxes.

Executory costs may be included as part of the rental payment or a pass through expense paid directly by the lessee.

2 Sales-Type Lease

다음 5가지 조건 중 하나를 충족하면 리스제공자(lessor)는 sales-type lease로 분류하며, 리스이용자(lessee)는 finance lease로 분류한다.

5가지 조건 중 하나라도 충족하지 못하면 리스제공자(lessor)는 direct financing lease 또는 operating lease로 분류하며 리스이용자(lessee)는 operating lease로 분류한다.

(1) Transfer of ownership test (소유권이전 약정기준)

The lease transfers ownership of the underlying asset to the lessee by the end of the lease term.

(2) Purchase option test (매수선택권 약정기준)

The lease grants the lessee an option to purchase the underlying asset that the lessee is reasonably certain to exercise.

(3) Lease term test (리스기간 기준)

The lease term is for the major part of the remaining economic life of the underlying asset.
(리스기간이 경제적 내용연수의 75% 이상인 경우)

(4) Present value test (공정가치 회수기준)

The present value of the sum of the lease payments and residual value guaranteed by the lessee equals or exceeds substantially all of the fair value of the underlying asset.
(리스료 및 리스이용자 보증잔존가치의 현재가치가 기초자산 공정가치의 90% 이상인 경우)

→ 공정가치 회수기준을 판단할 때 GRV는 포함하지만 URV는 포함하지 않는다.

(5) Alternative use test (범용성 없는 자산)

The underlying asset is of such a specialized nature that it is expected to have no alternative use to the lessor at the end of the lease term.

3 Direct Financing Lease

다음 2가지 조건을 모두 충족하면 direct financing lease로 분류한다. 조건 중 하나라도 충족하지 못하면 operating lease로 분류한다.

(1) 공정가치 회수기준

The present value of the sum of the lease payments and any residual value guaranteed by the lessee and any other third party unrelated to the lessor equals or exceeds substantially all of the fair value of the underlying asset.

(2) 회수 가능성 기준

It is probable that the lessor will collect the lease payments plus any amount necessary to satisfy a residual value guarantee.

⟨Treatment of residual value⟩

		GRV	URV
Lessee	Classification test	O	X
	Measurement of liability	?	X
Lessor	Classification test	O	X
	Measurement of receivable	O	O

Example-1

Lessor enters into a 6-year lease of equipment with Lessee, receiving annual lease payments of $9,500, payable at the end of each year.

Lessee provides a residual value guarantee of $13,000.

Lessor concludes that it is probable it will collect the lease payments and any amount necessary to satisfy the residual value guarantee provided by Lessee.

The equipment has a 9-year estimated remaining economic life, a carrying amount of $54,000, and a fair value of $62,000 at the commencement date.

Lessor expects the residual value of the equipment to be $20,000 at the end of the 6-year lease term.

The lease does not transfer ownership of the underlying asset to Lessee or contain an option for Lessee to purchase the underlying asset.

Lessor incurs $2,000 in initial direct costs in connection with obtaining the lease.

How should Lessor classify the lease?

• Answer •

(1) Rate implicit in the lease

[EXCEL] 함수선택 RATE

Nper =6, PMT = 9,500, PV = −62,000, FV = 20,000

Rate = 5.4839%

The rate implicit in the lease is 5.4839 percent.

(2) Present value test

[EXCEL] 함수선택 PV

Rate = 5.4839%, Nper =6, PMT = 9,500, FV = 13,000

PV = −56,919 (92% of fair value)

Lessor classifies the lease as a sales−type lease because the sum of the present value of the lease payments and the present value of the residual value guaranteed by the lessee amounts to substantially all of the fair value of the equipment.

02 Lessor Accounting

1 Sales-Type Lease

(1) At the commencement date

1) Recognition

① derecognize the underlying asset

② recognize a net investment in the lease → "Lease receivable"

③ recognize selling profit or selling loss arising from the lease

　※ Inventory : profit/loss = sales revenue − CGS

　※ PPE : profit/loss = Gain/Loss on sales of PPE

④ recognize Initial direct costs as an expense if the FV of the underlying asset is different from its CA. If the FV of the underlying asset equals its CA, initial direct costs are deferred at the commencement date and included in the measurement of the net investment in the lease.

　※ profit/loss =0 → initial direct costs are deferred

　※ profit/loss ≠0 → initial direct costs are recognized as expense

2) if collectibility of the lease payments is not probable at the commencement date,

the lessor should not derecognize the underlying asset but should recognize lease payments received as a deposit liability.

3) Initial measurement

net investment in the lease

= PV of lease payment not yet received + PV of RV + deferred initial direct cost

At the commencement date		
Accounts	DR	CR
Lease receivable ②	xxx	
Lease expense ④	xxx	
Underlying asset ①		xxx
Gain on sales of PPE ③		xxx
Cash ④		xxx

At the commencement date		
Accounts	DR	CR
Lease receivable ②	xxx	
Lease expense ④	xxx	
COGS ①	xxx	
Inventory ①		xxx
Sales revenue ②		xxx
Cash ④		xxx

(2) After the commencement date

1) Recognition

a) recognize interest income on the net investment in the lease

b) recognize variable lease payments as income in profit or loss

c) recognize credit losses on the net investment in the lease

→ 기초자산이 유형자산(PPE)인 경우 감가상각은 하지 않는다.

2) Subsequent measurement

a) Interest income

= discount rate x beginning net investment

b) Ending net investment

= beginning net investment - (lease payment – interest income)

c) Not remeasure the net investment in the lease unless the lease is modified

After the commencement date		
Accounts	DR	CR
Cash	xxx	
Lease receivable		xxx
Interest income		xxx

Example-2

On January 2, 20X1, Tesla leases a cybertruck to Amazon for four years at $5,000 per year with payment due at the end of the year, with initial direct costs of $450 and an implicit rate of 6 percent. On the date of the lease commencement date, the carrying amount and fair value of the truck are $22,000 and $24,216, respectively. The lease contract requires the lease to guarantee the residual value at the end of the lease for $8,700.

Present value of $1 for four years at 6 percent is 0.792
Present value of an ordinary annuity of $1 for four years at 6 percent is 3.465

If the lease is appropriately treated as a sales-type lease and assuming that collection of all amounts owed is probable. prepare Tesla's journal entries.

• Answer •

FV of underlying asset = PV of lease payments + PV of RV
$24,216 = 5,000 \times 3.465 + 8,700 \times 0.792$

Accounts	DR	CR
On January 2, 20X1		
Lease receivable	24,216	
Lease expense	450	
Underlying asset (PPE)		22,000
Gain on sales of PPE		2,216
Cash		450
On December 31, 20X1		
Cash	5,000	
Lease receivable		3,547
Interest income		1,453
On December 31, 20X4		
Cash	5,000	
Lease receivable		4,224
Interest income		776
Underlying asset (PPE)	xxx	
Cash	xxx	
Lease receivable		8,700

⟨amortization schedule⟩

Year	A Beginning Balance	B Lease Payment	C Interest	D Payment of Principal	E Ending Balance
1	24,216	5,000	1,453	3,547	20,670
2	20,670	5,000	1,240	3,760	16,910
3	16,910	5,000	1,015	3,985	12,925
4	12,925	5,000	776	4,224	8,700
Total		20,000	4,484	15,516	

$C1 = A1 \times 6\%$, $D1 = B1 - C1$, $E1 = A1 - D1$, $A2 = E1$

2 Direct Financing Lease

(1) At the commencement date

1) Recognition

① derecognize the underlying asset

② recognize a net investment in the lease → "Lease receivable"

③ recognize selling loss arising from the lease

④ selling profit and initial direct costs are deferred and included in the measurement of the net investment in the lease.

2) Initial measurement

net investment in the lease

= PV of lease payment + PV of RV + initial direct cost − selling profit

At the commencement date		
Accounts	DR	CR
Lease receivable ②④	xxx	
Loss on sales of PPE ③	xxx	
Underlying asset ①		xxx
Cash ④		xxx

(2) After the commencement date

리스개시일 이후의 인식 및 측정은 판매형 리스와 동일하다.

Example-3

On January 2, 20X1, Tesla leases a cybertruck to Amazon for four years at $5,000 per year with payment due at the end of the year, with initial direct costs of $450 and an implicit rate of 6 percent. On the date of the lease commencement date, the carrying amount and fair value of the truck are $22,000 and $24,216, respectively. The lease contract requires the lease to guarantee the residual value at the end of the lease for $8,700.

If the lease is appropriately treated as a direct financing lease, Tesla's journal entries.

• Answer •

이연된 손익을 고려하여 implicit rate를 다시 계산하여야 한다.

FV of the underlying asset + initial direct costs – selling profit

  = PV of lease payments + PV of RV

  $24,216 + 450 - 2,216 = 5,000 \times PVIFA + 8,700 \times PVIF$

[EXCEL] 함수선택 RATE

Nper =4, PMT = 5,000, PV = −22,450, FV = 8,700

Rate = 8.85%

Accounts	DR	CR
On January 2, 20X1		
Lease receivable	22,450	
Underlying asset (PPE)		22,000
Cash		450
On December 31, 20X1		
Cash	5,000	
Lease receivable		3,013
Interest income		1,987

On December 31, 20X4		
Cash	5,000	
Lease receivable		3,887
Interest income		1,113
Underlying asset (PPE)	xxx	
Cash	xxx	
Lease receivable		8,700

⟨amortization schedule⟩

Year	A Beginning Balance	B Lease Payment	C Interest	D Payment of Principal	E Ending Balance
1	22,450	5,000	1,987	3,013	19,437
2	19,437	5,000	1,720	3,280	16,157
3	16,157	5,000	1,430	3,570	12,587
4	12,587	5,000	1,113	3,887	8,700
Total		20,000	6,250	13,750	

$C1 = A1 \times 8.85\%$, $D1 = B1 - C1$, $E1 = A1 - D1$, $A2 = E1$

3 Operating Lease

(1) At the commencement date

1) initial direct costs are deferred

2) continue to measure the underlying asset

(2) After the commencement date

1) recognize lease payments as income in profit or loss over the lease term on a straight-line basis

2) recognize variable lease payments as income in profit or loss

3) recognize Initial direct costs as an expense over the lease term on the same basis as lease income

4) continue to measure the underlying asset

→ 기초자산이 유형자산(PPE)인 경우 감가상각을 한다.

> **Example-4**

On January 2, 20X1, Tesla leases a cybertruck to Amazon for four years at $5,000 per year with payment due at the end of the year, with initial direct costs of $450 and an implicit rate of 6 percent. On the date of the lease commencement date, the carrying amount and fair value of the truck are $22,000 and $24,216, respectively. The lease contract does not require the lease or third party to guarantee the residual value at the end of the lease. The cybertruck has a 10-year estimated remaining economic life at the commencement date. Lessor expects the residual value of the equipment to be $2,000 at the end of the 10-year economic life.

If the lease is appropriately treated as an operating lease, Tesla's journal entries.

> **• Answer •**

Accounts	DR	CR
On January 2, 20X1		
Deferred initial direct costs	450	
Cash		450
On December 31, 20X1		
Cash	5,000	
Lease revenue		5,000
initial direct cost expense	113	
Deferred initial direct costs		113
Depreciation expense	2,200	
Accumulated depreciation		2,200

리스개설비 상각 = 450/4 = 113
감가상각 = (22,000 − 2,000)/10 = 2,000

4 Presentation and Disclosure

(1) Sales-Type and Direct Financing Leases

1) present lease assets separately from other assets in the statement of financial position in classification as current or non-current assets in a classified balance sheet.

2) In the statement of cash flows, a lessor should classify cash receipts from leases within operating activities.

(2) Operating Leases

1) present the underlying asset subject to an operating lease.

2) In the statement of cash flows, a lessor should classify cash receipts from leases within operating activities.

(3) Disclosure

1) A lessor should disclose both of the following:

   a) Information about the nature of its leases

   b) Information about significant assumptions and judgments

2) Sales-Type and Direct Financing Leases

   A lessor should disclose a maturity analysis of its lease receivables, showing the undiscounted cash flows to be received on an annual basis for a minimum of each of the first five years and a total of the amounts for the remaining years.
   A lessor should disclose a reconciliation of the undiscounted cash flows to the lease receivables

3) Operating Leases

   A lessor should disclose a maturity analysis of lease payments, showing the undiscounted cash flows to be received on an annual basis for a minimum of each of the first five years and a total of the amounts for the remaining years.

03　Sale-Leaseback Transaction

1　General

(1) 판매후리스

　　판매후리스(sale-leaseback)는 판매자(the seller-lessee)가 구매자(the buyer-lessor)에게 자산을 이전하고 그 자산을 다시 리스하는 거래를 말한다.

　　판매후리스는 자산 이전이 자산의 판매에 해당되는 경우와 판매에 해당하지 않는 경우로 구분하여 회계처리를 한다.

Is the transfer of the asset as a sale?	
Yes	No
Sale transaction	Financing transaction

(2) Determining whether the transfer of the asset is a sale

> Apply the following requirements on revenue from contracts with customers when determining whether the transfer of an asset shall be accounted for as a sale of the asset:
> 1) On the existence of a contract
> 2) On when an entity satisfies a performance obligation by transferring control of an asset.

(3) Failed sale

　　자산 이전이 수익인식 조건을 충족하였지만 다음 상황에서는 실패한 자산 판매이므로 자산의 판매에 해당하지 아니한다.

1) Repurchase option

　　An option for the seller-lessee to repurchase the asset would preclude accounting for the transfer of the asset as a sale of the asset unless both of the following criteria are met:

a) The exercise price of the option is the fair value of the asset at the time the option is exercised.

b) There are alternative assets, substantially the same as the transferred asset, readily available in the marketplace.

2) Guarantee of the residual value

A significant residual value guarantee by the seller-lessee may affect an entity's consideration of the transfer of control indicator.

3) Finance lease

The buyer-lessor is not considered to have obtained control of the asset if the leaseback would be classified as a finance lease.

리스계약이 다음 조건인 경우 자산의 이전은 financing transaction으로 분류한다.

> 1) Finance lease
> 2) Seller가 보증한 잔존가치 금액이 큰 경우
> 3) 매수선택권의 행사가격과 행사시점의 기초자산의 공정가치가 다른 경우

2 Transfer of the Asset Is a Sale

자산 이전이 자산의 판매에 해당한다면 판매자와 구매자는 다음과 같이 회계처리 한다.

(1) 판매자 (the seller-lessee)

The seller-lessee should

① Recognize the transaction price for the sale

② Derecognize the carrying amount of the underlying asset

③ Account for the lease

(판매자는 이전한 자산을 제거하고 이전 대가를 인식하여 이전한 자산의 손익을 인식한다. 그리고 리스이용자의 회계처리를 적용한다.)

Accounts	DR	CR
Cash	xxxx	
Underlying asset		xxx
Gain on underlying asset sale		xxx
Right-of-use asset	xxx	
Lease liability		xxx

(2) 구매자 (the buyer-lessor)

The buyer-lessor should account for the purchase and for the lease.

(구매자는 자산의 매입에 대한 회계처리와 리스제공자 회계처리를 적용한다.)

Accounts	DR	CR
Underlying asset	xxx	
Cash		xxx
〈if direct financing lease〉		
Lease receivable	xxx	
Underlying asset		xxx
〈if operating lease〉		
No entry		

(3) Determine the sales transaction is at fair value

판매자는 판매거래가 공정가치인지를 판단하여 이전한 자산의 손익을 조정한다.

1) An entity should determine whether a sale and leaseback transaction is at fair value on the basis of the difference between either of the following, whichever is more readily determinable:

a) The sale price of the asset and the fair value of the asset

b) The PV of the lease payments and the PV of market rental payments.

(자산 판매대가가 그 자산의 공정가치와 같지 않거나 리스에 대한 지급액이 시장요율이 아니라면 판매거래가 공정가치가 아닌 것으로 판단한다.)

2) If the sale and leaseback transaction is not at fair value

① sale price of the asset ⟩ the fair value of the asset

시장조건을 웃도는 부분은 금융부채로 인식한다.

sale price of the asset =120

the fair value of the asset = 115

the carrying amount of the asset = 100

Accounts	DR	CR
Cash	120	
Underlying asset		100
Gain on underlying asset sale		15
Financing liability		5

② sale price of the asset ⟨ the fair value of the asset

시장조건을 밑도는 부분은 리스료의 선급금으로 인식한다.

sale price of the asset =120

the fair value of the asset = 125

the carrying amount of the asset = 100

Accounts	DR	CR
Cash	120	
Prepaid rent	5	
Underlying asset		100
Gain on underlying asset sale		25

3 Transfer of the Asset Is Not a Sale

자산 이전이 자산의 판매에 해당하지 아니하면 판매자와 구매자는 다음과 같이 회계처리 한다.

(1) 판매자 (the seller-lessee)

The seller-lessee should not derecognize the transferred asset and should account for any amounts received as a financial liability.

(판매자는 이전한 자산을 계속 인식하고, 이전 대가를 금융부채로 인식한다.)

Accounts	DR	CR
Cash	xxx	
Financing liability		xxx

The seller-lessee should adjust the interest rate on its financial liability as necessary to ensure that the carrying amount of the asset does not exceed the carrying amount of the financial liability at the earlier of the end of the lease term or the date at which control of the asset will transfer to the buyer-lessor.

(2) 구매자 (the buyer-lessor)

The buyer-lessor should not recognize the transferred asset and should account for the amounts paid as a receivable.

(구매자는 이전된 자산을 인식하지 않고, 이전 대가를 금융자산으로 인식한다.)

Accounts	DR	CR
Receivables	xxx	
Cash		xxx

Example-5

An entity (Seller) sells a piece of land to an unrelated entity (Buyer) for cash of $2 million. Immediately before the transaction, the land has a carrying amount of $1 million. The observable fair value of the land at the date of sale is $1.4 million.

At the same time, Seller enters into a contract with Buyer for the right to use the land for 10 years (the leaseback), with annual payments of $120,000 payable in arrears. Seller's incremental borrowing rate is 6 percent. The leaseback is classified as an operating lease.

Assuming that the criteria to qualify the transfer as a sale are met, prepare the journal entry.

• Answer •

(1) At the commencement date

Accounts	DR	CR
Cash	2,000,000	
Land		1,000,000
Gain on underlying asset sale		400,000
Financing liability		600,000

Seller recognizes a gain of $400,000 ($1.4 million − $1 million) on the sale of the land. The amount of the excess sale price of $600,000 ($2 million − $1.4 million) is recognized as additional financing from Buyer to Seller

Accounts	DR	CR
Right−of−use asset	283,210	
Lease liability		283,210

[EXCEL] 함수선택 PV

Rate = 6%, Nper =10, PMT = 120,000

PV = −883,210

[EXCEL] 함수선택 PMT

Rate = 6%, Nper =10, PV = −600,000

PMT= 81,521

The amount of $81,521 is the amount of each $120,000 annual payment that must be attributed to repayment of the principal of the financial liability

[EXCEL] 함수선택 PV

Rate = 6%, Nper =10, PMT = 38,479

PV = −283,210

Seller recognizes a lease liability for the leaseback at the present value of the portion of the 10 contractual leaseback payments attributable to the lease of $38,479 (= $120,000 − $81,521)

(2) At the end of Year 1

Accounts	DR	CR
Lease liability	*21,486	
Right−of−use asset		21,486
Lease expense	38,479	
Cash		38,479

* 38,479 − 283,210 × 6% = 21,486

Accounts	DR	CR
Financing liability	45,521	
Interest expense	*36,000	
Cash		81,521

* 600,000 × 6% = 36,000

the balance of the financial obligation is $554,479 (= $600,000 − $45,521)

Example-6

An entity (Seller) sells an asset to an unrelated entity (Buyer) for cash of $2 million. Immediately before the transaction, the asset has a carrying amount of $1.8 million and has a remaining useful life of 21 years.

At the same time, Seller enters into a contract with Buyer for the right to use the asset for 8 years with annual payments of $200,000 payable at the end of each year and no renewal options. Seller's incremental borrowing rate at the date of the transaction is 4 percent. The contract includes an option to repurchase the asset at the end of Year 5 for $800,000.

Seller imputes an interest rate of 4.23 percent to ensure that the carrying amount of the asset will not exceed the financial liability at the point in time the repurchase option expires.

Prepare the journal entry for seller and buyer.

• Answer •

(1) 판매자(the seller–lessee)

1) At the commencement date

The exercise price of the repurchase option is fixed and, therefore, is not the fair value of the asset on the exercise date of the option. Consequently, the repurchase option precludes accounting for the transfer of the asset as a sale.

Accounts	DR	CR
Cash	2,000,000	
Financing liability		2,000,000

2) At the end of Year 1

Accounts	DR	CR
Financing liability	115,400	
Interest expense	*84,600	
Cash		200,000

* $2,000,000 \times 4.23\% = 84,600$

Accounts	DR	CR
Depreciation expense	*85,714	
Accumulated depreciation		85,714

* 1,800,000 / 21 years = 85,714

(2) 구매자(the buyer-lessor)

1) At the commencement date

Accounts	DR	CR
Receivables	2,000,000	
Cash		2,000,000

2) At the end of Year 1

Accounts	DR	CR
Cash	200,000	
Interest revenue		*80,000
Receivables		120,000

* 2,000,000 × 4% = 80,000

04 Tasked-Based Simulation

[Q 4-1] Lessor accounting

Lessor leases a building to Lessee on January 1, 20X1.
The following facts pertain to the lease agreement.

1. The lease term is 10 years with equal annual rental payments of $3,449 at the end of each year.
2. Ownership does not transfer at the end of the lease term, there is no bargain purchase option, and the asset is not of a specialized nature.
3. The building has a fair value of $34,000, a book value to Lessor of $22,000, and a useful life of 15 years.
4. At the end of the lease term, Lessor and Lessee expect the residual value of the building to be $12,000, and this amount is guaranteed by Money, Inc., a third party.
5. Lessor wants to earn a 5% return on the lease, and collectibility of the payments is probable.

• Instructions •

(1) Describe the nature of this lease to both Lessor and Lessee,
(2) Assume the present value of lease payments and third-party guarantee is $34,000 and the rate of return to amortize the net lease receivable to zero is 13.24%. Prepare the amortization schedules Lessor would use to amortize the net lease receivable to zero.
(3) Prepare the journal entries to record the entries for Lessor for 20X1 and 20X2.
(4) Suppose the leased asset had a shorter economic life of 8 years, the lease agreement was only for 5 years, and the residual value of $12,000 guaranteed by Money, Inc. remained the same. Would the rate of return required to amortize the net lease receivable to zero increase, decrease, or stay the same?
(5) Suppose, instead of Money, Inc., Lessee guarantees the residual value itself. How would this affect the classification of this lease agreement for both Lessor and Lessee?

[Q 4-2] Sales-Type Lease

General Electric manufactures an X-ray machine with an estimated life of 12 years and leases it to National Medical Center for a period of 10 years. The normal selling price of the machine is $495,678, and its guaranteed residual value at the end of the non-cancelable lease term is estimated to be $15,000.

The hospital will pay rents of $60,000 at the beginning of each year. General Electric incurred costs of $300,000 in manufacturing the machine and $14,000 in legal fees directly related to the signing of the lease. General Electric has determined that the collectibility of the lease payments is probable and that the implicit interest rate is 5%.

• Instructions •

(1) Discuss the nature of this lease in relation to the lessor and compute the amount of each of the following items.
  1. Lease receivable at commencement of the lease.
  2. Sales price.
  3. Cost of sales.
(2) Prepare a 10—year lease amortization schedule for General Electric, the lessor.
(3) Prepare all of the lessor's journal entries for the first year.

[Q 4-3] Sales-Type Lease

Panasonic Company manufactures a check-in kiosk with an estimated economic life of 12 years and leases it to National Airlines for a period of 10 years. The normal selling price of the equipment is $299,140, and its unguaranteed residual value at the end of the lease term is estimated to be $20,000. National will pay annual payments of $40,000 at the beginning of each year.

Panasonic incurred costs of $180,000 in manufacturing the equipment and $4,000 in sales commissions in closing the case. Panasonic has determined that the collectibility of the lease payments is probable and that the implicit interest rate is 8%.

• Instructions •

(1) Discuss the nature of this lease in relation to the lessor and compute the amount of each of the following items.

　1. Lease receivable.

　2. Sales price.

　3. Cost of goods sold.

(2) Prepare a 10–year lease amortization schedule for Panasonic, the lessor.

(3) Prepare all of the lessor's journal entries for the first year.

[Q 4-4] Residual Values

Nestle Dairy leases its milking equipment from Morgan Finance Company under the following lease terms.

1. The lease term is 10 years, non-cancelable, and requires equal rental payments of $30,300 due at the beginning of each year starting January 1, 20X1.
2. The equipment has a fair value at the commencement of the lease (January 1, 20X1) of $242,741 and a cost of $180,000 on Morgan Finance's books. It also has an estimated economic life of 15 years and an expected residual value of $45,000, though Nestle Dairy has guaranteed a residual value of $50,000 to Morgan Finance.
3. The lease contains no renewal options, and the equipment reverts to Morgan Finance upon termination of the lease. The equipment is not of a specialized use.
4. Nestle Dairy's incremental borrowing rate is 8% per year. The implicit rate is also 8%.
5. Nestle Dairy depreciates similar equipment that it owns on a straight-line basis.
6. Collectibility of the payments is probable.

• Instructions •

(1) Evaluate the criteria for classification of the lease, and describe the nature of the lease. In general, discuss how the lessee and lessor should account for the lease transaction.

(2) Prepare the journal entries for the lessee and lessor at January 1, 20X1, and December 31, 20X2.

(3) What would have been the amount of the initial lease liability recorded by the lessee upon the commencement of the lease if:
  1. The residual value of $50,000 had been guaranteed by a third party, not the lessee?
  2. The residual value of $50,000 had not been guaranteed at all?

(4) On the lessor's books, what would be the amount recorded as the lease receivable at the commencement of the lease, assuming:
  1. The residual value of $50,000 had been guaranteed by a third party?
  2. The residual value of $50,000 had not been guaranteed at all?

[Q 4-5] Sale-Leaseback

Assume that on January 1, 20X1, Burger King sells a computer system to Morgan Fi - nance Co. for $680,000 and immediately leases back the computer system. The relevant information is as follows.

1. The computer was carried on Burger King's books at a value of $600,000.
2. The term of the non-cancelable lease is 3 years; title will not transfer to Burger King and the expected residual value at the end of the lease is $450,000, all of which is un-guaranteed.
3. The lease agreement requires equal rental payments of $115,970 at the beginning of each year.
4. The incremental borrowing rate for Burger King is 8%. Burger King is aware that Morgan Finance set the annual rental to ensure a rate of return of 8%.
5. The computer has a fair value of $680,000 on January 1, 20X1, and an estimated economic life of 10 years.

• Instructions •

Prepare the journal entries for both the lessee and the lessor for 20X1 to record the sale and leaseback agreement.

[Q 4-6] Lessee-Lessor Entries

Lessor and Lessee enter into an agreement that requires Lessor to build three die-sel-electric engines to Lessee's specifications. Upon completion of the engines, Lessee has agreed to lease them for a period of 10 years and to assume all costs and risks of ownership. The lease is non-cancelable, becomes effective on January 1, 20X1, and re-quires annual rental payments of $384,532 each January 1, starting January 1, 20X1. Lessee's incremental borrowing rate is 8%. The implicit interest rate used by Lessor and known to Winston is 6%. The total cost of building the three engines is $2,600,000. The economic life of the engines is estimated to be 10 years, with residual value set at zero. Lessee depreciates similar equipment on a straight-line basis. At the end of the lease, Lessee assumes title to the engines. Collectibility of the lease payments is proba- ble.

• Instructions •

(1) Discuss the nature of this lease transaction from the viewpoints of both lessee and lessor.
(2) Prepare the journal entry or entries to record the transaction on January 1, 20X1, on the books of Lessee.
(3) Prepare the journal entry or entries to record the transaction on January 1, 20X1, on the books of Lessor.
(4) Prepare the journal entries for both the lessee and lessor to record the first rental payment on January 1, 20X1.

Accounting and Reporting **For the** **US CPA** **E**xam

Accounting and Reporting

Chapter

05

Derivatives and Hedge Accounting

Chapter 05 Derivatives and Hedge Accounting

01　Derivatives

1　파생상품의 종류

일반적인 파생상품은 선도계약, 선물, 옵션 및 스왑이 있다.

(1) Forward contract (선도계약)

A forward is an agreement between two counter parties—a buyer and seller.

The buyer agrees to buy an underlying asset from the other party (the seller).

미래 일정 시점에 약정된 가격에 의해 계약상의 특정 대상을 사거나 팔기로 계약 당사자 간에 합의한 거래.

※ 기초자산 (underlying asset)

1) 상품 : 원유, 금, 은, 농산물, 축산물 등

2) 주가지수 또는 개별 주식

3) 통화 (환율)

4) 채권 (금리)

(2) Futures (선물)

수량 · 규격 · 품질 등이 표준화되어 있는 특정 대상에 대하여 현재 시점에서 결정된 가격에 의해 미래 일정 시점에 인도 · 인수할 것을 약정한 계약으로서 조직화된 시장에서 정해진 방법으로 거래되는 것

(3) Option

A contract that gives one party (the option holder) the right, but not the obligation to perform a specified transaction with another party (the option issuer or option writer) according to specified terms.

계약 당사자 간에 정하는 바에 따라 일정한 기간 내에 미리 정해진 가격으로 외화나 유가 증권 등을 사거나 팔 수 있는 권리에 대한 계약

(4) Swap

특정 기간 동안에 발생하는 일정한 현금흐름을 다른 현금흐름과 교환하는 선도거래

	Forward	Futures	Option	Swap
장내거래		✓	✓	
장외거래	✓		✓	✓

☞ 장외거래는 채무불이행위험이 발생하며, 장내거래는 채무불이행위험이 없다.

2 파생상품의 정의 (ASC 815)

(1) 파생상품의 정의

A derivative instrument is a financial instrument or other contract with all of the following characteristics.

파생상품은 다음의 요건을 모두 충족하는 금융상품 또는 유사한 계약을 말한다.

1) Underlying, notional amount, payment provision.

The contract has both of the following terms.

a) One or more underlyings

b) One or more notional amounts or payment provisions or both.

기초변수 및 계약단위의 수량(또는 지급규정)이 있어야 한다.

2) Initial net investment

The contract requires no initial net investment or an initial net investment that is smaller than would be required for other types of contracts that would be expected to have a similar response to changes in market factors.

최초 계약시 순투자금액을 필요로 하지 않거나 시장가격변동에 유사한 영향을 받는 다른 유형의 거래보다 적은 순투자금액을 필요로 해야 한다.

3) Net settlement

The contract can be settled net.

차액결제가 가능해야 한다.

(2) Underlying (기초변수)

파생상품의 가치를 결정하는 기초변수의 사례는 다음과 같다.

1) A security price or security price index

2) A commodity price

3) An interest rate

4) A credit rating

5) An exchange rate

6) A climatic or geological condition

(3) Notional amount (계약단위의 수량)

A notional amount is a number of currency units, shares, bushels, pounds, or other units specified in the contract.

3 파생상품의 기초

(1) Forward contract or futures

1) Long position (선물매수)

An agreement to buy an underlying asset from the other party. A long forward or futures investor profits when the underlying asset increases in price.

☞ 선물매수 손익 $y = x - a$ (x : 기초자산의 시장가격, a : 행사가격)

➌ 1년 후에 주식 1주를 \$100에 매입하기로 계약하면 1년 후의 주가에 따라 계약서의 손익은 다음과 같다.

주가	85	90	95	100	105	110	115
P/L	−15	−10	−5	0	5	10	15

2) Short position (선물매도)

1년 후에 주식 1주를 $100에 매도하기로 계약하면 1년 후의 주가에 따라 계약서의 손익은 다음과 같다.

주가	85	90	95	100	105	110	115
P/L	15	10	5	0	−5	−10	−15

선물매도 손익 $y = a - x$ (x : 기초자산의 가격, a : 행사가격)

(2) Option

1) Call option (콜옵션)

A call option is an agreement that gives the option buyer the right to buy the underlying asset at a specified price within a specific time period. A call buyer profits when the underlying asset increases in price.

콜옵션 투자자 만기손익 $y = \max[x - a, 0]$

x : 기초자산의 시장가격, a : 옵션의 행사가격

※ 콜옵션 발행자의 손익 + 콜옵션 투자자의 손익 = 0

ex 1년 후에 주식 1주를 $100에 매입할 수 있는 권리를 가지고 있으면 1년 후의 주가에 따라 계약서의 손익은 다음과 같다.

주가	85	90	95	100	105	110	115
P/L	0	0	0	0	5	10	15

2) Put option (풋옵션)

A put option is an agreement that gives the option buyer the right to sell the underlying asset at a specified price within a specific time period. A put buyer profits when the underlying asset decreases in price.

풋옵션 투자자 만기손익 $y = \max[a - x, 0]$

x : 기초자산의 시장가격, a : 옵션의 행사가격

※ 풋옵션 발행자의 손익 + 풋옵션 투자자의 손익 = 0

🌑 1년 후에 주식 1주를 $100에 매도할 수 있는 권리를 가지고 있으면 1년 후의 주가에 따라 계약서의 손익은 다음과 같다.

주가	85	90	95	100	105	110	115
P/L	15	10	5	0	0	0	0

3) European option (유럽형 옵션)

can only be exercised on the maturity date.

특정한 만기에만 권리를 행사할 수 있는 옵션

4) American option (미국형 옵션)

can be exercised anytime before the maturity date.

특정한 만기 이전에 언제라도 자유롭게 권리행사가 가능한 옵션

(3) Moneyness

옵션은 보유자가 유리한 경우에만 행사하기 때문에 다음과 같이 행사가능 구간을 구별한다.

	call option	put option
In-the-money (내가격)	x 〉 a	x 〈 a
At-the-money (등가격)	x = a	x = a
Out-of-the-money (외가격)	x 〈 a	x 〉 a

x : 기초자산의 시장가격, a : 옵션의 행사가격

내가격(In-the-money)은 옵션의 행사가격과 기초자산의 시장가격과의 관계를 나타내는 말로서 콜옵션은 기초자산의 시장가격이 옵션의 행사가격보다 높은 경우, 풋 옵션은 기초자산의 시장가격이 옵션의 행사가격보다 낮은 경우를 지칭한다.

(4) Option value

옵션의 가치를 옵션가격 또는 프리미엄이라 하며 옵션의 가치는 다음과 같이 내재가치와 시간가치로 구성이 된다.

Option value = Intrinsic value + Time value

1) Intrinsic value (내재가치)

현재 주가와 행사가격과의 차이를 말한다. 예를 들면 현재주가가 $107인 경우 행사가격이 $100인 콜옵션의 내재가치는 $7이지만 행사가격이 $100인 풋옵션의 내재가치는 $0이다.

2) Time value (시간가치)

옵션의 공정가치와 내재가치와의 차이를 의미한다. 예를 들면 현재주가가 $107인 경우 행사가격이 $100인 콜옵션의 현재가격이 $10라면 시간가치는 $3(=10-7)이며 행사가격이 $100인 풋옵션의 현재가격이 $3라면 시간가치는 $3(=3-0)이다.

(5) Swap

An agreement between two or more parties to exchange cash flows over a period in the future. (A type of forward contract)

1) Interest Rate Swap (IRS, 금리스왑)

일정 기간 동안 두 당사자가 고정금리이자(fixed interest)와 변동금리이자(floating interest)를 교환하는 계약으로 원금은 교환하지 않고 이자만 교환한다.

2) Currency Swap (CS, 통화스왑)

일정 기간 동안 두 당사자가 서로 다른 통화의 이자와 원금을 교환하는 계약

1년 후에 원금 $10,000를 기준으로 고정금리 5%를 지급하고 LIBOR로 이자를 수취하는 이자율 스왑계약을 체결한 경우 1년 후의 LIBOR에 따라 계약서의 손익은 다음과 같다.

LIBOR	3.5%	4%	4.5%	5%	5.5%	6%	6.5%
P/L	-150	-100	-50	0	+50	+100	+150

✓ LIBOR [London inter-bank offered rate]

런던의 금융시장에 있는 은행 중에서도 유로달러를 취급하는 가장 신용도가 있는 국제은행들이 대규모 대부시 서로 부과하는 이자율

02 Hedging accounting

1 파생상품의 회계처리

(1) Classification

파생상품은 보유목적에 따라 다음과 같이 분류한다.

> 1) Non-hedge derivatives
> 2) Fair value hedge derivatives
> 3) Cash flow hedge derivatives
> 4) Hedge of a net investment in a foreign operation

(2) Measurement

파생상품은 재무제표에 자산 및 부채로 인식하여 공정가치로 측정하며 공정가치의 변동에
의한 평가손익은 파생상품의 분류에 따라 보고방법을 달리한다.

(3) Criteria to qualify for hedge accounting

다음 요건을 모두 충족하여야 위험회피회계를 적용할 수 있다.

1) Formal designation and documentation at hedge inception

위험회피수단을 최초 지정하는 시점에 위험회피 종류, 위험관리의 목적, 위험회피전략을
공식적으로 문서화하여야 한다.

2) Eligibility of hedged items and transactions

위험회피대상이 적격요건을 만족하여야 한다.

3) Eligibility of hedging instruments

위험회피수단이 적격요건을 만족하여야 한다.

4) Hedge effectiveness

위험회피수단으로 최초 지정된 이후에 높은 위험회피효과를 기대할 수 있어야 한다.

2 Fair Value Hedge

(1) Definition

> A hedge of the exposure to changes in the fair value of a recognized asset or liability, or of an unrecognized firm commitment, that are attributable to a particular risk

공정가치위험회피는 특정위험으로 인한 자산, 부채 및 확정계약의 공정가치변동위험을 상계하기 위하여 파생상품 등을 이용하는 것이다.

(2) An unrecognized firm commitment

제3자간에 이루어진 이행의 법적 강제력을 가지는 약정으로서 거래수량, 거래가격, 거래시기 및 거래이행을 강제하기에 충분한 거래불이행시의 불이익 등이 구체적으로 포함되는 약정

(3) Changes in fair value

공정가치위험회피의 조건을 충족하는 경우에는, 다음과 같이 회계처리한다.

> Gain/loss on the hedging instrument ⟹ net income

위험회피수단의 평가손익을 해당 회계연도에 당기손익으로 처리한다.

> Gain/loss on the hedged item ⟹ net income

특정위험으로 인한 위험회피대상항목의 평가손익은 전액을 해당 회계연도에 당기손익으로 처리한다. 위험회피대상항목이 매도가능금융자산인 경우에도 회피대상위험으로 인한 손익은 당기손익으로 인식한다.

Example-1

On 11/1/20X1, KIMCPA purchased one share of MS for $500 as an FVTNI investment and purchased an at-the-money put option for $30. The put option gives KIMCPA the rights to sell one share of MS at $500 and option expires on 1/31/20X2. KIMCPA designates the hedge as fair value hedge. The market value of the stock and time value of put option follow:

	11/1/20X1	12/31/20X1	1/31/20X2
Investment-FVTNI	500	430	400
Put option-time value	30	10	0

11/1/20X1	Investment-FVTNI	500	
	Put option (Asset)	30	
	Cash		530
12/31/20X1	Unrealized loss on FVTNI	70	
	Investment-FVTNI		70
	Put option (Asset)	50*	
	Unrealized gain on put option		50
1/31/20X2	Unrealized loss on FVTNI	30	
	Investment-FVTNI		30
	Put option (Asset)	20	
	Unrealized gain on put option		20
Settlement	Cash	100	
	Put option (Asset)		100

* 풋옵션의 내재가치는 70(=500−430)이 증가하였지만 시간가치는 20이 감소하였기 때문에 평가이익은 50이다.

Example-2

On 7/1/20X1, KIMCPA agreed to take delivery of 100,000 gallons of fuels in one year at $15 per gallon. In order to hedge its firm commitment, KIMCPA entered into forward contract on 7/1/20X1, to sell 100,000 gallons at $15 per gallon on 7/1/20X2. KIMCPA designates the hedge as fair value hedge. The market price of fuel per gallon follows:

	7/1/20X1	12/31/20X1	7/1/20X2
fuel	15	13	12

7/1/20X1	No entry		
12/31/20X1	Unrealized loss on purchase commitment	200,000	
	Firm purchase commitment (Liability)		200,000
	Forward contract (Asset)	200,000	
	Unrealized gain on forward contract		200,000
7/1/20X2	Unrealized loss on purchase commitment	100,000	
	Firm purchase commitment (Liability)		100,000
	Forward contract (Asset)	100,000	
	Unrealized gain on forward contract		100,000
Settlement	Cash	300,000	
	Forward contract(Asset)		300,000
	Inventory	1,200,000	
	Firm purchase commitment (Liability)	300,000	
	Cash		1,500,000

Example-3

On 12/1/20X1, KIMCPA purchased goods from foreign company. The purchase in the amount of 1,000 EUR is to paid for on 2/1/20X2 in EUR. On that date, KIMCPA entered into forward contract to purchase 1,000 EUR. The exchange rates for EUR are as follows:

USD per EUR	12/1/20X1	12/31/20X1	2/1/20X2
spot rate	1.20	1.30	1.35
30-day forward	1.21	1.31	1.36
60-day forward	1.22	1.32	1.37

12/1/20X1	Inventory	1,200	
	Account payable		1,200
12/31/20X1	Exchange loss	100	
	Account payable		100
	Forward contract (Asset)	90	
	Exchange gain on forward contract		90*
2/1/20X2	Exchange loss	50	
	Account payable		50
	Forward contract (Asset)	40	
	Exchange gain on forward contract		40**
Settlement	Cash	130	
	Forward contract(Asset)		130
	Account payable	1,350	
	Cash		1,350

* 1,000 EUR × (1.31-1.22) = $90
** 1,000 EUR × (1.35-1.31) = $40

Example-4

On 12/1/20X1, KIMCPA sold goods to foreign company. The sale in the amount of 1,000 EUR is to paid for on 2/1/20X2 in EUR. On that date, KIMCPA entered into forward contract to sell 1,000 EUR. The exchange rates for EUR are as follows:

USD per EUR	12/1/20X1	12/31/20X1	2/1/20X2
spot rate	1.20	1.10	1.05
30-day forward	1.19	1.09	1.04
60-day forward	1.18	1.08	1.03

12/1/20X1	Account receivable	1,200	
	Sales revenue		1,200
12/31/20X1	Exchange loss	100	
	Account receivable		100
	Forward contract(Asset)	90	
	Exchange gain on forward contract		90*
2/1/20X2	Exchange loss	50	
	Account receivable		50
	Forward contract(Asset)	40	
	Exchange gain on forward contract		40**
Settlement	Cash	130	
	Forward contract(Asset)		130
	Cash	1,050	
	Account receivable		1,050

* 1,000 EUR × (1.18-1.09) = $90

** 1,000 EUR × (1.09-1.05) = $40

3 Cash Flow Hedge

(1) Definition

> A hedge of the exposure to variability in the cash flows of a recognized asset or liability, or of a forecasted transaction, that is attributable to a particular risk.

인식된 자산이나 부채 또는 발생가능성이 매우 높은 예상거래의 현금흐름 변동에 대한 위험회피이다. 인식된 부채에서 발생한 미래현금흐름의 변동의 예로는 변동금리부 채무상품에서 발생한 미래이자지급액을 들 수 있다.

(2) Changes in fair value

> Gain/loss on the hedging instrument
> the effective portion of the gain or loss ⇒ other comprehensive income
> the ineffective portion of the gain or loss ⇒ net income

The effective portion of the gain or loss on a derivative instrument designated as a cash flow hedge is reported in other comprehensive income, and the ineffective portion is reported in earnings.

위험회피수단의 손익 중 위험회피에 효과적인 부분은 기타포괄손익으로 인식하며, 비효과적인 부분은 당기손익으로 인식하며 현금흐름 위험회피대상항목의 평가손익은 인식하지 않는다.

If the effectiveness of a hedging relationship with an option is assessed based on changes in the option's intrinsic value, the changes in the option's time value would be recognized in earnings.

옵션의 내재가치 변동금액은 OCI에 보고하며, 시간가치 변동금액은 NI에 보고한다.

(3) Reclassifications from AOCI into net income

> Amounts in accumulated other comprehensive income shall be reclassified into earnings in the same periods during which the hedged **forecasted transaction affects earnings**. (such as in the periods that depreciation expense, interest expense, or cost of sales is recognized).

기타포괄손익으로 인식된 관련 손익은 위험회피대상인 예상현금흐름이 당기손익에 영향을 미치는 회계기간에 재분류조정으로 자본에서 당기손익으로 재분류한다.

(예: 예상매출이 발생한 때, 감가상각비나 매출원가가 인식되는 기간)

(4) Accumulated other comprehensive income

AOCI는 다음 중 작은 금액으로 보고한다.

1) 위험회피수단의 손익누계액

2) 위험회피대상항목의 미래예상현금흐름의 공정가치 변동누계액

(5) Hedge accounting for interest rate swap

1) Fair value hedge

이자율 변동으로 인한 고정금리부 채무상품의 공정가치 변동위험을 회피하는 경우

✔ Fixed- rate borrowing + IRS as a floating-rate payer

✔ Fixed- rate lending + IRS as a fixed-rate payer

2) Cash flow hedge

변동금리조건 채무상품을 고정금리조건 채무상품으로 전환하기 위하여(위험회피대상 미래현금흐름이 미래이자지급액인 미래 거래의 위험회피) 스왑을 사용하는 경우

✔ Floating -rate borrowing + IRS as a fixed -rate payer

✔ Floating -rate lending + IRS as a floating -rate payer

Example-5

On 11/1/20X1, an airline entered into forward contract to purchase 100,000 gallons at $15 per gallon on 2/1/20X2. The company designates the hedge as cash flow hedge. The market price of fuel per gallon follows:

	11/1/20X1	12/31/20X1	2/1/20X2
fuel	15	17	18

11/1/20X1	No entry		
12/31/20X1	Forward contract(Asset)	200,000	
	Other comprehensive income		200,000
2/1/20X2	Forward contract(Asset)	100,000	
	Other comprehensive income		100,000
Settlement	Cash	300,000	
	Forward contract(Asset)		300,000
	Inventory	1,800,000	
	Cash		1,800,000
When the fuel is consumed	Other comprehensive income	300,000	
	COGS		300,000
	COGS	1,800,000	
	Inventory		1,800,000

Example-6

On 11/1/20X1, an airline purchased an at-the-money call option for $9,000 to purchase 100,000 gallons at $15 per gallon on 2/1/20X2. The company designates the hedge as cash flow hedge and the effectiveness of a hedging relationship with an option is assessed based on changes in the option's intrinsic value. The market price of fuel and time value of the call option follow:

	11/1/20X1	12/31/20X1	2/1/20X2
fuel	15	17	18
call option-time value	9,000	3,000	0

11/1/20X1	Call option(Asset)	9,000	
	Cash		9,000
12/31/20X1	Call option(Asset)	194,000	
	Loss on call option	6,000	
	Other comprehensive income		200,000
2/1/20X2	Call option(Asset)	97,000	
	Loss on call option	3,000	
	Other comprehensive income		100,000
Settlement	Cash	300,000	
	Call option(Asset)		300,000
	Inventory	1,800,000	
	Cash		1,800,000
When the fuel is consumed	Other comprehensive income	300,000	
	COGS		300,000
	COGS	1,800,000	
	Inventory		1,800,000

4 Non-hedge derivatives

단기매매목적이거나 위험회피요건을 충족하지 못한 경우에 적용되며 공정가치의 변동으로 인한 평가손익은 당기손익에 보고한다.

Example-7

On 11/1/20X1, AIFA purchased an at-the-money call option for $9,000 to purchase 100,000 gallons at $15 per gallon on 2/1/20X2. AIFA designates the derivatives as speculation. The market price of fuel and time value of the call option follow:

	11/1/20X1	12/31/20X1	2/1/20X2
fuel	15	17	18
call option—time value	9,000	3,000	0

11/1/20X1	Call option(Asset)	9,000	
	Cash		9,000
12/31/20X1	Call option(Asset)	194,000	
	Gain on call option		194,000
2/1/20X2	Call option(Asset)	97,000	
	Gain on call option		97,000
Settlement	Cash	300,000	
	Call option(Asset)		300,000

Example-8

On 11/1/20X1, AIFA issued an at-the-money call option for $9,000 to purchase 100,000 gallons at $15 per gallon on 2/1/20X2. AIFA designates the derivatives as speculation. The market price of fuel and time value of the call option follow:

	11/1/20X1	12/31/20X1	2/1/20X2
fuel	15	17	18
call option-time value	9,000	3,000	0

11/1/20X1	Cash	9,000	
	Call option(Liability)		9,000
12/31/20X1	Loss on call option	194,000	
	Call option(Liability)		194,000
2/1/20X2	Loss on call option	97,000	
	Call option(Liability)		97,000
Settlement	Call option(Liability)	300,000	
	Cash		300,000

Example-9

On 11/1/20X1, AIFA purchased an at-the-money call option for $9,000 to purchase 100,000 gallons at $15 per gallon on 2/1/20X2. AIFA designates the derivatives as speculation. The market price of fuel and time value of the call option follow:

	11/1/20X1	12/31/20X1	2/1/20X2
fuel	15	13	14
call option–time value	9,000	3,000	0

11/1/20X1	Call option(Asset)	9,000	
	Cash		9,000
12/31/20X1	Loss on call option	6,000	
	Call option(Asset)		6,000
2/1/20X2	Loss on call option	3,000	
	Call option(Asset)		3,000
Settlement	No entry		

Example-10

On 11/1/20X1, AIFA issued an at-the-money call option for $9,000 to purchase 100,000 gallons at $15 per gallon on 2/1/20X2. AIFA designates the derivatives as speculation. The market price of fuel and time value of the call option follow:

	11/1/20X1	12/31/20X1	2/1/20X2
fuel	15	13	14
call option—time value	9,000	3,000	0

11/1/20X1	Cash	9,000	
	Call option(Liability)		9,000
12/31/20X1	Call option(Liability)	6,000	
	Gain on call option		6,000
2/1/20X2	Call option(Liability)	3,000	
	Gain on call option		3,000
Settlement	No entry		

5 A hedge of a net investment in a foreign operation

> The gain or loss on the hedging derivative or non—derivative instrument in a hedge of a net investment in a foreign operation shall be reported in other comprehensive income as part of the cumulative translation adjustment to the extent it is effective as a hedge.

해외사업장순투자의 위험회피는 위험회피수단의 손익 중 위험회피에 효과적인 부분은 기타포괄손익으로 인식하며 비효과적인 부분은 당기손익으로 인식한다. 위험회피수단의 손익 중 위험회피에 효과적이어서 기타포괄손익으로 인식한 부분은 향후 해외사업장의 처분시점에 재분류조정으로 자본에서 당기손익으로 재분류한다.

6 Statement of cash flow

파생상품계약에서 식별가능한 거래에 대하여 위험회피회계를 적용하는 경우, 그 계약과 관련된 현금흐름은 위험회피대상 거래의 현금흐름과 동일하게 분류한다.

7 Disclosures

파생상품에 대한 주석사항은 그 거래목적에 따라 구분하여 공시하며 상세한 내용은 실무적이고 전문적인 내용이기 때문에 수험목적으로는 생략한다.

Example-11

The treasurer of Apple Co. has read on the Internet that the stock price of Tesla is about to take off. In order to profit from this potential development, Apple Co. purchased a call option on Tesla common shares on July 7, 20X1, for $240. The call option is for 200 shares (notional value), and the strike price is $70. (The market price of a share of Tesla stock on that date is $70.) The option expires on January 31, 20X2. The following data are available with respect to the call option.

Date	Market price of Tesla Shares	Time Value of Call Option
September 30, 20X1	$77 per share	$180
December 31, 20X1	75 per share	65
January 31, 20X2	76 per share	0

What amount of gain or loss from these investments should Apple report in its 20X1 and 20X2 net income?

Solution

Underlying : $70/share

Notional amount : 200 shares of Tesla stock

Initial net investment : $240

Settlement amount : $70 × 200 shares = $14,000

12/31/20X1 FV of call option = 200 shares × ($75 − $70) + $65 = $1,065

1/4/20X2 FV of call option = 200 shares × ($76 − $70) = $200

Unrealized gain in 20X1 = 1,065 − 240 = $825

Realized loss in 20X2 = 200 − 1,065 = −$865

Net settlement = $200

The option writer would pay Apple $200 to settlement the contract.

Example-12 IRS designated as a Fair Value Hedge

On January 1, Year 1, East Co. issued a $1,000,000 three-year, 8%, fixed-rate note payable. The interest is due annually on December 31. The principal is due at maturity on December 31, Year 3.

East Co. faces the risk that changes in the benchmark interest rate will cause unfavorable changes in the fair value of the note payable.

To manage the risk that changes in the benchmark interest rate will cause unfavorable changes in the fair value of the note payable, East Co. concurrently entered into an interest rate swap and designated it as a fair value hedge. As the hedge terms are in line with the terms of the hedged item (note payable), the hedge is expected to be highly effective.

⟨Interest rate swap terms⟩

Date of Designation: January 1, Year 1
Term: 3 years
Counter party: West Co.

⟨Swap Arrangement⟩

East Co. agrees to make to West Co. a series of future payments equal to a variable interest rate of SOFR + 1% on a principal amount of $1,000,000.

In exchange, West Co. agreed to make to East Co. a series of future payments equal to a fixed interest rate of 8% on the principal amount of $1,000,000.

The swap settlements occur concurrently with the interest payment dates annually on December 31.

Assume the following at inception on January 1, Year 1, and the first settlement date on December 31, Year 1.

Date	SOFR	Swap Fair Value	Fair Value of N/P
January 1, Year 1	7%	$0	$1,000,000
December 31, Year 1	8.5%	$150,000	$850,000

Prepare the journal entries East Co. must record on January 1, Year 1 and on December 31, Year 1.

Solution

Underlying: East.: SOFR + 1%; West.: 8%

SOFR at inception: 7%

Notional amount: $1,000,000

Initial net investment: $0 (no cost to enter into the swap contract)

Initial fair value of swap: $0

Date	Hedged items	Hedging instruments
1/1	Dr) Cash 1,000,000 Cr) Notes payable 1,000,000	No entry

12/31	Dr) Notes payable 150,000
	   Cr) Interest expense 150,000
		Dr) Interest expense 150,000
		   Cr) Swap(liability) 150,000

	Dr) Interest expense 80,000
	   Cr) Cash 80,000
		Dr) Interest expense 15,000*
		   Cr) Cash 15,000

*net settlement $= (8\% - (\text{SOFR} + 1\%)) \times \$1,000,000$

$\qquad\qquad\qquad = (8\% - (8.5\% + 1\%)) \times \$1,000,000 = -\$15,000$

Example-13 IRS designated as a Cash Flow Hedge

On January 1, Year 1, East Co. issued a $1,000,000 three-year, variable-rate note payable. The variable rate is based on SOFR+1% and interest payment dates and rate resets occur annually. The principal is due at maturity on December 31, Year 3.

East Co. faces the risk that the variable rate of SOFR + 1% could rise causing an increase in the required interest-related cash outflows.

To manage the risk that interest rates may increase and cause variability in the cash flows related to interest payments, East Co. concurrently entered into an interest rate swap and designated it as a cash flow hedge. As the hedge terms are in line with the terms of the hedged item (note payable), the hedge is expected to be highly effective.

〈Interest rate swap terms〉

Date of Designation: January 1, Year 1
Term: 3 years
Counter party: West Co.

〈Swap Arrangement〉

East Co. agrees to make to West Co. a series of future payments equal to a fixed interest rate of 8% on a principal amount of $1,000,000. In exchange, West Co. agreed to make to East Co. a series of future payments equal to a floating interest rate of SOFR + 1% on the principal amount of $1,000,000. The swap settlements occur concurrently with the interest payment dates annually on December 31.

Assume the following at inception on January 1, Year 1, and the first settlement date on December 31, Year 1.

Date	SOFR	Swap Fair Value
January 1, Year 1	7%	$0
December 31, Year 1	8.5%	$150,000

Prepare the journal entries East Co. must record on January 1, Year 1 and on December 31, Year 1.

Solution

Underlying: East.: 8% ; West.: SOFR + 1%

SOFR at inception: 7%

Notional amount: $1,000,000

Initial net investment: $0 (no cost to enter into the swap contract)

Initial fair value of swap: $0

Date	Hedged items	Hedging instruments
1/1	Dr) Cash 1,000,000 Cr) Notes payable 1,000,000	No entry
12/31	No entry	Dr) Swap(asset) 150,000 Cr) OCI 150,000

	Dr) Interest expense 95,000
	  Cr) Cash 95,000
		Dr) OCI 15,000
		  Cr) Interest expense 15,000
		Dr) Cash 15,000*
		  Cr) Swap(asset) 15,000

*net settlement = ((SOFR+1%) − 8%) × $1,000,000

= ((8.5% + 1%) − 8%) × $1,000,000 = +$15,000

03 **Tasked-Based Simulation**

[Q 5-1] Call option

On 7/1/20X1, KIMCPA expected that steel prices may increase over the next one year and purchased call option to protect itself against that risk.

<Call option>
- Contract date : 7/1/20X1
- Maturity date : 7/1/20X2
- Exercise price : $500 per ton
- Quantities : 1,000 tons

Steel prices on selected dates are as follows:

	7/1/20X1	12/31/20X1	7/1/20X2
Steel price	$500 per ton	$540 per ton	$570 per ton
Time value of call option	$20 per ton	$12 per ton	$0 per ton

· Instructions ·

1. Prepare the journal entries on KIMCPA's books to account for 20X1.
2. Prepare the journal entries on KIMCPA's books to account for 20X2.

[Q 5-2] Forward contract

Exchange rates on selected dates are as follows:

	11/1/20X1	12/31/20X1	2/1/20X2
Spot rate	1 EUR = $1.20	1 EUR = $1.10	1 EUR = $1.05
Forward rate − 90days	1 EUR = $1.23	1 EUR = $1.12	1 EUR = $1.07
Forward rate − 30days	1 EUR = $1.22	1 EUR = $1.11	1 EUR = $1.06

[Situation-1] On 11/1/20X1, KIMCPA purchased goods from foreign company. The purchase in the amount of 1,000 euros is to be paid for on 2/1/20X2 in euro.

[Situation-2] On 11/1/20X1, KIMCPA sold goods to foreign company. The sale in the amount of 1,000 euros is to be received for on 2/1/20X2 in euro.

[Situation-3] On 11/1/20X1, KIMCPA made a commitment to purchase goods of 1,000 euros from foreign company. Tile to the goods passed on December 31, 20X1 and the payment is to be made for on 2/1/20X2 in euro.

[Situation-4] On 11/1/20X1, KIMCPA entered into a 90-day forward contract to purchase 1,000 euros.

[Situation-5] On 11/1/20X1, KIMCPA entered into a 90-day forward contract to sell 1,000 euros.

[Instruction]

1. Prepare journal entries for situation 1 and situation 4
2. Prepare journal entries for situation 2 and situation 5
3. Prepare journal entries for situation 3 and situation 4

[Q 5-3] Swap

On January 1, 20X1, KIM borrows $400,000 from LEE. The five-year term note is a variable-rate one in which the 20X1 interest rate is determined to be 8 percent, the LIBOR rate at January 1, 20X1, + 2%. Subsequent years' interest rates are determined in a similar manner, with the rate set for a particular year equal to the beginning-of-the-year LIBOR rate + 2%. Interest payments are due on December 31 each year and are computed assuming annual compounding.

Also on January 1, 20X1, KIM decides to enter into a pay-fixed, receive-variable interest rate swap arrangement with SONG. KIM will pay 8 percent.

Assume that the LIBOR rate on December 31, 20X1, is 5 percent.

• Instructions •

1. Prepare the entry at December 31, 20X1, to account for this hedge as well as the December 31, 20X1, interest payment.

2. Assuming that the LIBOR rate is 5.5% on December 31, 20X2, prepare all the necessary entries to account for the interest rate swap at December 31, 20X2, including the 2012 interest payment.

[Q 5-4] Swap

On January 1, 20X1, KIM borrows $400,000 from LEE. The five-year term note is a fixed rate of 8 percent and interest payments are due on December 31 each year and are computed assuming annual compounding.

Also on January 1, 20X1, KIM decides to enter into a pay-variable, receive-fixed interest rate swap. The variable portion of the swap formula is LIBOR rate + 2%, determined at the end of the year to set the rate for the following year. The first year that the swap will be in effect is for interest payments in 20X2.

Assume that the LIBOR rate on December 31, 20X1, is 7 percent.

• Instructions •

1. Prepare the entry at December 31, 20X1, to account for this hedge as well as the December 31, 20X1, interest payment.

2. Assuming that the LIBOR rate is 6.5% on December 31, 20X2, prepare all the necessary entries to account for the interest rate swap at December 31, 20X2, including the 2012 interest payment.

[Q 5-5] Forward contract

On December 1, 20X1, KIM enters into a 90-day forward contract with a rice specu-lator to purchase 500 tons of rice at $1,000 per ton. KIM enters into this contract in order to hedge an anticipated rice purchase. The contract is to be settled net. The spot price of rice at December 1, 20X1, is $950.

On December 31, 20X1, the forward rate is $980 per ton. The contract is settled and rice is purchased on February 28, 20X2. The spot and forward rates when the contract is settled are $1,005. Assume that KIM purchases 500 tons of rice on the date of the forward contract's expiration. Assume that this contract has been documented to be an effective hedge. Also assume an appropriate interest rate is 6 percent.

• Instructions •

1. Prepare the required journal entries to account for this hedge situation and the subsequent rice purchase on:
   (1) December 1, 20X1
   (2) December 31, 20X1
   (3) The settlement date

2. Assume that the rice is subsequently sold by KIM on June 1, 20X2, for $1,200 per ton. What journal entries will KIM make on that date?

[Q 5-6] Forward contract

KIM has 100,000 units of widgets in its inventory on October 1, 20X1. KIM purchased them for $1 per unit one month ago. It hedges the value of the widgets by entering into a forward contract to sell 100,000 widgets on January 31, 20X2, for $2 each. The contract is to be settled net. Assume that a discount rate of 6 percent is reasonable.

• Instructions •

Prepare the journal entries to properly account for this hedge of an existing asset on the following dates:

1. October 1, 20X1, when the widget price is $1.50
2. December 31, 20X1, when the widget price is $2.50
3. January 31, 20X2, when the widget price is $2.30

[Multiple Choice Questions]

01. What is a characteristic of a forward?

    a. Traded on an exchange

    b. Negotiated with a counterparty

    c. Covers a stream of future payments

    d. Must be settled daily

02. What is a characteristic of a swap?

    a. Traded on an exchange

    b. Only interest rates can be the underlying

    c. Covers a stream of future payments

    d. Must be settled daily

03. What is a characteristic of a future?

    a. Gives the holder the right but not the obligation to buy or sell

    b. Negotiated with a counterparty

    c. Covers a stream of future payments

    d. Must be settled daily

04. What is a characteristic of an option?

    a. Gives the holder the right but not the obligation to buy or sell

    b. Negotiated with a counterparty

    c. Covers a stream of future payments

    d. Must be settled daily

05. Which is true about the seller of a put option?

    a. They have the right to buy the underlying

    b. They have the right to sell the underlying

    c. They have the obligation to buy the underlying

    d. They have the obligation to sell the underlying

06. Which is true about the holder of a call option?

    a. They have the right to buy the underlying

    b. They have the right to sell the underlying

    c. They have the obligation to buy the underlying

    d. They have the obligation to sell the underlying

07. Which is true about the seller of a call option?

    a. They have the right to buy the underlying

    b. They have the right to sell the underlying

    c. They have the obligation to buy the underlying

    d. They have the obligation to sell the underlying

08. Which is true about the holder of a put option?

    a. They have the right to buy the underlying

    b. They have the right to sell the underlying

    c. They have the obligation to buy the underlying

    d. They have the obligation to sell the underlying

Accounting and Reporting For the US CPA Exam

Volume
1

Accounting and Reporting

Chapter

Stock Compensation

Chapter 06 | Stock Compensation

01 Introduction

1 Share-based payment (주식기준보상)

(1) 의의

주식기준보상이란 기업이 종업원이나 다른 실체로부터 재화나 용역을 제공받고 그 대가로 지분상품을 매입할 수 있는 권리(stock option) 또는 지분상품에 기초하여 현금을 받을 수 있는 권리(SAR : stock appreciation right)를 부여하는 것이다.

(2) Share-based payment as equity (주식결제형)

기업이 재화나 용역을 제공받는 대가로 자신의 주식 또는 주식선택권을 부여하는 주식기준보상거래를 말하며 보상은 비용과 자본으로 인식한다.

(3) Share-based payment as liability (현금결제형)

기업이 재화나 용역을 제공받는 대가로 기업의 지분상품의 가격에 기초한 금액만큼 현금을 지급해야 하는 부채를 재화나 용역의 공급자에게 부담하는 주식기준보상거래를 말하며 보상은 비용과 부채로 인식한다.

2 Option value

(1) Fair value (공정가치)

주식을 기초자산으로 하는 콜옵션(매수옵션), 풋옵션(매도옵션)의 공정가치는 다음과 같이 측정된다.

- Fair value = Intrinsic value + Time value

(2) Intrinsic value (내재가치)

현재 옵션을 행사하면 얻을 수 있는 이익으로 옵션 보유자는 불리한 경우 행사를 하지 않기 때문에 항상 "0"이상의 금액이 된다.

1) 기초자산의 주가가 $150이고 행사가격이 $100인 경우

⇒ intrinsic value = $50 (in-the-money)

2) 기초자산의 주가가 $100이고 행사가격이 $100인 경우

⇒ intrinsic value = $0 (at-the-money)

3) 기초자산의 주가가 $80이고 행사가격이 $100인 경우

⇒ intrinsic value = $0 (out-of-the-money)

(3) Time value (시간가치)

옵션의 만기까지 기초자산의 가격변동으로 이익이 실현될 가능성에 대해 옵션매입자가 지불하는 가치를 말하는 것으로 만기일까지의 기간이 길면 길수록 높으며 만기일이 가까워지면서 지속적으로 감소하게 된다. 시간가치는 옵션의 가치(프리미엄)에서 내재가치를 뺀 금액이 된다.

3 Option pricing model (OPM ; 옵션가격결정모형)

(1) Fair value of option

1) Observable market price of an option with the same or similar terms.

2) Estimated using a valuation technique such as an option-pricing model.

(2) Option-pricing model

가장 대표적인 옵션가격결정모형은 블랙-숄즈 모형으로 다음 6가지 변수를 고려한다.

1) The exercise price of the option.

2) The current price of the underlying share.

3) The expected term of the option.

4) The expected volatility of the price of the underlying share for the option.

5) The expected dividends on the underlying share for the expected.

6) The risk-free interest rate(s) for the expected term of the option.

☞ 옵션 가격결정 요소 6가지는 US GAAP에서 기술하고 있기 때문에 시험목적으로도 반드시 암기를 하여야 한다.

4 Vesting period (가득기간)

주식기준보상약정에 따라 거래상대방이 현금, 그 밖의 자산 또는 기업의 지분상품을 받을 자격을 획득하게 하는 용역을 기업이 제공받는지를 결정짓는 조건의 기간으로 용역제공조건과 성과조건이 있다. 용역제공조건은 거래상대방이 특정기간동안 용역을 제공할 것을 요구한다. 성과조건은 거래상대방이 특정기간동안 용역을 제공하고, 특정 성과목표를 달성(예: 특정기간동안 정해진 기업이익의 증가)할 것을 요구한다.

02 Share-based payment as equity

1 Measurement methods

(1) Transactions with non-employees

If the fair value of goods or services received in a share-based payment transaction with non-employees is more reliably measurable than the fair value of the equity instruments issued, the fair value of the goods or services received.

(2) Transactions with employees

A share-based payment transaction with employees shall be measured based on the fair value of the equity instruments.

(3) Measurement date : Grant date (부여일)

주식결제형의 측정일은 부여일의 공정가치이며 회계연도말에 재측정하지 않는다.

2 Recognition of compensation cost

The compensation cost for an award of share-based employee compensation classified as equity should be recognized over the requisite service period. The requisite service period is the period during which an employee is required to provide service in exchange for an award, which often is the vesting period.

종업원에게 3년간 근무하는 조건으로 주식선택권을 부여하는 경우, 주식선택권의 대가에 해당하는 근무용역을 미래 3년의 가득기간에 걸쳐 제공받는 것으로 본다. 부여되는 즉시 가득되는 경우, 종업원에게서 이미 근무용역을 제공받은 것으로 보기 때문에 비용과 자본을 즉시 인식한다.

Previously recognized compensation cost should not be reversed if an employee share option for which the requisite service has been rendered expires unexercised.

3 Forfeiture

An entity should make an entity-wide accounting policy election for all share-based payment awards to do either of the following:

(1) Estimate the number of forfeitures expected to occur.

(2) Recognize the effect of forfeitures in compensation cost when they occur.

중도 퇴사의 경우 회계연도말의 변경된 추정치에 의거하여 누적보상원가를 측정하고 전기누적 보상원가와의 차이를 당기 비용으로 인식한다.

(1) 당기누적보상비용 = 당기 말 가득예측수량 × 부여일의 공정가치 × 누적 용역제공비율

(2) 당기보상비용 = 당기누적보상비용 − 전기누적보상비용

Example-1

On 1/1/20X1, KIMCPA granted an employee an option to acquire 100 shares of KIMCPA's $5 par value common stock at $20 per share. The option became exercisable on 12/31/20X4, after the employee completed four years of service. On 1/1/20X1, the market price of KIMCPA's stock was $25 and the fair value of the stock option was $8 per share.

01/01/20X1	No entry
12/31/20X1	Dr) Compensation Expense 200 Cr) APIC- stock option 200
12/31/20X2	Dr) Compensation Expense 200 Cr) APIC- stock option 200
12/31/20X3	Dr) Compensation Expense 200 Cr) APIC- stock option 200
12/31/20X4	Dr) Compensation Expense 200 Cr) APIC- stock option 200

Exercise	Dr) Cash 2,000
	    APIC- stock option 800
	    Cr) Common Stock 500
	        APIC-common stock 2,300 (Plug)

※법인세 비용

주식보상비용은 법인세법에서는 행사시점에서 공제된다. 따라서 매년 말 주식보상비용의 세무조정은 (+)이며 이연법인세 자산(DTA)을 인식한다.

※현금흐름표

주식선택권의 행사로 인한 현금유입액은 현금흐름표 재무활동에 보고한다.

Example-2

On January 1, 20X1, KIMCPA, a public entity, grants at-the-money employee share options with a contractual term of 10 years. All share options vest at the end of three years, which is an explicit service (and requisite service) period of three years. The following table shows assumptions and information about the share options granted.

Share options granted	90,000
Employees granted options	300
Share price at the grant date	$30
Excercise price	$30
Par value per share	$5

KIMCPA used a Black-Scholes-Merton option-pricing formula that produces a fair value of $14 per option at the grant date. In 20X2 and 20X3, share option forfeitures are 4,000, and 3,800, respectively.

정답

⟨20X1⟩

Number of share options expected to vest = 90,000

Total compensation cost = 90,000 × $14 = $1,260,000

Compensation cost during 20X1 = 1,260,000 × 1/3 = $420,000

⟨20X2⟩

Number of share options expected to vest = 90,000 − 4,000 = 86,000

Total compensation cost = 86,000 × $14 = $1,204,000

Compensation cost during 20X2 = 1,204,000 × 2/3 − 420,000 = $382,667

⟨20X3⟩

Number of share options expected to vest = 86,000 − 3,800 = 82,200

Total compensation cost = 82,200 × $14 = $1,150,800

Compensation cost during 20X2

= 1,150,800 × 3/3 − (420,000 + 382,667) = $348,133

⟨Exercise⟩

Cash $= 82,200 \times 30 = 2,466,000$

Common stock $= 82,200 \times 5 = 411,000$

APIC$-$CS $= 2,466,000 + 1,150,800 - 411,000 = 3,205,800$

01/01/20X1	No entry	

12/31/20X1	Dr) Compensation Expense
	    Cr) APIC-stock option
		$420,000
		        $420,000

12/31/20X2	Dr) Compensation Expense
	    Cr) APIC-stock option
		$382,667
		        $382,667

12/31/20X3	Dr) Compensation Expense
	    Cr) APIC-stock option
		$348,133
		        $348,133

Exercise	Dr) Cash
	    APIC-stock option
	    Cr) Common Stock
	        APIC-common stock
		2,466,000
		1,150,800
		    411,000
		    3,205,800 (Plug)

Example-3

On January 1, 20X1, KIMCPA, a public entity, grants at-the-money employee share options with a contractual term of 10 years. All share options vest at the end of three years, which is an explicit service period of three years.

Share options granted	90,000
Employees granted options	300
Expected forfeitures per year	3%
Share price at the grant date	$30
Excercise price	$30
Par value per share	$5

KIMCPA used a Black−Scholes−Merton option−pricing formula that produces a fair value of $14 per option at the grant date.

정답

Number of share options expected to vest = $90,000 \times 0.97^3 = 82,141$

Total compensation cost = $82,141 \times \$14 = \$1,149,974$

Compensation cost during 20X1 = $1,149,974 \times 1/3 = \$383,325$

01/01/20X1	No entry
12/31/20X1 12/31/20X2 12/31/20X3	Dr) Compensation Expense $383,325 Cr) APIC-stock option $383,325

03 Share-based payment as liability

1 Measurement methods

(1) Transactions with non-employees : Share-based payment as equity와 동일

(2) Transactions with employees : Share-based payment as equity와 동일

(3) Measurement date : Settlement date (결제일)

측정일은 결제일의 공정가치 또는 내재가치로 매년 재측정 하여야 한다. (remeasurement)

1) Public entity

상장기업은 주가가 명확하기 때문에 공정가치로 재측정한다.

2) Non-public entity

비상장기업은 주가가 불분명하기 때문에 공정가치 또는 내재가치 중 선택하여 재측정한다.

2 Recognition of compensation cost

Share-based payment as equity와 동일

3 Forfeiture

Share-based payment as equity와 동일

(1) 당기누적보상비용 = 당기 말 가득예측수량 × 회계연도말의 공정가치 × 누적 용역제공비율

(2) 당기보상비용 = 당기누적보상비용 − 전기누적보상비용

Example-4

On 1/1/20X1, KIMCPA granted an employee 100 stock appreciation rights (SAR) to receive cash for the excess of the stock's market price on the exercise date over the market price on the grant date. The SAR became exercisable on 12/31/20X3, after the employee completed three years of service. The market price and fair value of SAR were as follows:

Date	Stock price	Fair value of SAR per share
1/1/20X1	$20	$6
12/31/20X1	30	15
12/31/20X2	40	24
12/31/20X3	45	25

At grant date	No entry
12/31/20X1	Dr) Compensation Expense 500 Cr) Liability under SAR plan 500* * 100개 × $15 × 1/3 = $500
12/31/20X2	Dr) Compensation Expense 1,100 Cr) Liability under SAR plan 1,100* * 100개 × $24 × 2/3 − 500 = $1,100
12/31/20X3	Dr) Compensation Expense 900 Cr) Liability under SAR plan 900* * 100개 × $25 × 3/3 − 1,600 = $900
At exercise date	Dr) Liability under SAR plan xxx Cr) Cash xxx

Example-5

On January 1, 20X1, KIMCPA, a public entity, grants share appreciation rights with a contractual term of 10 years. All share options vest at the end of three years, which is an explicit service (and requisite service) period of three years. Each stock appreciation right entitles the holder to receive an amount in cash equal to the increase in value of 1 share of KIMCPA stock over $30. The following table shows assumptions and information about the share options granted.

Share options granted	90,000
Employees granted options	300
Share price at the grant date	$30
Excercise price	$30
Par value per share	$5

KIMCPA uses a Black-Scholes-Merton option-pricing formula and the fair values of each stock appreciation right are follows:

January 1, 20X1	$14
December 31, 20X1	21
December 31, 20X2	25
December 31, 20X3	30

In 20X2 and 20X3, share option forfeitures are 4,000, and 3,800, respectively.

정답

⟨20X1⟩

Number of share options expected to vest = 90,000

Total compensation cost = 90,000 × $21 = $1,890,000

Compensation cost during 20X1 = 1,890,000 × 1/3 = $630,000

⟨20X2⟩

Number of share options expected to vest = 90,000 − 4,000 = 86,000

Total compensation cost = 86,000 × $25 = $2,150,000

Compensation cost during 20X2 $= 2,150,000 \times 2/3 - 630,000 = \$803,333$

⟨20X3⟩

Number of share options expected to vest $= 86,000 - 3,800 = 82,200$

Total compensation cost $= 82,200 \times \$30 = \$2,466,000$

Compensation cost during 20X2

$= 2,466,000 \times 3/3 - (630,000 + 803,333) = \$1,032,667$

01/01/20X1	No entry
12/31/20X1	Dr) Compensation Expense \$630,000 Cr) Liability under SAR plan \$630,000
12/31/20X2	Dr) Compensation Expense \$803,333 Cr) Liability under SAR plan \$803,333
12/31/20X3	Dr) Compensation Expense \$1,032,667 Cr) Liability under SAR plan \$1,032,667

Example-6

On January 1, 20X1, KIMCPA, a public entity, grants share appreciation rights with a contractual term of 10 years. All share options vest at the end of three years, which is an explicit service (and requisite service) period of three years. Each stock appreciation right entitles the holder to receive an amount in cash equal to the increase in value of 1 share of KIMCPA stock over $30. The following table shows assumptions and information about the share options granted.

Share options granted	90,000
Employees granted options	300
Expected forfeitures per year	3%
Share price at the grant date	$30
Excercise price	$30
Par value per share	$5

KIMCPA uses a Black-Scholes-Merton option-pricing formula and the fair values of each stock appreciation right are follows:

January 1, 20X1	$14
December 31, 20X1	21
December 31, 20X2	25
December 31, 20X3	30

정답

Number of share options expected to vest $= 90,000 \times 0.97^3 = 82,141$

Compensation cost during 20X1 $= 82,141 \times \$21 \times 1/3 = \$574,987$

Compensation cost during 20X2 $= 82,141 \times \$25 \times 2/3 - 574,987 = \$794,030$

Compensation cost during 20X3 $= 82,141 \times \$30 \times 3/3 - 1,369,017 = \$1,095,213$

01/01/20X1	No entry
12/31/20X1	Dr) Compensation Expense $574,987 Cr) Liability under SAR plan $574,987
12/31/20X2	Dr) Compensation Expense $794,030 Cr) Liability under SAR plan $794,030
12/31/20X3	Dr) Compensation Expense $1,095,213 Cr) Liability under SAR plan $1,095,213

04 기타사항

1 Disclosures

(1) The nature and terms of such arrangements that existed during the period and the potential effects of those arrangements on shareholders.

(2) The method of estimating the fair value of the goods or services received, or the fair value of the equity instruments granted (or offered to grant), during the period.

2 Employee Stock Ownership Plans (ESOP)

(1) ESOP (우리사주신탁제도)

회사에서 설립한 펀드에 종업원 개인별 계좌가 개설되고 종업원의 급여 중 일정액과 회사의 기여금으로 회사 주식을 매입해 그 계좌에 예치하는 제도다. 종업원은 회사 퇴직 때 주식을 당시 시장가격으로 회사에만 되팔 수 있다.

(2) Compensation expense

⇨ the amount contributed or committed to be contributed by employer.
자산으로 기여하는 경우 자산의 공정가치(FV)로 보상비용을 측정한다.

05   Tasked-Based Simulation

[Q 6-1] Share-based payment as equity

On January 1, 20X1, KIMCPA, a public entity, grants at-the-money employee share options with a contractual term of 10 years. All share options vest at the end of three years, which is an explicit service (and requisite service) period of three years. The enacted tax rate is 30 percent. The following table shows assumptions and information about the share options granted.

Share options granted	90,000
Employees granted options	300
Expected forfeitures per year	3%
Share price at the grant date	$30
Excercise price	$30

KIMCPA uses a Black-Scholes-Merton option-pricing formula and the fair values of each stock option are follows:

January 1, 20X1	$14
December 31, 20X1	21
December 31, 20X2	25
December 31, 20X3	30

At the end of 20X2, management changes its estimated employee forfeiture rate from 3 percent to 6 percent per year.

• Instructions •

(1) Prepare journal entries for compensation cost and deferred tax during 20X1, 20X2 and 20X3.

(2) Prepare journal entries for exercise of share options.

[Q 6-2] Share-based payment as liability

On January 1, 20X1, KIMCPA, a public entity, grants share appreciation rights with a contractual term of 10 years. All share options vest at the end of three years, which is an explicit service (and requisite service) period of three years. The enacted tax rate is 30 percent. Each stock appreciation right entitles the holder to receive an amount in cash equal to the increase in value of 1 share of KIMCPA stock over $30. The following table shows assumptions and information about the share options granted.

Share options granted	90,000
Employees granted options	300
Expected forfeitures per year	3%
Share price at the grant date	$30
Excercise price	$30

KIMCPA uses a Black-Scholes-Merton option-pricing formula and the fair values of each stock appreciation right are follows:

January 1, 20X1	$14
December 31, 20X1	21
December 31, 20X2	25
December 31, 20X3	30

At the end of 20X2, management changes its estimated employee forfeiture rate from 3 percent to 6 percent per year.

• Instructions •

Prepare journal entries for compensation cost and deferred tax during 20X1, 20X2 and 20X3.

[Q 6-3] Stock Options

On January 1, 20X4, AIFA Corporation granted 10,000 options to key executives. Each option allows the executive to purchase one share of Nichols' $5 par value common stock at a price of $20 per share. The options were exercisable within a 2-year period beginning January 1, 20X6, if the grantee is still employed by the company at the time of the exercise. On the grant date, Nichols' stock was trading at $25 per share, and a fair value option-pricing model determines total compensation to be $400,000.

On May 1, 20X6, 8,000 options were exercised when the market price of Nichols' stock was $30 per share. The remaining options lapsed in 2028 because executives decided not to exercise their options.

• Instructions •

Prepare the necessary journal entries related to the stock option plan for the years 20X4 through 20X8.

[Q 6-4] Stock Options

Assume that Amazon.com has a stock-option plan for top management. Each stock option represents the right to purchase a share of Amazon $1 par value common stock in the future at a price equal to the fair value of the stock at the date of the grant. Amazon has 5,000 stock options outstanding, which were granted at the beginning of 20X5. The following data relate to the option grant.

- Exercise price for options $40
- Market price at grant date (January 1, 20X5) $40
- Fair value of options at grant date (January 1, 20X5) $ 6
- Service period 5 years

• Instructions •

(1) Prepare the journal entry (entries) for the first year of the stock-option plan.

(2) Prepare the journal entry (entries) for the first year of the plan assuming that, rather than options, 700 shares of restricted stock were granted at the beginning of 20X5.

(3) Prepare the journal entry (entries) for the first year of the plan, assuming that 700 shares of restricted stock units were granted at the beginning of 20X5 rather than options.

(4) Now assume that the market price of Amazon stock on the grant date was $45 per share. Repeat the requirements for (1), (2), and (3).

(5) Amazon would like to implement an employee stock-purchase plan for rank-and-file employees, but it would like to avoid recording expense related to this plan. Which of the following provisions must be in place for the plan to avoid recording compensation expense?

1. Substantially all employees may participate.

2. The discount from market is small (less than 5%).

3. The plan offers no substantive option feature.

4. There is no preferred stock outstanding.

[Q 6-5] Stock-Appreciation Rights

AIFA Company establishes a stock-appreciation rights program that entitles its new president Ben Davis to receive cash for the difference between the market price of the stock and a pre-established price of $30(also market price) on December 31, 20X1, on 30,000 SARs. The date of grant is December 31, 20X1 and the required employment (service) period is 4 years.

President Davis exercises all of the SARs in 20X7. The fair value of the SARs is estimated to be $6 per SAR on December 31, 20X2; $9 0n December 31, 20X3; $15 on December 31, 20X4; $16 on December 31, 20X5; and $18 0n December 31, 20X6.

• Instructions •

(1) Prepare a 5-year (20X2-20X6) schedule of compensation expense pertaining to the 30,000 SARs granted president Davis.

(2) Prepare the journal entry for compensation expense in 20X2, 20X5, and 20X6 relative to the 30,000 SARS.

[Q 6-6] Accounting for Restricted Stock

AIFA Company issues 4,000 shares of restricted stock to its CFO, Dane Yaping, on January 1, 20X5. The stock has a fair value of $120,000 on this date. The service period related to this restricted stock is 4 years. Vesting occurs if Yaping stays with the company for 4 years. The par value of the stock is $5. At December 31, 20X6, the fair value of the stock is $145,000.

• Instructions •

(1) Prepare the journal entries to record the restricted stock on January 1, 20X5 (the date of grant), and December 31, 20X6.

(2) On March 4, 20X7, Yaping leaves the company. Prepare the journal entry (if any) to account for this forfeiture,

(3) Prepare the journal entries on January 1, 20X5, and December 31, 20X6, assuming that AIFA issued 4,000 shares of restricted stock units instead of 4,000 shares of restricted stock.

(4) On March 4, 20X7, Yaping leaves the company. Prepare the journal entry (if any) to account for this forfeiture of restricted stock units.

Accounting and Reporting For the **US CPA** Exam

Volume
1

Accounting and Reporting

Chapter

07

Revenue Recognition

Revenue Recognition

01 Revenue recognition

1 Concepts Statement #5

Revenue is recognized when realized or realizable and earned.

(1) Realized or realizable

when goods or services are converted in to cash or claims to cash.

(2) Earned

when the entity has substantially accomplished what it must do to been titled to the benefits

2 Revenue from contracts with customers (ASC 606)

When a performance obligation is satisfied, an entity should recognize as revenue the amount of the transaction price that is allocated to that performance obligation.

수익을 인식하기 위해서는 다음의 단계를 적용해야 한다.

Step 1	Identify the contract with a customer.
Step 2	Identify the performance obligations in the contract.
Step 3	Determine the transaction price.
Step 4	Allocate the transaction price to the performance obligations in the contract.
Step 5	Recognize revenue when the entity satisfies a performance obligation.

3 Identify the contract with a customer (계약의 식별)

(1) A contract (계약)

A contract is an agreement between two or more parties that creates enforceable rights and obligations.

(계약은 둘 이상의 당사자 사이에 집행 가능한 권리와 의무가 생기게 하는 합의이다.)

(2) A contract with a customer (고객과의 계약)

다음 기준을 모두 충족하는 때에만, 고객과의 계약으로 회계 처리한다.

1) The parties to the contract have approved the contract and are committed to perform their respective obligations.

(계약 당사자들이 계약을 승인하고 각자의 의무를 수행하기로 확약한다.)

2) The entity can identify each party's rights regarding the goods or services to be transferred.

(이전할 재화나 용역과 관련된 각 당사자의 권리를 식별할 수 있다.)

3) The entity can identify the payment terms for the goods or services to be transferred.

(이전할 재화나 용역의 지급조건을 식별할 수 있다.)

4) The contract has commercial substance.

계약에 상업적 실질이 있다. (계약의 결과로 미래 현금흐름의 위험, 시기, 금액이 변동될 것으로 예상된다).

5) It is probable that the entity will collect the consideration to which it will be entitled in exchange for the goods or services that will be transferred to the customer.

(고객에게 이전할 재화나 용역에 대하여 받을 권리를 갖게 될 대가의 회수 가능성이 높다.)

(3) 고객과의 계약 요건을 충족하지 못하지만 대가를 받은 경우 다음 사건 중 어느 하나가 일어난 경우에는 받은 대가를 수익으로 인식하며, 그렇지 못한 경우 고객에게서 받은 대가는 부채로 인식한다.

1) The entity has no remaining obligations to transfer goods/services and the consideration is non-refundable.

2) The contract has been terminated, and the consideration is non-refundable.

Example-1

On March 1, 20X1, KIMCPA enters into a contract to transfer a product to a customer on September 1, 20X1. The customer pays the consideration of $15,000 in advance on August 1, 20X1. KIMCPA transfers the product on September 1, 20X1. The cost of the product totaled $9,000.

Date	Account	Debit	Credit
March 1	No entry		
August 1	Cash	15,000	
	Contract liability		15,000
September 1	Contract liability	15,000	
	Revenue		15,000
	Cost of goods sold	9,000	
	Inventory		9,000

4 Identify the performance obligations in the contract(수행의무 식별)

(1) Performance Obligation (수행의무)

하나의 계약은 고객에게 재화나 용역을 이전하는 여러 약속을 포함한다. 그 재화나 용역들이 구별된다면 각 약속은 수행의무이고 별도로 회계처리 한다. 계약 개시시점에 고객과의 계약에서 약속한 재화나 용역을 검토하여 고객에게 다음 중 어느 하나를 이전하기로 한 각 약속을 하나의 수행의무로 식별한다.

1) A good or service (or a bundle of goods or services) that is distinct

2) A series of distinct goods or services that are substantially the same and that have the same pattern of transfer to the customer.

(2) If a promised good or service is not distinct

Combine that good or service with other promised goods and account for all the goods or services promised in a contract as a single performance obligation.

(3) A distinct good or service

다음 기준을 모두 충족한다면 고객에게 약속한 재화나 용역은 구별되는 것이다.

1) The customer can benefit from the good or service either on its own or together with other resources that are readily available to the customer.

2) The entity's promise to transfer the good or service to the customer is separately identifiable from other promises in the contract.

Example-2

A contractor enters into a contract to build a hospital for a customer. The entity is responsible for the overall management of the project and identifies various promised goods and services, including engineering, site clearance, foundation, procurement, construction of the structure, piping and wiring, installation of equipment, and finishing.

Identify the performance obligation in this contract

> Because both criteria are not met, the goods and services are not distinct. The entity accounts for all of the goods and services in the contract as a single performance obligation.

Example-3

A software developer enters into a contract with a customer to transfer a software license, perform an installation service, and provide unspecified software updates and technical support for a two-year period. The entity sells the license, installation service, and technical support separately. The installation service includes changing the web screen for each type of user (for example, marketing, inventory management, and information technology). The installation service is routinely performed by other entities and does not significantly modify the software. The software remains functional without the updates and the technical support.

Identify the performance obligation in this contract

Because both criteria are met, the goods and services are distinct. On the basis of this assessment, the entity identifies four performance obligations in the contract for the following goods or services:

a. The software license

b. An installation service

c. Software updates

d. Technical support.

5 Determine the transaction price (거래가격의 산정)

(1) Transaction price (거래가격)

The transaction price is the amount of consideration to which an entity expects to be entitled in exchange for transferring promised goods or services to a customer, excluding amounts collected on behalf of third parties (some sales taxes).

(거래가격은 고객에게 약속한 재화나 용역을 이전하고 그 대가로 기업이 받을 권리를 갖게 될 것으로 예상하는 금액이며, 제삼자를 대신해서 회수한 금액은 제외한다.)

The consideration promised in a contract with a customer may include fixed amounts, variable amounts, or both.

(고객과의 계약에서 약속한 대가는 고정금액, 변동금액 또는 둘 다를 포함할 수 있다.)

(2) Variable consideration (변동대가)

계약에서 약속한 대가에 변동금액이 포함된 경우에 고객에게 약속한 재화나 용역을 이전하고 그 대가로 받을 권리를 갖게 될 금액을 추정한다. 대가는 할인(discount), 리베이트, 환불, 공제(credits), 가격할인(price concessions), 장려금(incentives), 성과보너스, 위약금이나 그 밖의 비슷한 항목 때문에 변동될 수 있다.

An entity should estimate an amount of variable consideration by using either of the following methods, depending on which method the entity expects to better predict the amount of consideration to which it will be entitled:

① The expected value (the sum of probability-weighted amounts)
② The most likely amount (the single most likely amount)

(3) Significant financing component (계약에 있는 유의적인 금융요소)

An entity should adjust the promised amount of consideration for the effects of the time value of money if the timing of payments agreed to by the parties to the contract provides the customer.

(유의적인 금융 효익이 제공되는 경우에는 화폐의 시간가치가 미치는 영향을 반영하여 약속된 대가를 조정한다.)

An entity should recognize revenue at an amount that reflects the price that a customer would have paid for the promised goods or services if the customer had paid cash for those goods or services when they transfer to the customer (the cash selling price)
(재화나 용역 대금을 현금으로 결제했다면 지급하였을 가격을 반영하는 금액(현금판매가격)으로 수익을 인식한다.)

재화나 용역을 이전하는 시점과 대가를 지급하는 시점 간의 기간이 1년 이내일 것이라고 예상한다면 유의적인 금융요소의 영향을 반영하여 약속한 대가를 조정하지 않을 수 있다.

(4) Noncash consideration (비현금 대가)

An entity should measure the estimated fair value of the noncash consideration at contract inception.

If an entity cannot reasonably estimate the fair value of the noncash consideration, the entity should measure the consideration indirectly by reference to the standalone selling price of the goods or services promised to the customer.
(비현금 대가의 공정가치를 합리적으로 추정할 수 없는 경우에는, 그 대가와 교환하여 고객에게 약속한 재화나 용역의 개별 판매가격을 참조하여 간접적으로 그 대가를 측정한다.)

(5) Consideration payable to the customer (고객에게 지급할 대가)

고객에게 지급할 대가는 기업이 고객 또는 고객에게서 기업의 재화나 용역을 구매하는 다른 당사자에게 지급할 것으로 예상하는 현금 금액을 의미한다.

고객으로부터 제공받을 재화나 용역의 대가가 아닌 경우
⇨ 수익에서 차감하여 회계처리

고객으로부터 제공받을 재화나 용역의 대가인 경우
⇨ 별도의 구매거래로 회계처리하며 공정가치를 초과하는 경우 초과액은 수익에서 차감하여 회계처리

Example-4

KIMCPA enters into a contract with a customer on January 1, 20X1, to sell Product A for $100 per unit. If the customer purchases more than 1,000 units of Product A in a calendar year, the contract specifies that the price per unit is retrospectively reduced to $90 per unit. Consequently, the consideration in the contract is variable.

For the first quarter ended March 31, 20X1, the entity sells 75 units of Product A to the customer. The entity estimates that the customer's purchases will not exceed the 1,000-unit threshold required for the volume discount in the calendar year.

In May 20X1, the entity's customer acquires another company and in the second quarter ended June 30, 20X1, the entity sells an additional 500 units of Product A to the customer. In light of the new fact, the entity estimates that the customer's purchases will exceed the 1,000-unit threshold for the calendar year.

Identify revenue for the first quarter and second quarter.

> Revenue for the first quarter = 75 × $100 = $7,500
> Revenue for the second quarter = 575 × $90 - 7,500 = $44,250

6 Allocate the transaction price to the performance obligations in the contract (거래가격을 계약 내 수행의무에 배분)

(1) Allocation

An entity should allocate the transaction price to each performance obligation identified in the contract on a relative standalone selling price basis at contract inception.
(거래가격은 일반적으로 계약에서 약속한 각 구별되는 재화나 용역의 상대적 개별 판매가격을 기준으로 배분한다.)

(2) Discounts

A customer receives a discount for purchasing a bundle of goods or services if the sum of the standalone selling prices of those promised goods or services in the contract exceeds the promised consideration in a contract. The entity should allocate a discount proportionately to all performance obligations in the contract.
(할인액을 계약상 모든 수행의무에 비례하여 배분한다.)

(3) Transaction price changes

An entity should allocate to the performance obligations in the contract any subsequent changes in the transaction price on the same basis as at contract inception. But, an entity should not reallocate the transaction price to reflect changes in standalone selling prices after contract inception.
(거래가격의 후속 변동은 계약 개시시점과 같은 기준으로 계약상 수행의무에 배분한다.)

Example-5

KIMCPA enters into a contract with a customer to sell Products A, B, and C in exchange for $100. The entity will satisfy the performance obligations for each of the products at different points in time. The standalone selling prices of Products A, B and C are $50, 25 and 75 respectively.

Determine the allocated transaction prices.

The customer receives a discount for purchasing the bundle of goods because the sum of the standalone selling prices ($150) exceeds the promised consideration ($100).

Product A = $50 × 100 / 150 = $33
Product B = $25 × 100 / 150 = $17
Product C = $75 × 100 / 150 = $50

Example-6

KIMCPA enters into a contract with a customer to sell Products A, B, and C in exchange for $100. The entity will satisfy the performance obligations for each of the products at different points in time. The standalone selling prices of Products A, B and C are $40, 55 and 45 respectively. In addition, the entity regularly sells Products B and C together for $60.

Determine the allocated transaction prices.

Because the entity regularly sells Products B and C together for $60 and Product A for $40, it has evidence that the entire discount should be allocated to the promises to transfer Products B and C.

Product A = $100 − 60 = $40
Product B = $60 × 55 / 100 = $33
Product C = $60 × 45 / 100 = $27

7 Recognize revenue when the entity satisfies a performance obligation. (수행의무를 이행할 때 수익을 인식)

(1) Transfer of control

An entity should recognize revenue when the entity satisfies a performance obligation by transferring a promised good or service to a customer. An asset is transferred when the customer obtains control of that asset.

(2) Performance obligations satisfied over time

다음 기준 중 어느 하나를 충족하면, 재화나 용역에 대한 통제를 기간에 걸쳐 이전하므로, 기간에 걸쳐 수행의무를 이행하는 것이고 기간에 걸쳐 수익을 인식한다.

1) The customer simultaneously receives and consumes the benefits provided by the entity's performance as the entity performs.

2) The entity's performance creates or enhances an asset (work in process) that the customer controls.

3) The entity's performance does not create an asset with an alternative use to the entity, and the entity has an enforceable right to payment for performance completed to date.

(3) Measuring Progress (수행의무의 진행률)

For each performance obligation satisfied over time, an entity should recognize revenue over time by measuring the progress toward complete satisfaction of that performance obligation. As circumstances change over time, an entity should update its measure of progress to reflect any changes in the outcome of the performance obligation.

An entity should recognize revenue for a performance obligation satisfied over time only if the entity can reasonably measure its progress toward complete satisfaction of the performance obligation.

If an entity may not be able to reasonably measure the outcome of a performance obligation, but the entity expects to recover the costs incurred in satisfying the performance obligation. the entity should recognize revenue only to the extent of the costs incurred.

(4) Performance obligation satisfied at a point in time.

If a performance obligation is not satisfied over time, an entity satisfies the performance obligation at a point in time. Revenue should be recognized at the point in time when the customer obtains control of that asset.

(5) Indicators of the transfer of control

1) The entity has a present right to payment for the asset.

2) The customer has legal title to the asset.

3) The entity has transferred physical possession of the asset.

4) The customer has the significant risks and rewards of ownership of the asset.

5) The customer has accepted the asset.

Example-7

KIMCPA is developing a multi-unit residential complex. A customer enters into a binding sales contract with the entity for a specified unit that is under construction. Each unit has a similar floor plan and is of a similar size, but other attributes of the units are different.

The customer pays a deposit upon entering into the contract, and the deposit is refundable only if the entity fails to complete construction of the unit in accordance with the contract. The remainder of the contract price is payable on completion of the contract when the customer obtains physical possession of the unit. If the customer defaults on the contract before completion of the unit, the entity only has the right to retain the deposit.

Determine whether this performance obligation is satisfied over the time or at a point in time.

> Because the entity does not have a right to payment for work completed to date, the entity's performance obligation is not a performance obligation satisfied over time. Instead, the entity accounts for the sale of the unit as a performance obligation satisfied at a point in time.

Example-8

KIMCPA is developing a multi-unit residential complex. A customer enters into a binding sales contract with the entity for a specified unit that is under construction. Each unit has a similar floor plan and is of a similar size, but other attributes of the units are different.

The customer pays a nonrefundable deposit upon entering into the contract and will make progress payments during construction of the unit. The contract has substantive terms that preclude the entity from being able to direct the unit to another customer. If the customer defaults on its obligations by failing to make the promised progress payments as and when they are due, the entity would have a right to all of the consideration promised in the contract if it completes the construction of the unit.

Determine whether this performance obligation is satisfied over the time or at a point in time.

> The entity's performance obligation is a performance obligation satisfied over time because the unit does not have an alternative use to the entity and The entity also has a right to payment for performance completed to date.

8 Presentation

(1) Receivable (수취채권)

A receivable is an entity's right to consideration that is unconditional. A right to consideration is unconditional if only the passage of time is required before payment of that consideration is due.

(2) Contract liability (계약부채)

If a customer pays consideration, or an entity has a right to an amount of consideration that is unconditional, before the entity transfers a good or service to the customer, the entity should present the contract as a contract liability when the payment is made or the payment is due (whichever is earlier).

Example-9

On January 1, 20X1, KIMCPA enters into a cancellable contract to transfer a product to a customer on March 31, 20X1. The contract requires the customer to pay consideration of $1,000 in advance on January 31, 20X1. The customer pays the consideration on March 1, 20X1. KIMCPA transfers the product on March 31, 20X1.

Date	Account	Debit	Credit
January 31	No entry		
March 1	Cash	1,000	
	Contract liability		1,000
March 31	Contract liability	1,000	
	Revenue		1,000

Example-10

On January 1, 20X1, KIMCPA enters into a noncancellable contract to transfer a product to a customer on March 31, 20X1. The contract requires the customer to pay consideration of $1,000 in advance on January 31, 20X1. The customer pays the consideration on March 1, 20X1. KIMCPA transfers the product on March 31, 20X1.

Date	Account	Debit	Credit
January 31	Receivable	1,000	
	Contract liability		1,000
March 1	Cash	1,000	
	Receivable		1,000
March 31	Contract liability	1,000	
	Revenue		1,000

(3) Contract asset (계약자산)

If an entity performs by transferring goods or services to a customer before the customer pays consideration or before payment is due, the entity should present the contract as a contract asset, excluding any amounts presented as a receivable.

Example-11

On January 2, 20X1, KIMCPA enters into a contract to transfer Products A and B to a customer in exchange for $1,000. The contract requires Product A to be delivered first and states that payment for the delivery of Product A is conditional on the delivery of Product B. KIMCPA identifies the promises to transfer Products A and B as performance obligations and allocates $400 to the performance obligation to transfer Product A and $600 to the performance obligation to transfer Product B. On March 1, 20X1, KIMCPA satisfies the performance obligation to transfer Product A. On April 1, 20X1, KIMCPA satisfies the performance obligation to transfer Product B.

Date	Account	Debit	Credit
January 2	No entry		
March 1	Contract asset	400	
	Revenue		400
April 1	Receivable	1,000	
	Revenue		600
	Contract asset		400

9 Sale with a right of return (반품권이 있는 판매)

일부 계약에서는 기업이 고객에게 제품에 대한 통제를 이전하고, 다양한 이유(예: 제품 불만족)로 제품을 반품할 권리를 고객에게 부여한다. 반품기간에 언제라도 반품을 받기로 하는 기업의 약속은 환불할 의무에 더하여 수행의무로 회계처리하지 않는다. 반품권이 있는 제품의 이전을 회계처리하기 위하여, 다음 사항을 모두 인식한다.

1) Revenue for the transferred products in the amount of consideration to which the entity expects to be entitled (기업이 받을 권리를 갖게 될 것으로 예상하는 대가)

2) A refund liability (환불부채)

3) An asset for its right to recover products from customers on settling the refund liability (환불부채를 결제할 때, 고객에게서 제품을 회수할 기업의 권리)

보고기간 말마다 반품 예상량의 변동에 따라 환불부채의 측정치를 새로 수정하며, 이에 따라 생기는 조정액을 수익으로 인식한다.

Example-12

An entity enters into 100 contracts with customers. Each contract includes the sale of 1 product for $100 (100 total products × $100 = $10,000 total consideration). Cash is received when control of a product transfers. The entity's customary business practice is to allow a customer to return any unused product within 30 days and receive a full refund. The entity's cost of each product is $60. Using the expected value method, the entity estimates that 97 products will not be returned.

Account	Debit	Credit
Cash	10,000	
Refund liability		300
Revenue		9,700
Cost of sales	5,820	
Asset	180	
Inventory		6,000

Cash = $100 × 100 products = $10,000

Revenue = $100 × 97 products = $9,700

Refund liability = $100 × 3 products = $300

Cost of sales = $60 × 97 products = $5,820

Asset = $60 × 3 products = $180

Inventory = $60 × 100 products = $6,000

10 Warranty

(1) An assurance-type warranty

관련 제품이 합의된 규격에 부합하므로 당사자들이 의도한 대로 작동할 것이라는 확신을 고객에게 주는 보증으로 충당부채(warranty obligation)로 회계처리 한다.

(2) A service-type warranty

제품이 합의된 규격에 부합한다는 확신에 더하여 고객에게 용역을 제공하는 보증으로 별도의 수행의무(performance obligation)로 회계처리 한다.

(3) If a customer has the option to purchase a warranty separately

고객이 보증을 별도로 구매할 수 있는 선택권이 있는 경우

⇨ a service-type warranty

(4) If a customer does not have the option to purchase a warranty separately

고객에게 보증을 별도로 구매할 수 있는 선택권이 없는 경우

1) if the warranty provides the customer with an assurance

⇨ an assurance-type warranty

2) if the warranty provides the customer with a service in addition an assurance and can reasonably account for them separately

⇨ allocate the warranty to an assurance-type warranty and a service-type warranty

3) if the warranty provides the customer with a service in addition an assurance but cannot reasonably account for them separately

⇨ a service-type warranty

Example-13

KIMCPA, a manufacturer, provides its customer with a warranty with the purchase of a product. The warranty provides assurance that the product complies with agreed-upon specifications and will operate as promised for one year from the date of purchase. The contract also provides the customer with the right to receive up to 20 hours of training services on how to operate the product at no additional cost.

(1) The product and training services are each distinct and therefore give rise to two separate performance obligations. As a result, KIMCPA allocates the transaction price to the two performance obligations and recognizes revenue when those performance obligations are satisfied.

(2) The warranty that provides the customer with the assurance that the product will function as intended for one year. → an assurance-type warranty

(3) the two performance obligations = the product and the training services

11 Repurchase agreements

(1) 재매입약정

재매입약정은 자산을 판매하고, 그 자산을 다시 사기로 약속하거나 다시 살 수 있는 선택권을 갖는 계약으로 세 가지 형태로 나타난다.

1) An entity's obligation to repurchase the asset (a forward)

2) An entity's right to repurchase the asset (a call option)

3) An entity's obligation to repurchase the asset at the customer's request (a put option).

(2) A Forward or a Call Option

1) 기업이 자산을 다시 사야 하는 의무나 다시 살 수 있는 권리가 있다면, 고객은 자산을 통제하지 못하기 때문에 그 계약을 다음 중 어느 하나로 회계 처리한다.

① Lease

자산을 원래 판매가격보다는 낮은 금액으로 다시 사야 하는 경우

② Financing arrangement (금융약정)

자산을 원래 판매가격 이상의 금액으로 다시 사야 하는 경우

2) If the repurchase agreement is a financing arrangement

the entity should continue to recognize the asset and also recognize a financial liability for any consideration received from the customer. The entity should recognize the difference between the amount of consideration received from the customer and the amount of consideration to be paid to the customer as interest expense.

(3) A Put Option

1) 고객이 요청하면 기업이 원래 판매가격보다 낮은 가격으로 자산을 다시 사야 하는 의무가 있는 경우에는 그 계약을 다음 중 어느 하나로 회계 처리한다.

① Lease

if the customer has a significant economic incentive to exercise that right

② A sale with a right of return

if the customer does not have a significant economic incentive to exercise its right

2) 고객이 요청하면 기업이 원래 판매가격보다 높은 가격으로 자산을 다시 사야 하는 의무가
있는 경우에는 그 계약을 다음 중 어느 하나로 회계 처리한다.

① Financing arrangement

if the repurchase price is more than the expected market value of the asset

② A sale with a right of return

if the repurchase price is less than or equal to the expected market value of the asset

Example-14

KIMCPA enters into a contract with a customer for the sale of a tangible asset on January 1, 20X1, for $350,000. The contract includes a call option that gives the entity the right to repurchase the asset for $385,000 on or before December 31, 20X1. On December 31, 20X1, the option lapses unexercised.

Date	Account	Debit	Credit
January 1	Cash	350,000	
	Financial liability		350,000
December 31	Interest expense	35,000	
	Financial liability		35,000
December 31	Financial liability	385,000	
	Revenue		385,000

Example-15

KIMCPA enters into a contract with a customer for the sale of a tangible asset on January 1, 20X1, for $1,000,000. The contract includes a put option that obliges the entity to repurchase the asset at the customer's request for $900,000 on or before December 31, 20X1. The market value is expected to be $750,000 on December 31, 20X1.

Determine whether KIMCPA should account for this transaction as a lease, a financing arrangement or a sale with a right of return.

> The customer has a significant economic incentive to exercise the put option because the repurchase price significantly exceeds the expected market value of the asset at the date of repurchase. Therefore, KIMCPA accounts for the transaction as a lease.

12 Consignment arrangements

(1) 위탁판매

최종 고객에게 판매하기 위해 기업이 제품을 다른 당사자에게 인도하는 경우에 다른 당사자가 그 제품을 통제하지 못하는 경우에는 다른 당사자에게 인도한 제품을 위탁약정에 따라 보유하는 것이므로, 인도된 제품이 위탁물로 보유된다면 제품을 다른 당사자에게 인도할 때 수익을 인식하지 않는다.

(2) Indicators that an arrangement is a consignment arrangement

1) The product is controlled by the entity until a specified event occurs.

   정해진 사건이 일어날 때까지 기업이 자산을 통제한다.

   (예 : 중개인의 고객에게 자산을 판매하거나 정해진 기간이 만료될 때까지)

2) The entity is able to require the return of the product or transfer the product to a third party.

   기업은 제품의 반환을 요구하거나 제품을 제삼자에게 이전할 수 있다.

3) The dealer does not have an unconditional obligation to pay for the product.

   중개인은 제품에 대해 지급해야 하는 무조건적인 의무는 없다.

13 Bill-and-hold arrangement

(1) 미인도청구약정

미인도청구약정은 기업이 고객에게 제품의 대가를 청구하지만 미래 한 시점에 고객에게 이전할 때까지 기업이 제품을 물리적으로 점유하는 계약이다.

㉆ 고객이 제품을 보관할 수 있는 공간이 부족하거나 생산 일정이 지연되는 경우

(2) Revenue cannot be recognized until the customer obtains control of the product.

고객이 제품을 통제하기 위해서는 다음 기준을 모두 충족하여야 한다.

1) The reason for the bill-and-hold arrangement must be substantive.

미인도청구약정의 이유가 실질적이어야 한다(예: 고객의 요구).

2) The product must be identified separately as belonging to the customer.

제품은 고객의 소유물로 구분하여 식별되어야 한다.

3) The product currently must be ready for physical transfer to the customer.

고객에게 제품을 물리적으로 이전할 준비가 현재 되어 있어야 한다.

4) The entity cannot have the ability to use the product or to direct it to another customer.

기업이 제품을 사용할 능력을 가질 수 없거나 다른 고객에게 이를 넘길 능력을 가질 수 없다.

Example - 16

KIMCPA enters into a contract with a customer on January 1, 20X1, for the sale of a machine and spare parts. The manufacturing lead time for the machine and spare parts is two years. Upon completion of manufacturing, KIMCPA demonstrates that the machine and spare parts meet the agreed-upon specifications in the contract. The promises to transfer the machine and spare parts are distinct and result in two performance obligations that each will be satisfied at a point in time. On December 31, 20X2, the customer pays for the machine and spare parts but only takes physical possession of the machine. Although the customer inspects and accepts the spare parts, the customer requests that the spare parts be stored at the entity's warehouse because of its close proximity to the customer's factory. The customer has legal title to the spare parts, and the parts can be identified as belonging to the customer. Furthermore, KIMCPA stores the spare parts in a separate section of its warehouse, and the parts are ready for immediate shipment at the customer's request. KIMCPA expects to hold the spare parts for three years, and the entity does not have the ability to use the spare parts or direct them to another customer.

Determine when revenue is recognized on each performance obligation.

KIMCPA accounts for three performance obligations in the contract (the promises to provide the machine, the spare parts, and the custodial services). The transaction price is allocated to the three performance obligations and revenue is recognized when control transfers to the customer.

KIMCPA recognize revenue for the machine and the spare parts on December 31, 20X2 when control transfers to the customer.

KIMCPA recognize revenue for the custodial services over the three years that the services are provided.

---

14 Principal versus agent considerations

(1) 본인 및 대리인

고객에게 재화나 용역을 제공하는 데에 다른 당사자가 관여할 때, 기업은 약속의 성격이 정해진 재화나 용역 자체를 제공하는 수행의무인지(Principal)아니면 다른 당사자가 재화나 용역을 제공하도록 주선하는 수행의무인지(Agent)를 판단하여야 한다.

(2) Principal (본인)

An entity is a principal if it controls the specified good or service before that good or service is transferred to a customer. When a principal satisfies a performance obligation, the entity recognizes revenue in the gross amount of consideration to which it expects to be entitled in exchange for the specified good or service transferred.

(3) Agent (대리인)

An entity is an agent if the entity's performance obligation is to arrange for the provision of the specified good or service by another party. An entity that is an agent does not control the specified good or service provided by another party before that good or service is transferred to the customer. When an agent satisfies a performance obligation, the entity recognizes revenue in the amount of any fee or commission.

(4) Indicators that an entity controls the specified good or service

1) The entity is primarily responsible for fulfilling the promise to provide the specified good or service.

2) The entity has inventory risk

3) The entity has discretion in establishing the price for the specified good or service.

Example-17

KIMCPA sells vouchers that entitle customers to future meals at specified restaurants, and the sales price of the voucher provides the customer with a significant discount when compared with the normal selling prices of the meals (for example, a customer pays $100 for a voucher that entitles the customer to a meal at a restaurant that would otherwise cost $200). KIMCPA does not purchase or commit itself to purchase vouchers in advance of the sale of a voucher to a customer; instead, it purchases vouchers only as they are requested by the customers. KIMCPA sells the vouchers through its website, and the vouchers are non-refundable.

KIMCPA and the restaurants jointly determine the prices at which the vouchers will be sold to customers. Under the terms of its contracts with the restaurants, KIMCPA is entitled to 30% of the voucher price when it sells the voucher.

KIMCPA also assists the customers in resolving complaints about the meals and has a buyer satisfaction program. However, the restaurant is responsible for fulfilling obligations associated with the voucher, including remedies to a customer for dissatisfaction with the service.

Determine whether KIMCPA is acting as principal or agent.

> KIMCPA is an agent in the arrangement with respect to the vouchers because it does not control the voucher (right to a meal) at any time. KIMCPA recognizes revenue in the net amount of consideration, which is the 30 percent commission it is entitled to upon the sale of each voucher.

15 Licensing

(1) 라이선스

라이선스는 기업의 지적재산에 대한 고객의 권리를 정하는 것으로 다음과 같다.

a. Software and technology

b. Motion pictures, music, and other forms of media and entertainment

c. Franchises

d. Patents, trademarks, and copyrights

(2) Right to use the entity's intellectual property (사용권)

1) as it exists at the point in time at which the license is granted.

2) a license transfers to a customer at a point in time

(3) Right to access the entity's intellectual property (접근권)

1) throughout the license period (or its remaining economic life, if shorter)

2) a license transfers to a customer over time

(4) Sales-based or usage-based royalties

An entity should recognize revenue for a sales-based or usage-based royalty promised in exchange for a license of intellectual property only when the later of the following events occurs:

1) The subsequent sale or usage occurs.

2) The performance obligation to which some or all of the sales-based or usage-based royalty has been allocated has been satisfied.

Example-18

A well-known sports team licenses the use of its name and logo to a customer. The customer, an apparel designer, has the right to use the sports team's name and logo on items including t-shirts, caps, mugs, and towels for one year. In exchange for providing the license, the entity will receive fixed consideration of $2 million and a royalty of 5% of the sales price of any items using the team name or logo. The customer expects that the entity will continue to play games and provide a competitive team.

> The entity's promise in granting the license provides the customer with the right to access the entity's intellectual property throughout the license period and the entity accounts for the promised license as a performance obligation satisfied over time.
>
> The entity recognizes the fixed consideration allocable to the license performance obligation and recognizes revenue from the sales-based royalty when the customer's subsequent sales of items using the team name or logo occur is.
>
> Ratable recognition of the fixed consideration of $2 million plus recognition of the royalty fees as the customer's subsequent sales occur reasonably depict the entity's progress toward complete satisfaction of the license performance obligation.

Example-19

KIMCPA enters into a contract with a customer and promises to grant a franchise license that provides the customer with the right to use the entity's trade name and sell the entity's products for 10 years. In addition to the license, the entity also promises to provide the equipment necessary to operate a franchise store. In exchange for granting the license, the entity receives a fixed fee of $1 million, as well as a sales-based royalty of 5% of the customer's sales for the term of the license. The fixed consideration for the equipment is $150,000 payable when the equipment is delivered.

The entity has two performance obligations:

  a. The franchise license

  b. The equipment.

The entity should allocate $150,000 to the equipment and allocating the sales-based royalty as well as the additional $1 million in fixed consideration to the franchise license.

Ratable recognition of the fixed $1 million franchise fee plus recognition of the periodic royalty fees as the customer's subsequent sales occur reasonably depict the entity's performance toward complete satisfaction of the franchise license performance obligation to which the sales-based royalty has been allocated.

02 Long-Term Construction Contracts

T!he revenue from long-term construction contracts may be recognized over time or at a point in time.

(장기건설계약은 기간에 걸쳐 수익을 인식하거나 한 시점에 수익을 인식한다.)

1 Recognize revenue Over Time

(1) Recognize revenue Over Time (기간에 걸쳐 수익 인식)

An entity transfers control of a good or service over time and,satisfies a performance obligation and recognizes revenue over time if one of the following criteria is met:

1) The customer simultaneously receives and consumes the benefits provided by the entity's performance as the entity performs (예: 건물관리용역, 청소용역 등)

2) The entity's performance creates or enhances an asset (work in process) that the customer controls as the asset is created or enhanced

3) The entity's performance does not create an asset with an alternative use to the entity, and the entity has an enforceable right to payment for performance completed to date (예 : 고객만이 사용할 특수기계)

(2) Completion measures

1) Output methods (산출법)

recognize revenue on the basis of direct measurements of the value to the customer of the goods or services transferred to date relative to the remaining goods or services promised under the contract.

- surveys of performance completed to date
- appraisals of results achieved
- milestones reached

    — time elapsed

    — units produced or units delivered

2) Input methods

recognize revenue on the basis of the entity's efforts or inputs to the satisfaction of a performance obligation relative to the total expected inputs to the satisfaction of that performance obligation.

    — resources consumed

    — labor hours expended

    — costs incurred

    — time elapsed

    — machine hours used

If the entity's efforts or inputs are expended evenly throughout the performance period, it may be appropriate for the entity to recognize revenue on a straight-line basis.

(3) Formula for cost-to-cost basis

⟨Step 1⟩ Compute percentage of completion
  Percent complete = Cost incurred to date / Most recent estimated total costs

⟨Step 2⟩ Compute revenue (or gross profit) to be recognized to date
  = percentage of completion x estimated total revenue (or total gross profit)

⟨Step 3⟩ Compute revenue (or gross profit) for current year
  = revenue (or gross profit) to be recognized to date
    — revenue (or gross profit) to be recognized in prior periods

(4) Accounting

Transactions	Accounts	DR	CR
1) Costs incurred	CIP	xxx	
	Materials, Cash etc.		xxx
2) Billing on contract	A/R	xxx	
	Billings on CIP		xxx
3) Collections	Cash	xxx	
	A/R		xxx
4) Recognize revenue (year-end)	Construction expense	xxx	
	CIP	xxx	
	Revenue from LT contracts		xxx
5) Completion of the contract	Billings on CIP	xxx	
	CIP		xxx

* CIP (construction in progress) account (an inventory account)

= accumulated construction costs and estimated gross profit earned

* Billings on CIP (a contra-inventory account)

= accumulated billings on construction

(5) Presentation

The two accounts (CIP and Billing on CIP) are netted against each other for balance sheet reporting.

CIP $>$ Billing on CIP

→ Current asset (Costs and recognized profit in excess of billings)

CIP $<$ Billing on CIP

→ Current liability (Billings in excess of costs and recognized profit)

(6) Unprofitable projects

An estimated loss on the total contract is recognized immediately in the year it is discovered. However, any previous gross profit or loss reported in prior years must be adjusted for when calculating the total estimated loss.

Hyundai Construction Company has a contract to construct a $4,500,000 bridge at an estimated cost of $4,000,000. The contract is to start in July 20X1 and the bridge is to be completed in October 20X3. By the end of 20X2, Hyundai has revised the estimated total cost from $4,000,000 to $4,050,000.

The following data pertain to the construction period.

	20X1	20X2	20X3
Cost to date	$1,000,000	$2,916,000	$4,050,000
Estimated costs to complete	3,000,000	1,134,000	0
Progress billings during the year	900,000	2,400,000	1,200,000
Cash collected during the year	750,000	1,750,000	2,000,000

⟨Step 1⟩ Compute percentage of completion

20X1 진행률 = 1,000,000/4,000,000 = 25%

20X2 진행률 = 2,916,000/4,050,000 = 72%

20X3 진행률 = 4,050,000/4,050,000 = 100%

⟨Step 2⟩ Compute revenue to be recognized to date

20X1 revenue to date = 4,500,000 × 25% = 1,125,000

20X2 revenue to date = 4,500,000 × 72% = 3,240,000

20X3 revenue to date = 4,500,000 × 100% = 4,500,000

⟨Step 3⟩ Compute revenue for current year

20X1 revenue = 1,125,000 − 0 = 1,125,000

20X2 revenue = 3,240,000 − 1,125,000 = 2,115,000

20X3 revenue = 4,500,000 − 3,240,000 = 1,260,000

⟨Step 2⟩ Compute gross profit to be recognized to date

20X1 gross profit to date = 500,000 × 25% = 125,000

20X2 gross profit to date = 450,000 × 72% = 324,000

20X3 gross profit to date = 450,000 × 100% = 450,000

⟨Step 3⟩ Computer gross profit for current year

20X1 gross profit = 125,000 − 0 = 125,000

20X2 gross profit = 324,000 − 125,000 = 199,000

20X3 gross profit = 450,000 − 324,000 = 126,000

(Dollars in thousands)

Accounts	20X1 DR	20X1 CR	20X2 DR	20X2 CR	20X3 DR	20X3 CR
1) Costs incurred						
CIP	1,000		1,916		1,134	
Materials, Cash etc.		1,000		1,916		1,134
2) Billing on contract						
A/R	900		2,400		1,200	
Billings on CIP		900		2,400		1,200
3) Collections						
Cash	750		1,750		2,000	
A/R		750		1,750		2,000
4) Recognize revenue (year−end)						
Construction expense	1,000		1,916		1,134	
CIP	125		199		126	
Revenue		1,125		2,115		1,260
5) Completion of the contract						
Billings on CIP	N/A	N/A	N/A	N/A	4,500	
CIP						4,500

Balance Sheet			
	20X1	20X2	20X3
A/R	$150,000	$800,000	$0
Inventory (CIP 〉 Billings)	225,000	0	0
Current liability (CIP 〈 Billings)	0	60,000	0

Income Statement			
	20X1	20X2	20X3
Revenue from long−term contracts	$1,125,000	$2,115,000	$1,260,000
Costs of construction	1,000,000	1,916,000	1,134,000
Gross profit	125,000	199,000	126,000

Assume that at December 31, 20X2, Hyundai Construction Company estimates the costs to complete the bridge contract at $1,640,250 instead of $1,134,000.

Estimated total costs $= 2,916,000 + 1,640,250 = 4,556,250$
Estimated total gross profit $= 4,500,000 - 4,556,250 = (56,250)$

⟨Step 1⟩ Compute percentage of completion
20X2 진행률 $= 2,916,000/4,556,250 = 64\%$

⟨Step 2⟩ Compute revenue to be recognized to date
20X2 revenue to date $= 4,500,000 \times 64\% = 2,880,000$

⟨Step 3⟩ Compute revenue for current year
20X2 revenue $= 2,880,000 - 1,125,000 = 1,755,000$

⟨Step 4⟩ Compute loss and construction expense for current year

Loss recognized in 20X2 = reversal of 20X1 gross profit + estimated total loss

$$= 125,000 + 56,250 = 181,250$$

Construction costs recognized in 20X2 = 1,755,000 + 181,250 = 1,936,250

Transactions	Accounts	DR	CR
	Construction expense	1,936,250	
12/31/20X2	CIP		181,250
	Revenue from LT contracts		1,755,000

2 Recognize revenue at a Point in Time

(1) Recognize revenue at a Point in Time (수행의무를 이행하는 시점에 수익인식)

When a long-term construction contract does not meet the criteria for recognizing revenue over time, revenue and gross profit are recognized when the contract is completed.

(2) Presentation

1) CIP (construction in progress) account (an inventory account)

= accumulated construction costs

2) Billings on CIP (a contra-inventory account)

= accumulated billings on construction

The two accounts (CIP and Billing on CIP) are netted against each other for balance sheet reporting.

CIP ⟩ Billing on CIP

→ Current asset (Costs in excess of billings)

CIP ⟨ Billing on CIP

→ Current liability (Billings in excess of costs)

(3) Cost–recovery method (Zero–profit method)

(Dollars in thousands)

Accounts	20X1 DR	20X1 CR	20X2 DR	20X2 CR	20X3 DR	20X3 CR
1) Costs incurred						
CIP	1,000		1,916		1,134	
Materials, Cash etc.		1,000		1,916		1,134
2) Billing on contract						
A/R	900		2,400		1,200	
Billings on CIP		900		2,400		1,200
3) Collections						
Cash	750		1,750		2,000	
A/R		750		1,750		2,000
4) Recognize revenue (year–end)						
Construction expense	1,000		1,916		1,134	
CIP	0		0		450	
Revenue		1,000		1,916		1,584
5) Completion of the contract						
Billings on CIP	N/A				4,500	
CIP						4,500

Balance Sheet	20X1	20X2	20X3
A/R	$150,000	$800,000	$0
Inventory (CIP 〉 Billings)	100,000	0	0
Current liability (CIP 〈 Billings)	0	384,000	0

Income Statement	20X1	20X2	20X3
Revenue from long–term contracts	$1,000,000	$1,916,000	$1,584,000
Costs of construction	1,000,000	1,916,000	1,134,000
Gross profit	0	0	450,000

(4) Completed-contract method

(Dollars in thousands)

Accounts	20X1 DR	20X1 CR	20X2 DR	20X2 CR	20X3 DR	20X3 CR
1) Costs incurred						
CIP	1,000		1,916		1,134	
Materials, Cash etc.		1,000		1,916		1,134
2) Billing on contract						
A/R	900		2,400		1,200	
Billings on CIP		900		2,400		1,200
3) Collections						
Cash	750		1,750		2,000	
A/R		750		1,750		2,000
4) Recognize revenue (year-end)						
Construction expense						
CIP			N/A			
Revenue						
5) Completion of the contract						
Billings on CIP					4,500	
Revenue			N/A			4,500
Construction expenses					4,050	
CIP						4,050

Balance Sheet			
	20X1	20X2	20X3
A/R	$150,000	$800,000	$0
Inventory (CIP 〉 Billings)	100,000	0	0
Current liability (CIP 〈 Billings)	0	384,000	0

Income Statement			
	20X1	20X2	20X3
Revenue from long−term contracts	$0	$0	$4,500,000
Costs of construction	0	0	4,050,000
Gross profit	0	0	450,000

(5) Unprofitable projects

An estimated loss on the total contract is recognized immediately in the year it is discovered.

03 Tasked-Based Simulation

[Q 7-1] Recognition of Profit on Long-Term Contracts

During 20X5, AIFA Company started a construction job with a contract price of $1,600,000. The job was completed in 20X7. The following information is available.

	20X5	20X6	20X7
Costs incurred to date	$400,000	$825,000	$1,070,000
Estimated costs to complete	600,000	275,000	–0–
Billings to date	300,000	900,000	1,600,000
Collections to date	270,000	810,000	1,425,000

• Instructions •

a. Compute the amount of gross profit to be recognized each year, assuming the percentage–of–completion method is used.

b. Prepare all necessary journal entries for 20X6.

c. Compute the amount of gross profit to be recognized each year, assuming the cost–recovery method is used.

[Q 7-2] Analysis of Percentage-of-Completion Financial Statements

n 20X5, AIFA Construction Corp. began construction work under a 3-year contract. The contract price was $1,000,000. AIFA uses the percentage-of-completion method for financial accounting purposes. The income to be recognized each year is based on the proportion of cost incurred to total estimated costs for completing the contract. The financial statement presentations relating to this contract at December 31, 20X5, are shown below.

Balance Sheet		
Accounts receivable		$18,000
Construction in process	$65,000	
Less: Billings	61,500	
Costs and recognized profit in excess of billings		3,500
Income Statement		
Income (before tax) on the contract recognized in 20X5		$19,500

• Instructions •

a. How much cash was collected in 20X5 on this contract?

b. What was the initial estimated total income before tax on this contract?

[Q 7-3] Recognition of Revenue on Long-Term Contract and Entries

AIFA Construction Company uses the percentage-of-completion method of accounting. In 20X5, Hamilton began work under contract #E2-D2, which provided for a contract price of $2,200,000. Other details follow:

	20X5	20X6
Costs incurred during the year	$640,000	$1,425,000
Estimated costs to complete, as of December 31	960,000	–0–
Billings during the year	420,000	1,680,000
Collections during the year	350,000	1,500,000

• Instructions •

a. What portion of the total contract price would be recognized as revenue in 20X5? In 20X6?

b. Assuming the same facts as those above except that Hamilton uses the cost–recovery method of accounting, what portion of the total contract price would be recognized as revenue in 20X6?

c. Prepare a complete set of journal entries for 20X5 (using the percentage–of–completion method).

[Q 7-4] Revenue recognition

Eames Company enters into a contract with Leather Corporation to install a new general ledger system and provide IT services or the ledger system for five years. Eames Company incurs commission costs of $25,000 to obtain the contract. Design costs of $40,000 are incurred to modify the system according to Leather's specific requests. $10,000 is spent on printed materials, which includes $5,000 for the original printing of ledger handbooks and $5,000 for a reprint of ledger handbooks due to errors in the first printing.

• Instructions •

What amount is the incremental cost of obtaining the contract with Leather Corporation that will be recognized as an asset?

[Q 7-5] Revenue recognition

Cheap Tickets Now (CTN) is a company that specializes in offering deeply discounted tickets on major airlines and cruise ships. According to the agreement that CTN has with the transportation companies, CTN receives 5 percent of the ticket price as commission. CTN collects the full ticket price from the purchaser and remits the ticket price less the commission to the airline or cruise ship company. The airline and cruise ship conpanies are responsible for fulfilling the contract by providing the transportation. During the month of January, CTN's airline and cruise ship ticket sales totaled $250,000.

• Instructions •

According to the revenue rules in a principal–agent relationship, what is the total revenue that CTN will record for January ticket sales?

[Q 7-6] Revenue recognition

Jojo Roasters manufactures and sells coffee bean roasters. JoJo entered into an agreement with Smooth and Bold Coffee Company(S&B) to manufacture five roasters for S&B's new production facility. The roasters were manufactured to S&B's specifications and were completed on September 1, Year 2. Due to delays in the construction of S&B's new facility, JoJo agreed to maintain the coffee roasters in a separate section of its warehouse until the S&B facility opened on January 10, Year 3. S&B paid for the roasters on October 1, Year 2.

• Instructions •

On which date can JoJo recognize the revenue from this bill–and–hold arrangement?

[Q 7-7] Revenue recognition

Oriental Rug Company ships five handmade rugs valued at $5,000 each on consignment to Consign Design. Oriental Rug Company pays $1,000 of shipping costs and agrees to accept the return of any rugs within six months of the shipping date. Oriental Rug Company also agrees to pay Consign Design a commission of 10 percent for any rug sold. At the end of five months, Consign Design has sold four of the rugs for a total price of $38,000.

• Instructions •

What amount is the total inventory and revenue value reported by Consign Design at the end of the five months ?

[Q 7-8] Revenue recognition

On April 15, Year 3, Landon Co. signed a contract that entailed providing a specialized piece of scientific equipment for $215,000 to Jacobs Inc., with delivery expected to occur on August 31, Year3. Per the terms of the contract, Jacobs will pay Landon for the full amount on July 31, Year 3. Landon's cost to produce the equipment is $175,000.

• Instructions •

Assuming delivery occurs as expected, prepare the August 31 journal entry for Landon.

[Q 7-9] Revenue recognition

A country club charges its members $15,000 per year for full rights to use the club, which includes access to dining facilities, tennis courts, two golf courses, and the swimming pool. The club operates with a fiscal year ending June 30. The annual fee is automatically collected from all members on July 1 of each year and covers the upcoming period July 1-June With 350 members as of June 30, Year 3.

• Instructions •

What amount of Year 4 revenue will be reflected on the interim Year 4 income statement through December 31?

[Q 7-10] Recognition of Profit and Balance Sheet Amounts for Long-Term Contracts

AIFA Construction Company began operations on January 1, 20X5. During the year, AIFA Construction entered into a contract with ELK Corp. to construct a manufacturing facility. At that time, AIFA estimated that it would take 5 years to complete the facility at a total cost of $4,500,000. The total contract price for construction of the facility is $6,000,000. During the year, AIFA incurred $1,185,800 in construction costs related to the construction project. The estimated cost to complete the contract is $4,204,200. ELK Corp. was billed and paid 25% of the contract price.

• Instructions •

Prepare schedules to compute the amount of gross profit to be recognized for the year ended December 31, 20X5, and the amount to be shown as "costs and recognized profit in excess of billings" or "billings in excess of costs and recognized profit" at December 31, 20X5, under each of the following methods. Show supporting computations in good form.

a. Cost−recovery method.

b. Percentage−of−completion method.

[Q 7-11] Franchise Entries

AIFA Inc. charges an initial franchise fee of $70,000. Upon the signing of the agreement (which covers 3 years after commencement of operations), a payment of $28,000 is due. Thereafter, three annual payments of $14,000 are required. The credit rating of the franchisee is such that it would have to pay interest at 10%to borrow money. The franchise agreement is signed on May 1, 20X5, and the franchise commences operation on July 1, 20X5.

• Instructions •

Prepare the journal entries in 20X5 for the franchisor under the following assumptions. (Round to the nearest dollar.)

a. No future services are required by the franchisor once the franchise starts operations.

b. The franchisor has substantial services to perform, once the franchise begins operations, to maintain the value of the franchise.

c. The total franchise fee includes training services (with a value of $2,400) for the period leading up to the franchise opening and for 2 months following opening.

[Q 7-12] Repurchase Agreement

MARS Inc. enters into an agreement on March 1, 20X5, to sell VENUS Metal Company aluminum ingots. As part of the agreement, MARS also agrees to repurchase the ingots on May 1, 20X5, at the original sales price of $200,000 plus 2%.

• Instructions •

a. Prepare MARS's journal entry necessary on March 1, 20X5.

b. Prepare MARS's journal entry for the repurchase of the ingots on May 1, 20X5.

[Q 7-13] Bill and Hold

AIFA Company is involved in the design, manufacture, and installation of various types of wood products for large construction projects. AIFA recently completed a large contract for Stadium Inc., which consisted of building 35 different types of concession counters for a new soccer arena under construction. The terms of the contract are that upon completion of the counters, Stadium would pay $2,000,000. Unfortunately, due to the depressed economy, the completion of the new soccer arena is now delayed. Stadium has therefore asked Wood-Mode to hold the counters for 2 months at its manufacturing plant until the arena is completed. Stadium acknowledges in writing that it ordered the counters and that they now have ownership. The time that AIFA Company must hold the counters is totally dependent on when the arena is completed. Because Wood-Mode has not received additional progress payments for the counters due to the delay, Stadium has provided a deposit of $300,000.

• Instructions •

a. Explain this type of revenue recognition transaction.

b. What factors should be considered in determining when to recognize revenue in this transaction?

c. Prepare the journal entry(ies) that AIFA should make, assuming it signed a valid sales contract to sell the counters and received at the time the $300,000 deposit.

[Q 7-14] Consignment Sales

On May 3, 20X5, AIFA Company consigned 80 freezers, costing $500 each, to Saturn Company. The cost of shipping the freezers amounted to $840 and was paid by AIFA Company. On December 30, 20X5, a report was received from the consignee, indicating that 40 freezers had been sold for $750 each. Remittance was made by the consignee for the amount due after deducting a commission of 6%, advertising of $200, and total installation costs of $320 on the freezers sold.

• Instructions •

a. Compute the inventory value of the units unsold in the hands of the consignee.
b. Compute the profit for the consignor for the units sold.
c. Compute the amount of cash that will be remitted by the consignee.

[Q 7-15] Warranty Arrangement

On January 2, 20X5, AIFA Company sells production equipment to Fargo Inc. for $50,000. AIFA includes a 2-year assurance warranty service with the sale of all its equipment. The customer receives and pays for the equipment on January 2, 20X5. During 20X5, AIFA incurs costs related to warranties of $900. At December 31, 20X5, AIFA estimates that $650 of warranty costs will be incurred in the second year of the warranty.

• Instructions •

a. Prepare the journal entry to record this transaction on January 2, 20X5, and on December 31, 20X5 (assuming financial statements are prepared on December 31, 20X5).
b. Repeat the requirements for (a), assuming that in addition to the assurance warranty, AIFA sold Fargo an extended warranty (service–type warranty) for an additional 2 years (20X7–20X8) for $800.

Accounting and Reporting For the US CPA Exam

Volume
1

Accounting and Reporting

Chapter

Financial Statements of Employee Benefit Plan

Financial Statements of Employee Benefit Plan

01 Introduction

1 Pension plan

(1) Pension plan

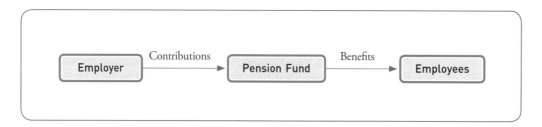

퇴직급여제도는 확정기여제도나 확정급여제도로 분류된다.

(2) Defined contribution pension plan (DC)

확정기여제도에서, 기업은 별도의 실체(기금)에 고정기여금을 납부하고, 그 기금이 당기와 과거 기간에 제공된 종업원 근무용역과 관련된 모든 종업원급여를 지급할 수 있을 정도로 충분한 자산을 보유하지 못하더라도 추가로 기여금을 납부해야 하는 법적의무나 의제의무가 없을 것이다. 기업은 확정기여제도에 대한 기여금을 그 기여금과 교환하여 종업원이 근무용역을 제공하는 때에 인식한다.

(3) Defined benefit pension plan (DB)

확정기여제도 이외의 모든 퇴직급여제도는 확정급여제도이다. 확정급여채무의 현재가치와 사외적립자산의 공정가치는 재무제표에 인식된 금액이 보고기간말에 결정될 금액과 중요한 차이가 나지 않을 정도의 주기를 두고 결정한다.
확정기여제도(DC)와 확정급여제도(DB)를 비교하면 다음과 같다.

	DC	DB
Risk taker	Employee	Employer
Benefit	확정(X)	확정(O)
Employer's obligation	Fixed	Variable

앞으로 기술하는 퇴직금 제도는 확정급여제도(DB)를 전제로 한다.

2 Terminology

(1) Actuarial Present Value

The value, as of a specified date, of an amount or series of amounts payable or receivable thereafter, with each amount adjusted to reflect the time value of money (through discounts for interest) and the probability of payment (by means of decrements for events such as death, disability, withdrawal, or retirement) between the specified date and the expected date of payment.

(2) Attribution

The process of assigning pension benefits or cost to periods of employee service.

(3) Pension benefit obligation

Vested Benefit Obligation (VBO)	− For vested benefits only − Based on current salary level
Accumulated Benefit Obligation (ABO)	− For vested and non−vested benefits − Based on current salary level
Projected Benefit Obligation (PBO)	− For vested and non−vested benefits − Based on futures salary level

※ 일반적으로 PBO 〉 ABO 〉 VBO이며, 퇴직급여를 측정을 위한 부채는 PBO이다.

(4) Vested Benefits

Benefits for which the employee's right to receive a pension benefit is no longer contingent on remaining in the service of the employer.

(5) Plan Assets

Assets—usually stocks, bonds, and other investments—that have been segregated and restricted, usually in a trust, to provide for pension benefits. The amount of plan assets includes amounts contributed by the employer, and by employees for a contributory plan, and amounts earned from investing the contributions, less benefits paid.

(6) Contributory Plan

A pension plan under which employees contribute part of the cost.

3 Basic journal entry

Contribution	Plan assets	xxx	
	Cash		xxx
Benefit paid	Projected benefit obligations (PBO)	xxx	
	Plan assets		xxx
Attribution	Pension expense	xxx	
	Projected benefit obligations (PBO)		xxx
Actual return on plan assets	Plan assets	xxx	
	Pension expense		xxx

4 T-account analysis

Plan assets			
Beginning balance (FV)	xxx	Benefit paid	xxx
Contribution	xxx		
Actual return	xxx	Ending balance (FV)	xxx

PBO			
Benefit paid	xxx	Beginning balance (PV)	xxx
Ending balance (PV)	xxx	Attribution	xxx

02 Financial Statements of Employee Benefit Plans

1 Defined benefit pension plans

The annual financial statements of a defined benefit pension plan should include all of the following :

(1) Statement of net assets available for benefits

(2) Statement of changes in net assets available for benefits

(3) Statement of accumulated plan benefits

(4) Statement of changes in accumulated plan benefits

⇨ 현금흐름표는 요구되지 않음

2 Defined contribution pension plans

The annual financial statements of a defined contribution pension plan should include all of the following :

(1) Statement of net assets available for benefits

(2) Statement of changes in net assets available for benefits

〈Statement of net assets available for benefits〉

Assets		
Investments, at fair value		
United States government securities	$	350,000
Corporate bonds and debentures		3,500,000
Common stock		
C&H Company		690,000
Other		2,250,000
Mortgages		480,000
Real estate		270,000
		7,540,000
Deposit administration contract, at contract value		1,000,000
Total investments		8,540,000
Receivables:		
Employees' contributions		40,000
Securities sold		310,000
Accrued interest and dividends		77,000
		427,000
Cash		200,000
Total assets		9,167,000
Liabilities:		
Accounts payable		70,000
Accrued expenses		85,000
Total liabilities		155,000
Net assets available for benefits	$	9,012,000

⟨Statement of changes in net assets available for benefits⟩

Investment income		
Net appreciation in fair value of investments	$	207,000
Interest		345,000
Dividends		130,000
Rents		55,000
		737,000
Less investment expenses		39,000
		698,000
Contributions		
Employer		780,000
Employees		450,000
		1,230,000
Total additions		1,928,000
Benefits paid directly to participants		740,000
Purchases of annuity contracts		257,000
		997,000
Administrative expenses		65,000
Total deductions		1,062,000
Net increase		866,000
Net assets available for benefits		
Beginning of year		8,146,000
End of year	$	9,012,000

⟨Statement of accumulated plan benefits⟩

Actuarial present value of accumulated plan benefits		
Vested benefits		
Participants currently receiving payments	$	3,040,000
Other participants		8,120,000
		11,160,000
Nonvested benefits		2,720,000
Total actuarial present value of accumulated plan benefits	$	13,880,000

⟨Statement of changes in accumulated plan benefits⟩

Actuarial present value of accumulated plan benefits at beginning of year	$	11,880,000
Increase (decrease) during the year attributable to:		
Plan amendment		2,410,000
Change in actuarial assumptions		(1,050,500)
Benefits accumulated		895,000
Increase for interest due to the decrease in the discount period		742,500
Benefits paid		(997,000)
Net increase		2,000,000
Actuarial present value of accumulated plan benefits at end of year	$	13,880,000

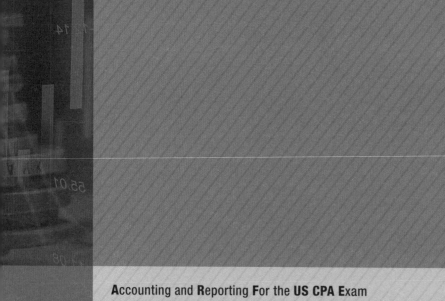

Accounting and Reporting For the **US CPA** Exam

Volume
1

Chapter

Public Company Reporting Topics

Chapter 09 | Public Company Reporting Topics

01 Segment reporting

1 Introduction

(1) Objectives

재무제표이용자가 public entity가 영위하는 사업활동의 내용 및 재무효과 그리고 영업을 영위하는 경제환경을 평가할 수 있도록 정보를 공시한다.

(2) Public entity

- It has issued debt or equity securities or is a conduit bond obligor for conduit debt securities that are traded in a public market.
- It is required to file financial statements with the SEC.
- It provides financial statements for the purpose of issuing any class of securities in a public market.

(3) Operating segment

영업부문은 다음 사항을 모두 충족하는 기업의 구성단위를 말한다.

1) 수익을 창출하고 비용을 발생 (내부거래 포함)시키는 사업활동을 영위한다.

2) 부문에 배분될 자원에 대한 의사결정을 하고 부문의 성과를 평가하기 위하여 최고영업의사결정자가 영업성과를 정기적으로 검토한다.

3) 구분된 재무정보의 이용이 가능하다.

영업부문은 아직까지 수익을 창출하지 않는 사업활동을 영위할 수 있다. 예를 들어, 신규 영업은 수익을 창출하기 전에도 영업부문이 될 수 있다.

2 Reportable segment

다음 조건을 모두 충족하는 각 영업부문에 대한 정보는 별도로 보고한다.

　　– 통합기준 (Aggregation Criteria)

　　– 양적기준 (Quantitative Thresholds)

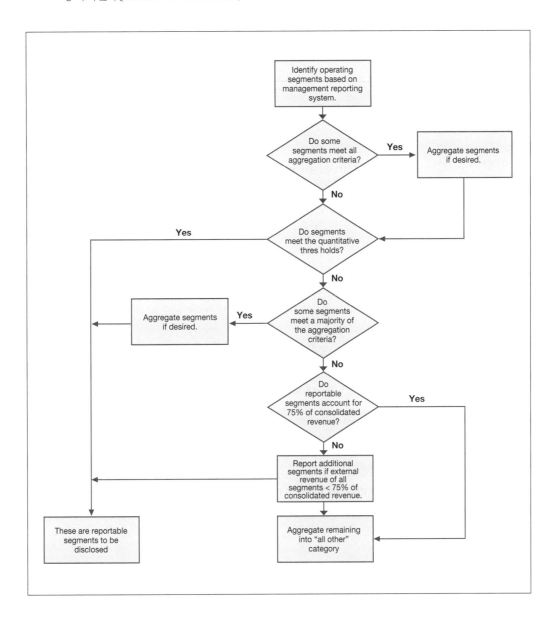

(1) 통합기준 (Aggregation Criteria)

다음 사항이 부문 간에 유사한 경우에는 둘 이상의 영업부문을 하나의 영업부문으로 통합할 수 있다.

a. The nature of the products and services
b. The nature of the production processes
c. The type or class of customer for their products and services
d. The methods used to distribute their products or provide their services
e. If applicable, the nature of the regulatory environment, for example, banking, insurance, or public utilities.

(2) 양적기준 (Quantitative Thresholds)

다음 양적기준 중 하나에 해당하는 영업부문에 대한 정보는 별도로 보고한다.

1) Its reported **revenue**, including both sales to external customers and inter-segment sales, is 10 percent or more of the combined revenue, internal and external, of all operating segments.
2) The absolute amount of its reported **profit or loss** is 10 percent or more of the greater, in absolute amount, of either:
   – The combined profit of all operating segments that did not report a loss
   – The combined loss of all operating segments that did report a loss.
3) Its **assets** are 10 percent or more of the combined assets of all operating segments

If total of external revenue reported by operating segments constitutes less than 75 percent of total consolidated revenue

⇒ additional operating segments shall be identified as reportable segments until at least 75 percent of total consolidated revenue is included in reportable segments.

Example-1

The following data pertain to Planet's operating segments for the current year.

Segment	external sales	inter-segment sales	Operating profit	segment assets
A	1,200	0	100	500
B	900	900	200	700
C	2,000	200	(370)	1,400
D	3,300	0	300	2,300
E	1,100	0	0	500
F	4,000	800	(30)	2,100
Totals	$12,500	1,900	200	7,500

Which operating segments are deemed to be reportable segment?

[10% revenue test]
 - threshold = $(12,500 + 1,900) \times 10\% = 1,440$
 - reportable segments : B, C, D, F

[10% profit test]
 - threshold = max $[600, 400] \times 10\% = 60$
 - reportable segments : A, B, C, D

[10% asset test]
 - threshold = $7,500 \times 10\% = 750$
 - reportable segments : C, D, F

[75% revenue test]
 - threshold = $12,500 \times 75\% = \$9,375$
 - final reportable segments : A, B, C, D, F

3 Disclosure Requirements

(1) General information

다음의 일반 정보를 공시한다.

1) 조직기준을 포함하여 보고부문을 식별하기 위하여 사용한 요소

  - 예 : 경영진이 제품과 용역의 차이, 지리적 위치의 차이, 규제환경의 차이

2) 각 보고부문이 수익을 창출하는 제품과 용역의 유형

(2) Information about profit or loss and assets

1) A public entity shall report a measure of profit or loss and total assets for each reportable segment.

2) A public entity also shall disclose all of the following about each reportable segment.

a. Revenues from external customers
b. Revenues from transactions with other operating segments
c. Interest revenue
d. Interest expense
e. Depreciation, depletion, and amortization expense
f. Unusual items
g. Equity in the net income of investees by the equity method
h. Income tax expense or benefit
i. Significant noncash items other than depreciation

※ IFRS는 total liabilities를 공시하지만 US GAAP은 공시하지 않는다.

	Auto parts	Motor Vessels	Soft ware	Elec tronics	Finance	All Other	Totals
Revenues from external customers	$ 3,000	$ 5,000	$ 9,500	$ 12,000	$ 5,000	$ 1,000	$ 35,500
Intersegment revenues	–	–	3,000	1,500	–	–	4,500
Interest revenue	450	850	1,000	1,500	–	–	3,750
Interest expense	350	600	700	1,100	–	–	2,750
Net interest revenue	–	–	–	–	1,000	–	1,000
Depreciation and amortization	200	100	50	1,500	1,100	–	2,950
Segment profit	200	70	900	2,300	500	100	4,070
Other significant noncash items:							
cost in excess of billings on long-term contracts	–	200	–	–	–	–	200
Segment assets	2.000	5,000	3,000	12,000	57,000	2,000	81,000
Expenditures for segment assets	300	700	500	800	600	–	2,900

(3) Reconciliations of reportable segment revenues, profit or loss, and assets, to the consolidated totals

Revenues	
Total revenues for reportable segments	$ 39,000
Other revenues	1,000
Elimination of intersegment revenues	(4,500)
Total consolidated revenues	$ 35,500
Profit or Loss	
Total profit or loss for reportable segments	$ 3,970
Other profit or loss	100
Elimination of intersegment profits	(500)
Unallocated amounts:	
Litigation settlement received	500
Other corporate expenses	(750)
Adjustment to pension expense in consolidation	(250)
Income before income taxes and extraordinary items	$ 3,070
Assets	
Total assets for reportable segements	$ 79,000
Other assets	2,000
Elimination of receivables from corporate headquarters	(1,000)
Goodwill not allocated to segments	4,000
Other unallocated amounts	1,000
Consolidated total	$ 85,000

(4) Interim period information

A public entity shall disclose all of the following about each reportable segment in condensed financial statements of interim periods:

a. Revenues from external customers

b. Intersegment revenues

c. A measure of segment profit or loss

d. Total assets for which there has been a material change from the amount disclosed in the last annual report

e. A description of differences from the last annual report in the basis of segmentation or in the basis of measurement of segment profit or loss

f. A reconciliation of the total of the reportable segments' measures of profit or loss to the public entity's consolidated income

(5) Restatement of previously reported information

내부조직의 구조를 변경하여 보고부문의 구성이 변한 경우 과거기간의 해당 부문정보를 재작성한다. 단, 필요한 정보를 이용할 수 없고 그 정보를 산출하는 비용이 과도한 경우에는 예외로 한다.

(6) Measurement

각 부문항목 금액은 부문에 대한 자원배분의 의사결정과 보고부문의 성과평가를 위하여 최고영업의사결정자에게 보고되는 측정치이어야 한다.

4 Entity-wide information

단 하나의 보고부문을 가진 기업을 포함하여 이 기준서의 적용대상인 모든 기업에 적용된다.

(1) Information about products and services

각각의 제품과 용역 또는 유사한 제품과 용역의 집단별로 외부고객으로부터의 수익을 보고한다.

(2) Information about geographic areas

지역에 대한 다음의 정보를 보고한다.

1) 다음과 같은 외부고객으로부터의 수익

 − 본사 소재지 국가에 귀속되는 금액

 − 수익이 발생하는 모든 외국에 귀속되는 금액의 총계

  (특정 외국에 귀속되는 수익이 중요한 경우에는 별도로 공시)

2) 다음과 같은 비유동자산 (금융상품은 제외)

 − 본사 소재지 국가에 소재하는 비유동자산 금액

 − 모든 외국에 소재하는 비유동자산 금액의 총계

  (특정 외국에 소재하는 자산이 중요한 경우에는 별도로 공시)

(3) Information about major customers

주요 고객에 대한 의존도에 관한 정보를 제공한다. 단일 외부고객으로부터의 수익이 기업 전체 수익의 10% 이상인 경우에는, 그 사실, 해당 고객별 수익금액 및 그러한 수익금액이 보고되는 부문의 명칭을 공시한다. 그러나 주요 고객의 신원이나 그 주요 고객으로부터의 각 부문의 수익금액을 공시할 필요는 없다.

※ 기업전체정보의 공시사항은 중간재무제표에는 요구되지 않는다.

CASE STUDY

Amazon's entity–wide information

Information about products and services

Net sales by groups of similar products and services is as follows (in millions):

		Year Ended December 31,				
		2015		2016		2017
Net Sales:						
Online stores (1)	$	76,863	$	91,431	$	108,354
Physical stores (2)		—		—		5,798
Third-party seller services (3)		16,086		22,993		31,881
Subscription services (4)		4,467		6,394		9,721
AWS		7,880		12,219		17,459
Other (5)		1,710		2,950		4,653
Consolidated	$	107,006	$	135,987	$	177,866

Information about geographic areas

Net sales generated from our internationally-focused websites are denominated in local functional currencies. Revenues are translated at average rates prevailing throughout the period. Net sales attributed to countries that represent a significant portion of consolidated net sales are as follows (in millions):

		Year Ended December 31,				
		2015		2016		2017
United States	$	70,537	$	90,349	$	120,486
Germany		11,816		14,148		16,951
United Kingdom		9,033		9,547		11,372
Japan		8,264		10,797		11,907
Rest of world		7,356		11,146		17,150
Consolidated	$	107,006	$	135,987	$	177,866

02 Regulation S-X

Regulation S-X is a set of rules issued by the SEC(Securities and Exchange Commission) that defines how financial statements will be prepared for various filings.

1 Interim financial statements

(1) Review requirements

Interim financial statements may be unaudited. However, before filing, interim financial statements included in quarterly reports on Form 10–Q must be reviewed by an independent public accountant and a report of the accountant on the review must be filed with the interim financial statements.

(2) Balance sheet

as of the end of the issuer's most recent fiscal quarter

as of the end of the preceding fiscal year

예) Year 2 second quarter

6/30/Year 2, 12/31/Year 1

(3) Statements of comprehensive income

for the most recent fiscal quarter

for the interim period up to the date of such balance sheet

for the comparable period of the preceding fiscal year

예) Year 2 second quarter

4/1/Year 2~ 6/30/Year 2, 1/1/Year 2~ 6/30/Year 2

4/1/Year 1~ 6/30/Year 1, 1/1/Year 1~ 6/30/Year 1

(4) Statements of cash flows

for the interim period up to the date of such balance sheet

for the comparable period of the preceding fiscal year

예) Year 2 second quarter

1/1/Year 2~ 6/30/Year 2, 1/1/Year 1~ 6/30/Year 1

(5) Condensed format

Interim financial statements may be condensed as follows:

1) Balance sheets

include separate captions for each balance sheet component presented in the annual financial statements that represents 10% or more of total assets.

2) Statements of comprehensive income

include net sales or gross revenue, each cost and expense category presented in the annual financial statements that exceeds 20% of sales or gross revenues, provision for income taxes, and discontinued operations.

3) Cash flow statements

include cash flows from operating, investing and financing activities as well as cash at the beginning and end of each period and the increase or decrease in such balance.

(6) Disclosure required

Footnote and other disclosures should be provided as needed for fair presentation and to ensure that the financial statements are not misleading.

2 Annual financial statements

(1) Audit requirements

Annual financial statements filed with the SEC must be audited by an independent public accountant, and the audit report must be filed with the financial statements.

(2) Balance sheet

as of the end of each of the two most recent fiscal years

(3) Statements of comprehensive income

for each of the three fiscal years preceding the date of the most recent audited balance sheet

(4) Statements of cash flows

for each of the three fiscal years preceding the date of the most recent audited balance sheet

(5) Changes in each caption of stockholders' equity

should be given in a note or separate statement

for each of the three fiscal years preceding the date of the most recent audited balance sheet

(6) Disclosure requirements

The following items must be disclosed in the financial statements or in the notes:

1) Dividends per share and in total for each class of shares

2) Principles of consolidation or combination

3) Assets subject to lien

4) Defaults with respect to any issue of securities or credit agreements if the default or breach existed at balance sheet date and has not been subsequently cured

5) Preferred shares disclosures

6) Restrictions that limit the payment of dividends

7) Significant changes in bonds, mortgages, or similar debt

8) Summarized financial information of subsidiaries not consolidated and 50 percent or less owned entities

9) Income tax expense

10) Warrants or rights outstanding

11) Related party transactions which affect the financial statements

12) Repurchase and reverse repurchase agreements

13) Accounting policies for derivative instruments

03 Regulation S-K

Regulation S-K is a SEC regulation that outlines how registrants should disclose material qualitative descriptors of their business on registration statements, periodic reports, and any other filings. Regulation S-K is generally focused on qualitative descriptions while the related Regulation S-X focuses on financial statements.

(1) Business (Items 100)

Includes descriptions of the business, property, legal proceedings, mine safety disclosures, and risk factors. A principles-based disclosure regime allowing registrants discretion to determine what merits disclosure based on materiality.

(2) Registrant Securities (Items 200)

Includes information on the market price of common equity, dividends on common equity, and security descriptions.

(3) Financial Information (Items 300)

Includes selected financial data, supplementary financial information, management's discussion and analysis (MD&A), changes in and disagreements with accountants, quantitative and qualitative disclosures about market risk, controls and procedures, and internal controls.

(4) Management and Certain Security Holders (Items 400)

Includes information on directors and executive officers, executive compensation, security ownership of certain beneficial owners and management, related person transactions, Exchange Act compliance, code of ethics, and corporate governance.

(5) Registration Statement and Prospectus Provisions (Items 500)

Includes cover pages, a prospectus summary, how proceeds will be used, offering price determination, dilution, selling security holders, distribution plan, interests of named experts and counsel, disclosure of commission positions, other expenses of issuance and distribution, and undertakings.

(6) Exhibits (Items 600)

Relates to the exhibits that typically accompany the filings of various SEC required forms.

(7) Industry Guides (Items 800)

Relates to the disclosure requirements for particular industries.

(8) Roll-up Transactions (Items 900)

These are less frequently seen situations involving private firms merging into larger companies.

04 XBRL Reporting Requirements

1 XBRL

XBRL (eXtensible Business Reporting Language) is a royalty-free, open specification for software that uses XML (eXtensible Markup Language) data tags to describe financial information for business and financial reporting.

(XBRL은 컴퓨터가 재무보고 수치의 의미 및 상관관계 등을 정의할 수 있어 회계수치 또는 재무보고 내용에 대한 정확성 검증 및 심층 분석이 가능하도록 설계된 재무보고 전용 국제표준 전산언어이다.)

XBRL is a next-generation language after HTML. HTML tells computers how to display text. XML and XBRL tell computers how to interpret the context of the text.

XBRL was designed to provide an electronic format for financial and business reporting, with an overall goal of improving the way in which data is communicated.

The application of XBRL tags (defined below) applied to financial statements allows computers to search and assemble information quickly so that data can be accessed and analyzed by financial statement users.

Through XBRL, machine-readable financial statements are available real-time in digital format.

This enables automated data collection, provides faster access to financial statement data, and facilitates more robust data analysis.

2 Terminology

(1) Tag

A machine-readable code that gives a standard definition for each line item in an income statement, cash flow statement, balance sheet, or other financial or nonfinancial data, including data contained in the notes to the financial statements. Tags include descriptive labels, definitions, references to U.S. GAAP, and other elements that provide contextual information that allow data to be recognized and processed by software.

(2) Taxonomy

A taxonomy defines the specific, computer-readable tags used for individual items of business and financial data. XBRL taxonomies include:

1) XBRL U.S. GAAP Financial Reporting Taxonomy

The XBRL U.S. GAAP taxonomy is maintained and updated by the FASB and the Financial Accounting Foundation to reflect changes in U.S. GAAP and SEC financial statement disclosure requirements, as well as changes in common reporting practices.

2) SEC Reporting Taxonomy:

A taxonomy that includes the elements necessary to meet SEC requirements for financial statements, schedules, and disclosures.

3) Global Ledger Taxonomy

A taxonomy independent of other reporting standards or system types that permits flexible, multinational consolidation.

4) Industry Specific Taxonomies

Taxonomies have been created to accommodate industry specific financial reporting needs. Industry specific taxonomies exist for the commercial and industrial, banking and savings, real estate, insurance, and broker/dealer industries.

5) Company Specific Tags

Companies can create their own tags when needed tags are not included in any existing taxonomy.

(3) Instance Document

An instance document is an XBRL formatted document that contains tagged data.

3 SEC Interactive Data Rule

The SEC's Interactive Data Rule requires U.S. public companies and foreign private issuers that use U.S. GAAP to present financial statements and any applicable financial statement schedules in an exhibit prepared using XBRL. This exhibit is required with the filers' SEC registration statements, quarterly and annual reports, and reports containing revised or updated financial statements.

(1) Data Tagging Details

Tagged disclosures must include the primary financial statements, notes, and financial statement schedules. A filer's primary financial statements are required to be tagged in detail.

Financial statement footnote and financial statement schedule tagging is broken into four different levels. Level 1 tagging is required for a company's first XBRL submission.

Level 1 through Level 4 tagging is required starting one year from the filer's initial submission.

(2) Level 1

Each complete footnote and schedule is tagged as a single block of text.

(3) Level 2

Each significant accounting policy within the significant accounting policies footnote is tagged as a single block of text.

(3) Level 3

Each table within each footnote or schedule is tagged as a separate block of text.

(4) Level 4

Within each footnote or schedule, each amount (i.e., monetary value, percentage, and number) is required to be separately tagged.

(5) Inline XBRL

An In line XBRL (iXBRL) format, which embeds XBRL data directly into HTML documents, is required by the SEC for periodic and interim financial reporting. The output is a single format that is readable by both humans and machines. The objectives of In line XBRL are to make financial information more usable and machine-readable, while providing more consistency in reporting and giving companies more of a platform to communicate their stories to financial statement users.

Accounting and Reporting For the **US CPA** Exam

Accounting and Reporting

Chapter

10

Governmental Accounting

Chapter 10 | Governmental Accounting

01 Introduction

1 정부회계의 의의

회계는 자본시장의 발달과 함께 투자 및 신용 의사결정에 유용한 정보를 제공하는 것으로 발전하고 있다. 회계는 회계실체에 따라 기업회계와 정부회계로 구분되는데 기업회계가 주주와 채권자의 경제적 의사결정을 위한 정보제공을 목적으로 한다면 정부회계는 정부(국가 또는 지방자치단체)의 경제적, 정치적 및 사회적 의사결정을 위한 다양한 이해관계자들에게 정보를 제공하는 것을 목적으로 한다.

정부회계는 중앙정부나 지방자치단체와 같은 정부조직의 재정활동에 대한 회계를 말한다. 정부조직의 재정활동은 국방, 치안, 교육과 같은 서비스를 제공하기 위하여 조세를 부과하거나 채권 등을 발행하여 재원을 조달하는 사용하는 활동을 말한다. 정부회계가 기업회계와 다른 특징은 다음과 같다.

(1) 비영리

정부조직은 민간기업과 달리 영리추구를 목적으로 하지 않고 공공서비스를 제공하는 것을 목적으로 한다. 정부는 기업처럼 수익이 비용을 초과하는 순이익을 보인다고 해서 정부의 기능을 잘 수행했다고 할 수 없다.

(2) 소유권

민간기업의 주인인 주주는 기업을 팔거나 해산할 수 있지만 정부의 주인인 국민은 정부를 팔거나 해산할 수 없다.

(3) 법령

정부의 서비스는 공권력에 의해 집행되기 때문에 법령에 의해서 강한 통제를 받는다. 정부 서비스를 위한 지출은 예산에 의하여 통제된다.

2 정부회계의 정보이용자

(1) Council

민간기업은 기업의 소유주인 주주가 재무제표를 가장 활발하게 이용하며, 정부회계는 국민을 대표하는 의회가 가장 중요한 정보이용자가 된다. 정부의 수탁책임과 서비스 활동의 효율적인 이행여부 등이 가장 중요한 정보인 것이다.

(2) Investors and creditors

정부에서 채권을 발행하어 사업을 추진하는 경우, 이를 취득하는 투자자는 해당 정부의 재무상태에 대한 정보를 필요로 한다.

(3) Citizenry (taxpayers and voters)

납세자는 자신이 납부한 세금이 정당하고 효율적으로 사용되는지에 대한 정보를 필요로 하며 유권자는 자신이 선출한 공직자가 임무를 유능하게 수행하는 지에 대한 정보를 필요로 한다.

(4) Legislative and oversight bodies

정부기관 중 상급기관은 자신이 감독하는 하급기관에 대한 재무적 정보를 필요로 한다. 특히 중앙정부는 지방자치단체에게 지원하는 국고보조금의 사용에 대한 정보를 필요로 한다.

3 미국 정부회계의 의의

미국 기업회계는 1930년대의 미국 대공황을 계기로 발전되었다면 미국의 정부회계는 1970년에 지방정부 중에서 재정규모가 가장 큰 뉴욕시의 파산위기를 계기로 발전하게 되었다. 1973년에 NCGA(National Council on Governmental Accounting)에서 정부의 재무제표에 대한 회계기준(GAAP)을 제정하였고 1984년부터는 미국 GASB (Governmental Accounting Standard Board)에서 회계기준(GAAP)을 제정하고 있다. 특히, GASB Statement No. 34는 미국 정부회계 역사상 가장 획기적인 내용으로, 정부도 기업과 마찬가지로 재무정보를 발생주의를 적용하여 엄격하게 보고하는 것을 강조하고 있다.

정부회계기준위원회(GASB)는 미국의 주정부 및 지방정부의 회계기준을 제정하고 있으며 미국의 기업, 정부 및 비영리단체의 회계기준을 제정하는 기관을 요약하면 다음과 같다. 단, 연방정부 회계는 본서의 범위에서 제외한다.

Corporation		FASB
State and local government		GASB
NFP	Private	FASB
	Public	GASB

미국정부가 적용하여야 할 회계기준의 체계순서는 다음과 같다.

GAAP hierarchy for all state and local governmental entities

Category A	GASB Statement(GASBS)
Category B	GASB technical bulletins GASB Implementation Guides Literature of the AICPA cleared by the GASB

※ GASB Interpretation : 2016년도부터 폐지

4 정부의 기초지식

(1) 대한민국 조세의 분류

1) 과세주체

- 국세 : 국가가 부과하는 세금
- 지방세 : 지방자치단체가 부과하는 세금

2) 세수의 용도가 정해져 있는가?

- 보통세 : 일반경비에 충당하는 세금
- 목적세 : 특정경비에 충당하는 세금

3) 납세의무자가 누구인가?

- 직접세 : 납세의무자와 세금부담자가 동일한 세금
- 간접세 : 납세의무자와 세금부담자가 다른 세금

	과세주체	세수용도	납세의무자
부가가치세	국세	보통세	간접세
종합소득세	국세	보통세	직접세
법인세	국세	보통세	직접세
취득세 및 등록면허세	지방세	보통세	직접세
재산세	지방세	보통세	직접세
교육세	국세	목적세	직접세
상속세 및 증여세	국세	보통세	직접세

(2) 미국 정부의 종류

미국 정부는 행정, 입법 및 사법권의 분리에 따라 다음 3가지로 구분된다.

1) Federal government (연방정부)

2) State government (주정부)

3) Local government (지방정부)

미국은 50개의 주(states)와 1개의 특별구(District of Columbia)로 이루어져 있으며, State 아래 단위의 행정구역은 County로 3,000개 이상이 있다.

(3) 정부의 수익구조

정부의 수익은 비교환수익과 교환수익으로 분류 된다.

1) Non-exchange transaction (비교환수익)

직접적인 반대급부 없이 발생하는 수익   ex) tax, penalty, grant, donation

2) Exchange transaction (교환수익)

정부가 재화용역을 공급하고 대가를 받은 수익   ex) user charge

(4) 미국 조세의 분류

Federal (연방세)	State (주세)	Local (지방세)
- Individual income tax - Corporate income tax - Estate & gift tax - FICA & Medicare tax	- Sales tax - Individual income tax - Corporate income tax	- Property tax - Sales tax - Consumption tax - Individual income tax - Corporate income tax

※ Sales tax는 재화의 판매에 수반되는 조세로서 한국의 부가가치세와 유사하며 보통 5%~9%의 범위
내에서 State마다 세율이 다르다.

(5) 정부회계의 보고실체

정부회계의 보고 실체는 일반목적정부(General government)와 특별목적정부(Special government)로 나누어 다음과 같이 분류한다.

General government	Special government
1) State 2) County 3) Sub-county ① Municipality : City, Borough, Village ② Township : Town, Township	1) School district 2) Special district

5 정부회계와 기업회계의 차이점

(1) Fund accounting

펀드회계란 정부의 자원을 펀드별로 구분하여 회계처리 및 재무보고를 하여야 한다.

(2) Modified accrual accounting

정부 펀드 중 일부는 발생주의가 아닌 수정발생주의로 회계처리를 하여 재무제표를 작성하여야 한다.

(3) Budgetary accounting

예산회계는 정부가 예산수립을 하여 그 내용을 회계처리 하여 보고하는 과정이다.

(4) Two-types financial statements

정부는 펀드 재무제표와 통합 재무제표의 두 종류 재무제표를 작성하여야 한다.

6 Accounting cycle

정부회계는 기업회계와 마찬가지로 다음과 같은 회계순환과정을 가진다.

1. Analyze each transaction
2. Journalizing
3. Posting : Transferring journal entries to the ledger account.
4. Unadjusted trial balance (수정전 시산표 작성)
5. Adjusting entries (수정분개)
6. Adjusted Trial balance (수정후 시산표 작성)
7. Financial statement (재무제표의 작성)
8. Closing Entries (마감분개)

정부회계는 기업회계와 마찬가지로 총 계정원장(general ledger)의 기록을 위하여 통계계정 (control accounts)을 사용한다.

A control account is a summary account in the general ledger. This account contains aggregated totals for transactions that are individually stored in subsidiary-level ledger accounts.

A/R subsidiary-level ledger	General ledger
Customer 1 : $200 Customer 2: 100 Customer 3: 150	A/R Control : $450

Revenue subsidiary-level ledger	General ledger
Taxes : $200 Fines : 100 Grant : 150	Revenue Control : $450

※ Closing Entries

마감분개는 수익과 비용 계정을 제거하여 자본에 기록하는 과정이다.

- Permanent or real account: assets, liabilities and equity
- Temporary or nominal account: revenues and expenses

	Dr	Cr
Revenue-control	100	
Expense-control		90
Retained earnings (plug)		10

ex) 수익 100, 비용 90의 마감분개는 다음과 같다.

▶ 정부회계는 Fund Balance 또는 Net Position에 마감한다.

7 GASB Concepts Statement

(1) Financial reporting objectives

Governmental financial reporting should provide information to assist users in assessing accountability and making economic, social, and political decisions.

(2) Accountability

재산의 관리를 위탁받은 경영자나 정부조직이 수탁책임(stewardship)을 회계정보로 보고하는 것을 회계보고책임(accountability)이라고 한다.

(3) Interperiod equity

Financial reporting should provide information to determine whether current-year revenues were sufficient to pay for current-year services.

기간 간의 형평성은 한 해의 세입이 그 해의 서비스제공을 위한 지출을 감당하기에 충분한지에 대한 여부와 그해의 납세자가 제공받은 서비스의 원가가 장래의 납세자에 게 떠넘겨졌는지에 대한 여부에 대한 정보이다.

(4) Fiscal accountability

Financial reporting should demonstrate whether resources were obtained and used in accordance with the entity's legally adopted budget.

적법성은 정부가 자원을 조달하고 지출한 내용이 예산에 따라 적법하게 이루어 졌는지를 나타내며, 법규나 계약의 내용과 합치되는지를 나타낸다.

(5) Operation accountability

Financial reporting should provide information to assist users in assessing the service efforts, costs, and accomplishments of the governmental entity.

운영의 효율성은 정부가 제공한 서비스의 원가가 얼마이며 각 부서가 업무를 얼마나 효율적으로 수행했는지를 판단할 수 있는 정부를 제공하는 것을 말한다.

(4) Basic characteristics of financial information

1) Understandability

Information in financial reports should be expressed as simply as possible

2) Reliability

Information in financial reports should be verifiable and free from bias and should faithfully represent what it purports to represent.

3) Relevance

Information is relevant if it is capable of making a difference in a user's assessment of a problem, condition, or event.

4) Timeliness

If financial reports are to be useful, they must be issued soon enough after the reported events to affect decisions.

5) Consistency

Financial reports should be consistent over time.

6) Comparability

Financial reports should be comparable. This does not imply that similarly designated governments perform the same functions.

(5) Elements of Financial statements

1) Assets

Assets are resources with present service capacity that the government presently controls.

2) Liabilities

Liabilities are present obligations to sacrifice resources that the government has little
or no discretion to avoid.

3) Deferred outflow of resources

A deferred outflow of resources is a consumption of net assets by the government that
is applicable to a future reporting period.

4) Deferred inflow of resources

A deferred inflow of resources is an acquisition of net assets by the government that
is applicable to a future reporting period.

5) Net position

Net position is the residual of all other elements presented in a statement of financial position.

> Assets + Deferred outflow of resources
> = Liabilities + Deferred inflow of resources + Net position

6) Outflow of resources

An outflow of resources is a consumption of net assets by the government that is applicable to the reporting period.

7) Inflow of resources

An inflow of resources is an acquisition of net assets by the government that is applicable to the reporting period.

> Inflow of resources − Outflow of resources = Changes in Net position

(6) Measurement of Elements of Financial statements

1) Two measurement approaches

- **Initial Amount**

  The transaction price or amount assigned when an asset was acquired or a liability was incurred, including subsequent modifications to that price or amount that are derived from the amount at which the asset or liability was initially reported.

- **Remeasured Amount**

  The amount assigned when an asset or liability is remeasured as of the financial statement date.

2) Four measurement attributes

- **Historical cost**

  Price paid to acquire an asset or the amount received pursuant to the incurrence of a liability in an actual exchange transaction.

- **Fair value**

  Price that would be received to sell an asset or paid to transfer a liability in an orderly transaction between market participants at the measurement date.

- **Replacement cost**

  Price that would be paid to acquire an asset with equivalent service potential in an orderly market transaction at the measurement date.

- **Settlement amount**

  The amount at which an asset could be realized or a liability could be liquidated with the counterparty, other than in an active market.

02 ⏵ Fund accounting

1 Definition

미국 정부회계에서 가장 중요한 개념이 펀드회계이다. 펀드회계는 자원의 사용목적과 제약에 따라 각각의 펀드를 설정하며, 설정된 각각의 펀드를 회계실체로 하여 수입과 지출 등의 회계처리를 별도로 하는 시스템이다. 각 펀드는 각 단위회계실체로서 자체적으로 복식부기 형태의 독립적인 장부체계를 갖는다.

> Fund is a sum of money or other resources segregated for the purpose of carrying on specific activities. Fund is an independent fiscal and accounting entity and each fund is self-balancing and is a separate entity having its own financial statements.

2 Types of funds

미국 주 및 지방 정부의 경우 펀드를 크게 정부형 펀드, 사업형 펀드, 수탁형 펀드로 구분하여 각 유형별 펀드는 다음과 같이 세분류한다.

Governmental fund	General fund (GF)
	Special revenue fund (SRF)
	Capital project fund (CPF)
	Debt service fund (DSF)
	Permanent fund (PF)
Proprietary fund	Enterprise fund (EF)
	Internal service fund (ISF)
Fiduciary fund	Pension trust fund (PTF)
	Investment trust fund (ITF)
	Private-purpose trust fund (PPTF)
	Custodial Fund (CF)

3 Governmental fund

Account for activities that provide public with services financed by taxes.

정부형 펀드는 주로 조세수입과 정부활동을 위한 세출을 기록하기 위한 펀드를 말하며, 다음의 다섯 종류의 펀드로 구성된다.

(1) General Fund (GF)

한국의 일반예산에 해당되는 펀드로 다른 펀드에서 특별히 규정하지 않는 모든 자금의 변동을 기록하고 관리하는 펀드이다.

- Accounts for ordinary operations which are financed from taxes and all transactions not accounted for in some other fund are accounted for in this fund

- Example: police department, fire department

(2) Capital Projects Fund (CPF)

정부형 자원 중에서 유형 자산의 취득 또는 건설목적으로 특정되어 있는 자원을 보고하는 펀드로서 다음과 같은 특징이 있다.

- Capital projects funds are used to account for and report financial resources that are restricted, committed, or assigned to expenditure for capital outlays, including the acquisition or construction of capital facilities and other capital assets.

- Capital projects funds exclude those types of capital-related outflows financed by proprietary funds or fiduciary funds

- Example : Bond proceeds for construction of new City Hall Building

(3) Debt Service Fund (DSF)

정부형 자원 중에서 지방채의 원금과 이자상환의 목적으로 특정되어 있는 자원을 보고하는 펀드로서 다음과 같은 특징이 있다.

- Debt service funds are used to account for and report financial resources that are restricted, committed, or assigned to expenditure for principal and interest on all general obligation debt. Financial resources that are being accumulated for principal and interest maturing in future years also should be reported in debt service funds.

- Debt service funds should be used to report resources if legally mandated.

- Example : Tax dedicated to servicing general obligation bonds

(4) Special Revenue Fund (SRF)

정부형 자원 중에서 capital project와 debt service 목적을 제외한 목적이 특정되어 있는 자원을 보고하는 펀드로서 다음과 같은 특징이 있다.

- Special revenue funds are used to account for and report the proceeds of specific revenue sources that are restricted or committed to expenditure for specified purposes other than debt service or capital projects.

- Earmarked taxes (목적세)

  ① Motor-fuel tax

  ② Hotel tax used to promote tourist

(5) Permanent fund (PF)

정부형 자원 중에서 원금은 그대로 유지하고 투자수익으로만 사용이 특정되어 있는 자원을 보고하는 펀드로서 다음과 같은 특징이 있다.

- Permanent funds should be used to account for and report resources that are restricted to the extent that only earnings, and not principal, may be used for purposes that support the reporting government's programs—that is, for the benefit of the government or its citizenry.

- Permanent funds do not include private-purpose trust funds, which should be used to report situations in which the government is required to use the principal or earnings for the benefit of individuals, private organizations, or other governments.

- Example : Citizen's gifts for maintenance of city's cemetery

4 Proprietary fund

Account for business—type activities that derive their revenue from user charge

사업형 펀드는 정부가 민간기업과 같은 사업을 하는 데 따르는 펀드로서 다음의 두 가지 종류의 펀드로 구성된다.

(1) Enterprise Funds (EF)

정부가 시민에게 민간기업과 같은 재화를 판매하거나 용역을 제공하는 데 따르는 자금을 관리하기 위한 펀드로서, 상수도나 하수도, 지하철 같은 서비스를 제공하는 데 필요한 자금을 관리하는 것이다.

- Account for the operation of governmental facilities and services that are intended to be primarily from user charges.
- Examples : water and sewer utilities, transportation systems, lottery

(2) Internal Service Funds (ISF)

한 정부기관이 다른 정부기관에 민간기업과 같은 서비스를 유상으로 제공하는 데 따르는 자금을 관리하기 위한 펀드로서, 예를 들면 한 정부기관에서 자동차를 구입한 후 이를 다른 정부기관에게 임차하는 서비스를 제공하는 데 필요한 자금을 관리하는 것이다.

- Account for goods and services provided to other departments within governmental unit on a cost reimbursement fee basis.
- Examples : Motor pool, EDP processing , Self insurance

5 Fiduciary funds (신탁형 펀드)

> The assets associated with the activity have one or more of the following characteristics:
>
> (1) The assets are administered through a trust in which the government itself is not a beneficiary (Trust)
>
> (2) The assets are for the benefit of individuals and the government does not have administrative involvement with the assets (Agent)

신탁형 펀드는 정부가 다른 수혜자를 위하여 자산을 관리하는 펀드로서 다음의 네 가지 종류의 펀드로 구성된다.

(1) Pension Trust Funds (PTF)

공무원 연금을 관리하는 펀드로서 다음과 같은 특징이 있다.

- Used to report fiduciary activities for pension plans and other post−employment benefit (OPEB) plans that are administered through trusts.
- Examples : Public Employees Retirement Systems (PERS)

(2) Investment Trust Funds (ITF)

타 정부기관의 투자업무를 대행하는 펀드로서 다음과 같은 특징이 있다.

- Used to report fiduciary activities from the external portion of investment pools that are held in a trust
- Examples : Investment pools for all cities within its borders.

(3) Private−purpose Trust Funds (PPTF)

pension trust와 investment trust를 제외한 trustee의 업무를 보고하는 펀드이다.

- Used to report all fiduciary activities that are not required to be reported in PTF or ITF and are held in a trust.
- May be non−expendable or expendable
- Non−expendable : The principal is intact and cannot be used

(4) Custodial funds (CF)

정부가 단기간 자산을 맡아 이를 다른 기관이나 민간부문에 분배하는 펀드이다.

- Used to report fiduciary activities that are not required to be reported in PTF, ITF, or PPTF.

- Examples : Property tax collections for other cities
  ⇨ replace an agency fund with a custodial fund (2019)

6 Financial Reporting (GASBS 34)

정부재무보고서의 양식은 다음과 같다.

(1) Management's discussion and analysis (MD &A)
(2) Government-wide F/S
(3) Fund F/S
    1) Governmental funds
    2) Proprietary funds
    3) Fiduciary funds
(4) Notes to F/S
(5) Required Supplementary Information (other than MD&A)

※ (1)과 (5)는 재무보고서의 필수사항이지만 재무제표는 아니다.

7 Measurement focus

펀드는 자원의 측정목적에 따라 spending과 capital maintenance로 분류된다.

(1) Spending

1) Financial resource

   기업회계의 운전자본과 유사한 개념으로 지출 가능한 자원을 의미하며 재무상태표에 fixed asset과 long-term debt은 보고하지 않는다.

2) 재무상태표의 자본을 "Fund balance"라고 한다.

3) 수익과 지출을 "Modified Accrual basis"로 측정한다.

4) Governmental funds (5개)가 여기에 해당된다.

(2) Capital maintenance

1) Economic resource

   기업회계의 자산 및 부채와 동일하며 정부의 모든 자원을 측정한 것으로 재무상태표에 fixed asset과 long-term debt를 보고한다.

2) 재무상태표의 자본을 "Net position"이라고 한다.

3) 수익과 비용을 "Accrual basis"로 측정한다.

4) Proprietary funds (2개) & fiduciary funds(4개)가 여기에 해당된다.

5) Government-wide F/S가 여기에 해당된다.

	Governmental	Proprietary	Fiduciary	G-wide F/S
Focus	Spending	Capital maintenance		
Resource	Financial resource	Economic resource		
Accounting	Modified Accrual basis	Accrual basis		

8 Financial statements

펀드별 재무제표와 통합 재무제표의 종류는 다음과 같다.

Governmental funds	1) Balance Sheet 2) Statement of Revenue, Expenditures and Changes in Fund Balances
Proprietary funds	1) Statement of Net Position 2) Statement of Revenue, Expenses and Changes in Net Position 3) Statement of Cash Flow
Fiduciary funds	1) Statement of Fiduciary Net Position 2) Statement of Changes in Fiduciary Net Position
Government-wide F/S	1) Statement of Net Position 2) Statement of Activities

※ 재무제표의 구체적인 사례는 부록을 참고한다.

03 Modified accrual accounting (수정발생주의)

1 Financial statements

수정발생주의를 사용하는 정부형 펀드의 재무제표를 요약하면 다음과 같다.

Governmental Fund Balance Sheet

(1) Assets (current assets)	xxx
(2) Deferred outflows of resources	xxx
(3) Liabilities (current liabilities)	xxx
(4) Deferred inflows of resources	xxx
(5) Fund Balance	xxx

Statement of Revenue, Expenditures and Changes in Fund Balances

(1) Revenues	xxx
(2) Expenditures	(xxx)
(3) Other Financing Sources	xxx
Other Financing Uses	(xxx)
(4) Special Items	xxx
(5) Changes in Fund Balance	xxx

2 Modified accrual accounting

	Modified accrual accounting	Accrual accounting
Revenue	Measurable and Available	Earned and Realized
Expense/ Expenditure*	Measurable and Incurred	Matching

* 수정발생주의에서는 expense가 아닌 expenditure로 용어를 사용한다.

수정발생주의는 재무적 자원을 이용하여 지출 가능한 자원을 측정하는 회계처리 방법으로 지출은 발생 즉시 인식하며 수익은 지출에 사용가능한 시점에 인식한다.

3 Capital assets

수정발생주의는 유형 자산의 취득시점에서 "expenditure"로 인식하고 감가상각을 하지 않으며 매각시의 매각대금은 "special items"로 회계처리한다.

Example

20X1년 1월 1일 내용연수 5년인 유형 자산을 $100에 취득하여 20X2년 1월1일에 $90에 처분하였다.

	Modified accrual	Accrual basis
1/1/20X1	Dr) Expenditure 100 　 Cr) Cash 100	Dr) Capital assets 100 　 Cr) Cash 100
12/31/20X1	No entry	Dr) Expense 20 　 Cr) Accumulated Depreciation 20
1/1/20X2	Dr) Cash 90 　 Cr) Special items 90	Dr) Cash 90 　 Accumulated Depreciation 20 　 Cr) Capital assets 100 　　 Special items 10

4 Bond payable

수정발생주의는 지방채권 발행시점에서 "other financing sources (OFS)"로 인식하고 이자와 원금의 상환시에는 "expenditure"로 회계처리한다. 지방채의 회계처리를 거래별로 수정발생주의와 발생주의를 비교하면 다음과 같다.

※ General Obligation Bonds(GOB) : 정부형 활동을 지원하기 위하여 발행한 채권

　Revenue Bonds(RB) : 사업형 활동을 지원하기 위하여 발행한 채권

20X1년 1월 1일 지방채를 $100에 액면 발행하였고 20X1년 12월31일에 이자 $10와 원금 $20를 상환하였다.

	Modified accrual		Accrual basis	

1/1/20X1	Dr) Cash 100
	   Cr) OFS 100
			Dr) Cash 100
			   Cr) Bond payable 100	

12/31/20X1	Dr) Expenditure 10
	   Cr) Cash 10
			Dr) Expense 10
			   Cr) Cash 10	

	Dr) Expenditure 20
	   Cr) Cash 20
			Dr) Bond payable 20
			   Cr) Cash 20	

※ 수정발생주의에서는 이자지급시기와 재무제표 작성시점이 불일치하여도 기간귀속에 따른 accrual을 하지 않는다.

5 Interfund transaction

펀드간의 자원의 이전은 각 펀드별로 회계처리를 하여야 하며 자원이 유입된 펀드는 "other financing sources (OFS)"로 인식하고 자원이 유출된 펀드는 "other financing uses (OFU)"로 인식한다.

general fund에서 capital project fund로 $100의 현금이 이전되었다.

General Fund		Capital Project Fund	

Dr) Transfer-out (OFU)   100
   Cr) Cash   100
		Dr) Cash 100
		   Cr) Transfer-in (OFS) 100	

6 Inflow of resources

수정발생주의는 자원의 유입을 다음 항목으로 분류하여 보고한다.

Revenue	Other Financing Sources	Special items
- Tax - Grant - Fines - User charge	- Proceeds from LT Debt - Operating transfer-in	- Proceeds from sale of capital assets

※ Long-term debt : General obligation bond, Lease liability, Bond anticipation payable

7 Outflow of resources

수정발생주의는 자원의 유출을 다음 항목으로 분류하여 보고한다.

Expenditures	Other Financing Uses
- Operating activities - Acquisition of capital asset - Payment of interest and principal for LT Debt	- Operating transfer-out

> **Example**

In the government-wide financial statement, the statement of net position, deferred outflows of resources are presented

a. As a part of liabilities.
b. As a part of equity.
c. In a separate section following assets.
d. In a separate section following liabilities.

> **정답** : c

Deferred outflows of resources는 자산과 별도로 표시한다.

> **Example**

At the end of the fiscal year, a state government reported capital assets of $20 million, accumulated depreciation of $5 million, current assets of $2 million, liabilities of $7 million, deferred inflows of resources of $3 million and deferred outflows of resources of $1 million. What amount should the government report as the total net position in its government-wide financial statements?

> **정답**

Assets = 20 − 5 + 2 = 17
Net position = 17 + 1 − (7 + 3) = $8 million

Example

The general fund of Seoul City acquired two police cars at the beginning of January 20X1, at a total cost of $50,000. The cars are expected to last five years and have a $10,000 salvage value. The City used the straight-line method to depreciate all of its capital assets. The City sold the cars for $35,000 in December 31, 20X2.

Q1) On the balance sheet for governmental fund at December 31, 20X1, what amount should be reported for assets related to the police cars?

Q2) On the government-wide statement of net position at December 31, 20X1, what amount should be reported for assets related to the police cars?

Q3) On the statement of revenues, expenditures and changes in fund balances for governmental fund for the ended December 31, 20X1, what amount should be reported for expenditures related to the police cars?

Q4) On the government-wide statement of activities for the ended December 31, 20X1, what amount should be reported for expenses related to the police cars?

Q5) On the statement of revenues, expenditures and changes in fund balances for governmental fund for the ended December 31, 20X2, what amount should be reported for special items related to the police cars?

Q6) On the government-wide statement of activities for the ended December 31, 20X2, what amount should be reported for special items related to the police cars?

정답

Q1) $0

Q2) depreciation = 40,000 / 5 = 8,000

   Capital asset = 50,000 − 8,000 = $42,000

Q3) $50,000

Q4) $8,000

Q5) $35,000

Q6) 35,000 − (50,000 −16,000) = $1,000

Example

Seoul City issued $10,000, 6%, general obligation bond (GOB) at par on April 1, 20X1 to build a new city hall. Interest is payable every six months.

Q1) On the balance sheet for governmental fund at December 31, 20X1, what amount should be reported for bond payable related to the GOB?

Q2) On the government-wide statement of net position at December 31, 20X1, what amount should be reported for bond payable related to the GOB?

Q3) On the statement of revenues, expenditures and changes in fund balances for governmental fund for the ended December 31, 20X1, what amount should be reported for other financing sources related to the GOB?

Q4) On the statement of revenues, expenditures and changes in fund balances for governmental fund for the ended December 31, 20X1, what amount should be reported for expenditures related to the GOB?

Q5) On the government-wide statement of activities for the ended December 31, 20X1, what amount should be reported for expenses related to the GOB?

Q6) On the balance sheet for governmental fund at December 31, 20X1, what amount should be reported for interest payable related to the GOB?

Q7) On the government-wide statement of net position at December 31, 20X1, what amount should be reported for interest payable related to the GOB?

정답

Q1) $0
Q2) $10,000
Q3) $10,000
Q4) $10,000 \times 6\% \times 6/12 = \$300$
Q5) $10,000 \times 6\% \times 9/12 = \$450$
Q6) $0
Q7) $10,000 \times 6\% \times 3/12 = \$150$

> **Example**

Seoul City issued $10,000, 6%, revenue bonds (RB) at par on April 1, 20X1 to build a new water line for the water enterprise fund. Interest is payable every six months.

Q1) On the statement of net position for proprietary fund at December 31, 20X1, what amount should be reported for bond payable related to the RB?

Q2) On the government-wide statement of net position at December 31, 20X1, what amount should be reported for bond payable related to the RB?

Q3) On the statement of revenues, expenses and changes in net position for proprietary fund for the ended December 31, 20X1, what amount should be reported for expenses related to the RB?

Q4) On the government-wide statement of activities for the ended December 31, 20X1, what amount should be reported for expenses related to the RB?

Q5) On the statement of net position for proprietary fund at December 31, 20X1, what amount should be reported for interest payable related to the RB?

Q6) On the government-wide statement of net position at December 31, 20X1, what amount should be reported for interest payable related to the RB?

> **정답**

Q1) $10,000

Q2) $10,000

Q3) $10,000 \times 6\% \times 9/12 = \$450$

Q4) $10,000 \times 6\% \times 9/12 = \$450$

Q5) $10,000 \times 6\% \times 3/12 = \$150$

Q6) $10,000 \times 6\% \times 3/12 = \$150$

04 Budgetary accounting (예산회계)

1 예산회계의 의의

예산회계는 단위별로 회계연도 초에 편성된 예산금액을 장부에 기록하고 실제 예산집행금액이 예산의 범위 내에서 이루어지도록 통제하는 회계시스템이다. 즉, 예산회계는 예산관리와 예산통제에 중점을 두고 있다.

예산회계는 정부 자원의 유입 및 유출을 법규에 의하여 통제하고자 만든 체계로서 정부형 펀드만 예산회계를 하고 영리성 펀드와 신탁형 펀드는 하지 않는다. 기업도 예산수립이라는 내부통제 과정이 있지만 이를 회계처리 하는 예산회계는 없기 때문에 예산회계는 기업회계와 정부회계의 가장 큰 차이점 중의 하나이다.

- Budgetary accounts are included for general fund, special revenue fund and other funds that have a legally adopted annual budget.
- Budgetary accounts are reported in budgetary comparison schedules in RSI (Required Supplementary Information)

예산회계는 회계의 계정과목을 예산과목으로 그대로 사용하여 처리하는데 이는 예산상의 정보를 요구할 때 실제 사용된 내용도 예산과목에 맞추어 보고해야 하기 때문이다. 단, 예산과목은 실제 계정과목의 반대 위치에 기입한다.

예를 들면 "Revenue"는 credit 계정이지만 "Estimated Revenue"는 debit 계정으로 기록하며, "Expenditure"는 debit 계정이지만 "Estimated Expenditure"는 credit 계정으로 기록한다.

2 기초시점의 예산회계

Example

For the budgetary year, Seoul city's general fund expects the following inflows and out-flows of resources:

- Property taxes and fines	$300,000
- Proceeds of general obligation bond	100,000
- Expenditures	290,000
- Interfund transfer to capital project fund	50,000

위의 자료를 이용한 기초의 예산회계처리는 다음과 같다.

At the beginning of the year		
Dr) Estimated Revenue	$300,000	
Estimated Other Financing Sources	100,000	
Cr) Appropriations		290,000
Estimated Other Financing Uses		50,000
Budgetary Fund Balance		60,000(plug)

- Property taxes and fines의 계정과목이 "Revenue"이므로 예산과목은 "Estimated Revenue"로 debit 계정으로 기록한다.

- Proceeds of general obligation bond의 계정과목이 "Other Financing Sources"이므로 예산과목은 "Estimated Other Financing Sources"로 debit 계정으로 기록

- 예상지출 $290,000의 경우 "Estimated Expenditures"라는 계정을 사용하지 않으며 "Appropriations"라는 계정을 사용하여야 한다.

- Interfund transfer out의 계정과목이 "Other Financing Uses" 이므로 예산과목은 "Estimated Other Financing Used"로 creit 계정으로 기록

- 기초시점의 예산 유입과 유출의 크기에 따라 "Budgetary Fund Balance"는 다음과 같이 기록된다.
    - 자원의 유입 〉 유출 : Credit Budgetary Fund Balance
    - 자원의 유입 〈 유출 : Debit Budgetary Fund Balance

3 기말시점의 예산회계

예산 계정은 손익계정과 마찬가지로 "temporary account"이므로 기말에 마감회계처리를 하여 다음연도에 기초 잔액이 발생하지 않도록 하여야 한다. 위의 자료를 이용한 예산 마감회계처리는 다음과 같다.

At the end of the year		
Dr) Appropriations	290,000	
Estimated Other Financing Uses	50,000	
Budgetary Fund Balance	60,000(plug)	
Cr) Estimated Revenue		300,000
Estimated Other Financing Sources		100,000

기초시점의 예산 회계처리를 기말에 모두 반대분개를 통하여 제거하기 때문에 예산계정은 대차대조표에 주는 영향은 없다.

실제손익계정의 마감 회계처리는 다음과 같다.

At the end of the year		
Dr) Revenue	xxx	
Other Financing Sources	xxx	
Cr) Expenditure		xxx
Other Financing Uses		xxx
Fund Balance-Unassigned		xxx(plug)

4 Encumbrance accounting

지출원인행위(encumbrance)는 예산통제를 하기 위하여 정부가 재화나 용역의 주문을 할 때 예산상의 금액을 차감하도록 하는 회계처리방식으로 예산상 얼마의 금액이 남아 있는지를 알 수 있게 하여 예산의 초과지출을 방지하고 예산의 관리를 원활하게 하는 것이 목적이다. 기업회계에서는 외부에서 재화를 구입하는 경우 계약을 하거나 주문서를 작성할 때 회계처리를 하지 않고 해당 재화가 도착하는 시점에서 회계처리를 한다. 하지만 예산회계에서는 지출을 통제하기 위해서 계약을 하거나 주문서를 작성하는 경우 예산배정액을 차감함으로써 예산상 얼마의 금액이 남아 있는지를 알 수 있게 한다. 즉, "encumbrances"는 기초에 기록한 "appropriations"의 한도내에서 "expenditures"를 통제하고자 만든 계정이므로 재화가 도착하는 시점에서는 제거하여야 한다.

주문 가능금액은 다음과 같이 계산된다.

Amount available for use (unencumbered amount)
= Appropriations − {Encumbrances + Expenditures}

Example

For 20X1, Seoul city ordered two police cars.
One was $50,000 and the other was $40,000.
The first police car was received along with an invoice for $49,000.

Issue the purchase order of the first car	
Dr) Encumbrance	50,000
Cr) Budgetary Fund Balance	50,000

Amount available for use = 290,000 − 50,000 = 240,000

Issue the purchase order of the second car	
Dr) Encumbrance	40,000
Cr) Budgetary Fund Balance	40,000

Amount available for use = 290,000 − 90,000 = 200,000

The arrival of the equipment and approval of the invoice		
Dr) Expenditure	49,000	
Cr) Vouchers Payable (Account payable)		49,000
Dr) Budgetary Fund Balance	50,000	
Cr) Encumbrance Control		50,000

Amount available for use = 290,000 − (49,000+40,000) = 201,000

The payment of the invoice		
Dr) Vouchers Payable (Account payable)	49,000	
Cr) Cash		49,000

Amount available for use = 290,000 − (49,000+40,000) = 201,000

Closing entries		
Dr) Budgetary Fund Balance	40,000	
Cr) Encumbrance Control		40,000
Dr) Fund Balance -Unassigned	40,000	
Cr) Fund Balance- Assigned (or committed)		40,000

⇨ Before GASBS 54

   Fund Balance : Unreserved, Reserved

   After GASBS 54

   Fund Balance : Non−spendable, Restricted, Committed, Assigned, Unassigned

(3) Appropriations lapse

전년도에 주문한 금액이 다음연도에 도착하는 경우 해당지출에 대한 예산대응의 문제가 발생한다. 20X1년도에 주문한 금액 $40,000이 20X2년도에 도착한 경우 20X1년도 예산에 대응하는 방법과 20X2년도 예산에 대응하는 방법이 있으며 다음과 같이 각각 회계처리 한다.

1) Appropriations remain open (20X1년도 예산에 대응하는 방법)

During 20X2, the arrival of the second police car		
Dr) Expenditure-20X1	40,000	
Cr) Vouchers Payable (Account payable)		40,000
Dr) Fund Balance- Assigned	40,000	
Cr) Fund Balance -Unassigned		40,000

2) Appropriations lapse (20X2년도 예산에 대응하는 방법)

At the beginning of 20X2		
Dr) Encumbrance Control	40,000	
Cr) Budgetary Fund Balance		40,000
Dr) Fund Balance- Assigned	40,000	
Cr) Fund Balance -Unassigned		40,000

During 20X2, the arrival of the second police car		
Dr) Expenditure	40,000	
Cr) Vouchers Payable (Account payable)		40,000
Dr) Budgetary Fund Balance	40,000	
Cr) Encumbrance Control		40,000

5 Budgetary comparison schedules

The budgetary comparison schedule should present both (a) the original and (b) the final appropriated budgets for the reporting period as well as (c) actual inflows, outflows, and balances, stated on the government's budgetary basis. A separate column to report the variance between the final budget and actual amounts is encouraged, but not required.

다음 자료를 바탕으로 예산비교표를 작성하면 다음과 같다.

- Estimated Revenue : $300,000
- Appropriations : 290,000
- Revenue : 305,000
- Expenditure : 240,000
- Outstanding encumbrance : 40,000

	Original budget	Final budget	Actual	Variance (Option)
Revenues	$300,000	300,000	305,000	5,000 (F)
Expenditure	290,000	290,000	*280,000	10,000 (F)

＊ 예산비교표의 Actual column 지출금액은 240,000이 아닌 encumbrance 40,000을 가산한 280,000을 제시하여야 한다.

05 General fund

1 Revenue

(1) 수익의 인식기준 및 종류

수정발생주의 수익의 인식기준은 "measurable & available"이다

> Available : to finance expenditures made during the current fiscal year

When an asset is recorded in governmental fund but the revenue is not available, the government should report a deferred inflow of resources until such time as the revenue becomes available. (GASBS 65)

정부형 펀드는 수익을 원천(by source)별로 표시하여야 한다.

1) Taxes : Property tax, sales tax, income tax

2) Intergovernmental : Grants, shared revenues, entitlements

3) Licences and permits : motor vehicle permits

4) Fines and forfeits : Traffic fines

5) Charge for service : User charge without self-supporting

6) Investment earnings

(2) Property taxes

재산세는 가장 중요한 지방세이며 부동산 및 중요 동산을 대상으로 지방정부가 부과하는 세금으로 수정발생주의에서는 수익의 인식기준을 다음과 같이 정하고 있다.

> Available : collected within the current period or expected to be collected in soon enough to pay liabilities of the current period(within 60-days after year-end)

재산세는 정부에서 부과(levy)하는 세금이며, 소득세와 판매세는 납세자가 신고납부(filing)하는 세금이다.

Example

For 20X1, Seoul city levied property taxes of $250,000, of which 4% is expected to be uncollectible. The following information pertains to the property taxes.

- Collections during 20X1	$130,000
- Expected collections by March 1, 20X2	60,000
- Expected collections during the remainder for 20X2	50,000
- Write-off property tax receivable during 20X1	8,000

재산세의 부과시점에서 충당금을 설정하고 나머지 회수가능액을 수익으로 인식한다.

To levy property tax of 20X1

Dr) Property taxes receivable-current	250,000	
Cr) Allowance for uncollectible taxes-current		10,000
Property taxes revenue		240,000

To record collections of property taxes of 20X1

Dr) Cash	130,000	
Cr) Property taxes receivable-current		130,000

To write-off property tax receivable during 20X1

Dr) Allowance for uncollectible taxes-current	8,000	
Cr) Property taxes receivable- current		8,000

20X1년도 회계연도말로부터 60일 이내에 회수가 되지 않는 재산세는 20X2년도 수익으로 이연시킨다.

To record deferral property that will not be collected until March 1, 20X2

Dr) Property taxes revenue	50,000	
Cr) Deferred inflows of resources		50,000

20X1년도 회계연도말까지 회수되지 않은 재산세는 "delinquent"로 계정 대체한다.

To reclassify 20X1 property taxes not collected by due date as delinquent.		
Dr) Property taxes receivable-delinquent	112,000	
Cr) Property taxes receivable-current		112,000
Dr) Allowance for uncollectible taxes-current	2,000	
Cr) Allowance for uncollectible taxes-delinquent		2,000

20X1년도 general fund의 재무제표를 작성하면 다음과 같다.

⟨Balance Sheet⟩

Cash	130,000
Property taxes receivable–delinquent	112,000
Allowance for uncollectible taxes–delinquent	(2,000)
	110,000
Deferred inflows of resources	50,000

⟨Statement of Revenue, Expenditures and Changes in Fund Balances⟩

Property taxes revenue	190,000

20X2년도에 회수되는 20X1년도 재산세의 회계처리는 다음과 같다.

Dr) Cash	110,000	
Cr) Property taxes receivable-delinquent		110,000
Dr) Deferred inflows of resources	50,000	
Cr) Property taxes revenue		50,000

※ Government–wide F/S (GASBS 33)

재산세를 발생주의 수익인식기준은 다음과 같다.

"Property taxes revenue is the amount levied net of allowance for estimated uncollectible taxes."

따라서 위의 사례에서는 20X1년도 발생주의에 의한 수익은 $240,000를 보고한다.

```
┌──────────────────────────────────────────────────────────────────┐
│ 〈Statement of Net Position〉                                       │
│ Cash                                              130,000           │
│ Property taxes receivable—delinquent              112,000           │
│ Allowance for uncollectible taxes—delinquent       (2,000)          │
│                                                   ─────────         │
│                                                   110,000           │
│                                                                    │
│ Deferred inflows of resources                           0          │
│ 〈Statement of Activities〉                                         │
│ Property taxes revenue                            240,000           │
└──────────────────────────────────────────────────────────────────┘
```

(3) Grant

1) If grants are unrestricted ⇨ recognize revenue when received.

Dr) Cash xxx   Cr) Revenue   xxx

2) If grants are restricted ⇨ recognize revenue **when expended.**

보조금은 재산세와는 달리 사용시점을 추적하여 수익을 인식한다.

When the restricted grant is received
Dr) Cash xxx   Cr) Deferred inflows of resources   xxx

When the restricted grant is spent
Dr) Expenditure   xxx   Cr) Cash   xxx
Dr) Deferred inflows of resources xxx   Cr) Revenue   xxx

3) Pass-through grant (cash conduit)

If it merely transmit moneys without administrative involvement ⇨ report the grant in Custodial Funds

(4) User charge revenues

1) With self-supporting ⇨ enterprise fund

사용자 수익이 해당 서비스 지출의 50%를 초과하는 경우

2) Without self-supporting ⇨ general fund

사용자 수익이 해당 서비스 지출의 50% 이하인 경우

(5) Fines, licenses and permits

Revenue are recorded when cash is collected.

벌과금은 세금보다는 징수율이 낮으므로 현금 수령시점에서 수익을 인식한다.

(6) Bond Anticipation Notes (BAN)

1) Bond Anticipation Notes (BAN)

Short-term notes issued with the expectation that they will soon be replaced by long-term bonds.

① if it were able to demonstrate the ability to refinance

Dr) Cash xxx	Cr) Other financing sources xxx

② if it were unable to demonstrate the ability to refinance

Dr) Cash xxx	Cr) BAN payable xxx

2) Tax Anticipation Notes (TAN)

Short-term notes issued in anticipation of future collection of taxes.

Dr) Cash xxx	Cr) Tax anticipation notes payable xxx

▷ ASC 470 : Short-term obligations expected to be refinanced

A short-term obligation should be excluded from current liabilities if the entity intends to refinance the obligation on a long-term basis and the intent to refinance the short-term obligation on a long-term basis is supported by an ability to consummate the refinancing demonstrated.

▷ ASC 210 : Current liabilities

Current liabilities is used principally to designate obligations whose liquidation is reasonably expected to require the use of existing resources properly classifiable as current assets, or the creation of other current liabilities.

2 GASB 33 : Non-exchange Transaction

GASB 33은 비교환거래 수익을 네 가지 유형으로 구분한다.

Derived tax	sales taxes, income taxes, motor fuel taxes
Imposed non-exchange	property taxes, fines, special assessments
Government-mandated	restricted grants
Voluntary non-exchange	unrestricted grants, donations

(1) Derived tax revenues

1) Examples: sales taxes, personal and corporate income taxes, motor fuel taxes, and similar taxes on earnings or consumption

2) Recognition : when underlying exchange has occurred.

> **Example**

For 20X1, the general fund of Seoul city received $50,000 of sales tax revenues from the state and was owed another $20,000 by the state for sales taxes collected in 20X1 that will not be remitted to the city until mid-March 20X2. The sales taxes expected to be received in March will be used to pay for expenditures incurred in 20X2.

General fund	Cash	50,000	
	Sales taxes receivable	20,000	
	Revenues-sales taxes		50,000
	Deferred inflows of resources		20,000
G-wide F/S	Cash	50,000	
	Sales taxes receivable	20,000	
	Revenues-sales taxes		70,000

(2) Imposed non-exchange revenues

1) Examples: property taxes, most fines and forfeitures

2) Recognition : the period for which levied, net of allowance

3) Deferred inflows of resources should be reported when resources associated with imposed nonexchange revenue transactions are received or reported as a receivable before the period for which property taxes are levied.

Example

For 20X1, police issued $400,000 in parking tickets. Of the fines assessed, $250,000 are paid without protest by the due date of December 31, 20X1.
The balance of $60,000 will be uncollectible.

General fund	Cash	250,000	
	Parking tickets receivable	150,000	
	Allowance for uncollectible tickets		60,000
	Revenue-parking fines		250,000
	Deferred inflows of resources		90,000
G-wide F/S	Cash	250,000	
	Parking tickets receivable	150,000	
	Allowance for uncollectible tickets		60,000
	Revenue-parking fines		340,000

(3) Government-mandated non-exchange transactions

1) Examples : federal government mandates on state and local governments

2) Recognition : Period when all eligibility requirements have been met.

3) Resources transmitted before the eligibility requirements are met should be reported as assets by the provider and as liabilities by the recipient.

4) Resources received before time requirements are met, but after all other eligibility requirements have been met, should be reported as a deferred inflow of resources by the recipient.

Example

For 20X1, the general fund of Seoul city received $50,000 grant from the state to be used for training its police force. The state recently passes legislation that requires training for all police departments in the state. The grant was received in cash on December 10, 20X1, and was used for training seminars during January 20X2.

General fund	Cash	50,000	
	Deferred inflows of resources		50,000
G-wide F/S	Cash	50,000	
	Revenue-state grant		50,000

(4) Voluntary non-exchange transactions

1) Examples : unrestricted grants and entitlements, most donations

2) Recognition : Period when all eligibility requirements have been met.

3) Resources transmitted before the eligibility requirements are met should be reported as assets by the provider and as liabilities by the recipient.

4) Resources received before time requirements are met, but after all other eligibility requirements have been met, should be reported as a deferred inflow of resources by the recipient.

Example

During 20X2, Seoul City levied property taxes of $200,000, of which 2% is expected to be uncollectible. The following amounts were collected during the current year or the subsequent year :
- Prior year taxes collected within the 60 days of the current year : $5,000
- Prior year taxes collected between 60 days and 90 days into the current year : 7,000
- Current year taxes collected in the current year : 150,000
- Current year taxes collected within the first 60 days of the subsequent year : 20,000

Q1) On the statement of revenues, expenditures and changes in fund balances for governmental fund for the ended December 31, 20X2, what amount should be reported for revenues related to the property taxes?

Q2) On the government-wide statement of activities for the ended December 31, 20X2, what amount should be reported for revenues related to the property taxes?

Q3) On the balance sheet for governmental fund at December 31, 20X2, what amount should be reported for property tax receivable net of allowance?

Q4) On the balance sheet for governmental fund at December 31, 20X2, what amount should be reported for deferred inflows of resources related to the property taxes?

Q5) On the government-wide statement of net position at December 31, 20X2, what amount should be reported for deferred inflows of resources related to the property taxes?

정답

Q1) $7,000 + 150,000 + 20,000 = \$177,000$
Q2) $200,000 \times (1-0.02) = \$196,000$
Q3) $196,000 - 150,000 = \$46,000$
Q4) $196,000 - 150,000 - 20,000 = \$26,000$
Q5) 0

Example

In November and December 20X1, merchants collected $20,000 in sales tax. Of these, $15,000 were remitted to the State, as due, by December 31, 20X1. The remaining amount were due on February 28, 20X2. The State remitted the taxes to the City 30 days after it received them.

Q1) On the statement of revenues, expenditures and changes in fund balances for governmental fund for the ended December 31, 20X1, what amount should be reported for revenues related to the sales taxes?

Q2) On the government-wide statement of activities for the ended December 31, 20X1, what amount should be reported for revenues related to the sales taxes?

Q3) On the balance sheet for governmental fund at December 31, 20X1, what amount should be reported for sales tax receivable net of allowance?

Q4) On the balance sheet for governmental fund at December 31, 20X1, what amount should be reported for deferred inflows of resources related to the sales taxes?

Q5) On the government-wide statement of net position at December 31, 20X1, what amount should be reported for deferred inflows of resources related to the sales taxes?

정답

Q1) $15,000
Q2) $20,000
Q3) $20,000
Q4) $5,000
Q5) $0

3 Expenditure

(1) Expenditure classification

1) Fund

2) Function (=program)

기능별 분류는 지출의 목적을 기준으로 분류한다.

Ex) health & welfare, education, public safety(police), general administration

3) Activity

A specific goal under a program

Ex) low−income healthcare, AIDS awareness

4) Nature (=Object)

성격별 분류는 지출로 취득한 재화 또는 용역의 성격으로 분류한다.

Ex) salaries, supplies, rent, utilities

5) Character

지출의 효익이 미치는 기간으로 분류한다.

① Current expenditure : benefits the current period only

② Capital outlay : benefits current and future periods

③ Debt service : benefits past periods

④ Intergovernmental transfer

F/S	Expense/Expenditure presentation
Statement of Revenue, Expenditures and Changes in Fund Balances	Character
Statement of Revenue, Expenses and Changes in Net Position	Object(Nature)
Statement of Activities	Program/Function

(2) Expenditure recognition

1) Capital assets

   ⇨ reported expenditure when received (not ordered)

2) Interest & principal payments

   ⇨ reported expenditure when matured (not accrued)

(3) Compensated absences, claims and litigation

1) vacation days, sick leave, injuries to employees, negligence of employees

2) The amount that would be liquidated with expendable available financial resources should be accounted as expenditure in governmental funds

   ⇒ The balance should not be reported in governmental fund, but reported in government-wide F/S

Example

For 20X1, City employees earn $80,000 in vacation leave. Of this amount, employees will use $60,000 in the next year. The leave vests and can be taken any time up to retirement or as additional compensation at the time of retirement.

General fund	Expenditures	60,000	
	Liability-compensated absences		60,000
G-wide F/S	Expenses	80,000	
	Liability-compensated absences		80,000

4 Inventory

Inventoriable supplies and prepaid items may be recognized as expenditures either when purchased (purchase method) or when used (consumption method).

Example

For 20X1, Pine City purchases $60,000 of inventoriable supplies during the year. Pine had $12,000 of supplies on hand at the end of the year.

Purchase method

Date	Entries	Dr	Cr
Purchase	Expenditures	60,000	
	Cash (or Account payable)		60,000
Year-end	Supplies inventory	12,000	
	Fund balance-nonspendable		12,000

Consumption method

Date	Entries	Dr	Cr
Purchase	Supplies inventory	60,000	
	Cash (or Account payable)		60,000
Year-end	Expenditures	48,000	
	Supplies inventory		48,000
	Fund balance-unassigned	12,000	
	Fund balance-nonspendable		12,000

5 Lease accounting (GASBS 87)

(1) Short-term leases

- A short-term lease is a lease that has a maximum possible term under the lease contract of 12 months (or less), including any options to extend, regardless of their probability of being exercised.

- A lessee should recognize short-term lease payments as expense based on the payment provisions of the lease contract. The lessee should not recognize an outflow of resources during any rent holiday period.

- A lessor should recognize short-term lease payments as revenue based on the payment provisions of the lease contract. The lessor should not recognize an inflow of resources during any rent holiday period.

(2) Contracts that transfer ownership

A contract that transfers ownership of the underlying asset to the lessee by the end of the contract should be reported as a financed purchase of the underlying asset by the lessee or sale of the asset by the lessor.

(3) Lessee recognition and measurement for leases other than short-term leases and contracts that transfer ownership

1) Recognition

At the commencement of the lease term, a lessee should recognize a lease liability and an intangible right-to-use lease asset (a capital asset).

2) Lease liability

- A lessee initially should measure the lease liability at the present value of payments expected to be made during the lease term.

- The future lease payments should be discounted using the interest rate the lessor charges the lessee, which may be the interest rate implicit in the lease. If the interest rate cannot be readily determined by the lessee, the lessee's estimated incremental borrowing rate should be used.

- A lessee should reduce the lease liability as payments are made and recognize an outflow of resources for interest on the liability.

3) Lease Assets

- A lessee initially should measure the lease asset as the sum of the following:
  ① The amount of the initial measurement of the lease liability.
  ② Lease payments made to the lessor at or before the commencement of the lease term, less any lease incentives.
  ③ Initial direct costs that are ancillary charges necessary to place the lease asset into service.

- The lessee should amortize the lease asset in a systematic and rational manner over the shorter of the lease term or the useful life of the underlying asset.

(4) Lessor recognition and measurement for leases other than short-term leases and contracts that transfer ownership

- At the commencement of the lease term, a lessor should recognize a lease receivable and a deferred inflow of resources, except as short-term leases and contracts that transfer ownership. A lessor should not derecognize the asset underlying the lease.

- Any initial direct costs incurred by the lessor should be reported as expense for the period.

- The lease receivable should be measured at the present value of lease payments expected to be received during the lease term.

- A lessor initially should measure the deferred inflow of resources as follows:
  ① The amount of the initial measurement of the lease receivable
  ② Lease payments received from the lessee at or before the commencement less any lease incentive paid to the lessee.

- A lessor subsequently should recognize the deferred inflow of resources as revenue in a systematic and rational manner over the term of the lease.

(5) Lessee accounting

FASB	IFRS	GASB
• Operating lease • Finance lease	• Short-term/Low-value lease • Lease	• Short-term lease • Contracts that transfer ownership • Lease

GASB 리스이용자 회계처리는 IFRS 리스이용자의 회계처리와 유사하다.

1) Short-term lease

Commencement	No entry
Amortization	No entry
Lease payment	Dr) Expense xxx Cr) Cash xxx

2) Contracts that transfer ownership

Commencement	Dr) Capital asset xxx Cr) Lease liability xxx
Depreciation	Dr) Depreciation expense xxx Cr) Accumulated depreciation xxx
Lease payment	Dr) Lease liability xxx Dr) Interest expense xxx Cr) Cash xxx

3) Leases (Accrual accounting)

Commencement	Dr) ROU xxx Cr) Lease liability xxx
Amortization	Dr) Amortization expense xxx Cr) Accumulated amortization xxx
Lease payment	Dr) Lease liability xxx Dr) Interest expense xxx Cr) Cash xxx

4) Leases (Modified accrual accounting)

Commencement	Dr) Expenditure-capital outlay xxx Cr) Other financing sources xxx
Amortization	No entry
Lease payment	Dr) Expenditure-debt service(principal) xxx Dr) Expenditure-debt service(interest) xxx Cr) Cash xxx

(6) Lessor accounting

1) Short-term lease

Commencement	No entry
Depreciation	Dr) Depreciation expense xxx Cr) Accumulated depreciation xxx
Lease payment	Dr) Cash xxx Cr) Revenue xxx

2) Contracts that transfer ownership

Commencement	Dr) Lease receivable xxx Cr) Capital assets xxx Cr) Gain on sale of assets xxx(plug)
Depreciation	No entry
Lease payment	Dr) Cash xxx Cr) Lease receivable xxx Cr) Interest revenue xxx

3) Leases (Accrual accounting)

Commencement	Dr) Lease receivable xxx Cr) Deferred inflows of resources xxx
Depreciation	Dr) Depreciation expense xxx Cr) Accumulated depreciation xxx
Lease payment	Dr) Cash xxx Cr) Lease receivable xxx Cr) Interest revenue xxx
Year–end	Dr) Deferred inflows of resources xxx Cr) Revenue xxx

4) Leases (Modified accrual accounting)

Commencement	Dr) Lease receivable xxx Cr) Deferred inflows of resources xxx
Depreciation	No entry
Lease payment	Dr) Cash xxx Cr) Lease receivable xxx Cr) Interest revenue xxx
Year–end	Dr) Deferred inflows of resources xxx Cr) Revenue xxx

Example

On 1/1/20X1, Lessee City leases computer from Lessor City.

Lease term : 5 years

economic life : 5 years

Interest rate : 8%

Annual lease payments : $20,000 payable on December 31, each year.

Present value of lease payments : $80,000

Lessee(Modified accrual accounting)

Date	Entries	Dr	Cr
1/1/20X1	Expenditure-capital outlay	80,000	
	Other financing source		80,000
Amortization	No entry		
12/31/20X1	Expenditure-debt service	20,000	
	Cash		20,000

Lessee(Accrual accounting)

Date	Entries	Dr	Cr
1/1/20X1	ROU(Capital asset)	80,000	
	Lease liability		80,000
Amortization	Amortization expense	*16,000	
	Accumulated amortization		16,000
12/31/20X1	Interest expense	**6,400	
	Lease liability	13,600	
	Cash		20,000

* 80,000 / 5 = 16,000

** 80,000 × 8% = 6,400

Lessor(Modified accrual accounting)

Date	Entries	Dr	Cr
1/1/20X1	Lease receivable	80,000	
	Deferred inflows of resources		80,000
Depreciation	No entry		
12/31/20X1	Cash	20,000	
	Lease receivable		13,600
	Interest revenue		6,400
12/31/20X1	Deferred inflows of resources	13,600	
	Revenue		13,600

Lessor(Accrual accounting)

Date	Entries	Dr	Cr
1/1/20X1	Lease receivable	80,000	
	Deferred inflows of resources		80,000
Depreciation	Depreciation expense	16,000	
	Accumulated depreciation		16,000
12/31/20X1	Cash	20,000	
	Lease receivable		13,600
	Interest revenue		6,400
12/31/20X1	Deferred inflows of resources	16,000	
	Revenue		16,000

Example

On 1/1/20X1, Seoul city leases computer from ABC Company.

Lease term : 5 years

economic life : 6 years

Interest rate : 8%

Annual lease payments : $20,000 payable on December 31, each year.

Present value of lease payments : $80,000

Lessee's initial direct cost : $5,000

Modified accrual accounting

Date	Entries	Dr	Cr
1/1/20X1	Expenditure-capital outlay	85,000	
	Other financing source		80,000
	Cash		5,000
Amortization	No entry		
12/31/20X1	Expenditure-debt service	20,000	
	Cash		20,000

Accrual accounting

Date	Entries	Dr	Cr
1/1/20X1	Capital asset	85,000	
	Lease liability		80,000
	Cash		5,000
Amortization	Amortization expense	17,000	
	Accumulated amortization		17,000
12/31/20X1	Interest expense	6,400	
	Lease liability	13,600	
	Cash		20,000

6 Fund balance reporting (GASBS 54)

Fund balance for governmental funds should be reported in classifications that comprise a hierarchy based primarily on the extent to which the government is bound to honor constraints on the specific purposes for which amounts in those funds can be spent.

(1) Non-spendable fund balance

- The non-spendable fund balance classification includes amounts that cannot be spent because they are either (a) not in spendable form or (b) legally or contractually required to be maintained intact.
- inventory

(2) Restricted fund balance

- Fund balance should be reported as restricted when constraints placed on the use of resources are either:
  a. Externally imposed by creditors, grantors, contributors, or laws or regulations of other governments; or
  b. Imposed by law through constitutional provisions or enabling legislation.

(3) Committed fund balance

- Amounts that can be used only for the specific purposes determined by a formal action of the government's highest level of decision-making authority.

(4) Assigned fund balance

- Amounts that are constrained by the government's intent to be used for specific purposes, but are neither restricted nor committed, should be reported as assigned fund balance.
- Assigned fund balance includes (a) all remaining amounts that are reported in governmental funds, other than the general fund, that are not classified as non-spendable and are neither restricted nor committed and (b) amounts in the general fund that are intended to be used for a specific purpose.

- In governmental funds other than the general fund, assigned fund balance represents the remaining amount that is not restricted or committed.

(5) Unassigned fund balance

- The residual classification for the government's general fund and includes all spendable amounts not contained in the other classifications.

- In other funds, the unassigned classification should be used only to report a deficit balance resulting from overspending for specific purposes for which amounts had been restricted, committed, or assigned.

Summary of fund balance categories

	GF	SRF	CPF	DSF	PF
Non-spendable	O	O			O
Restricted	O	O	O	O	
Committed	O	O	O	O	
Assigned	O	O	O	O	
Unassigned	O	(−)	(−)	(−)	(−)

7 Balance Sheet

(1) 의의

- Financial statements for governmental funds should be presented using the current financial resources measurement focus and the modified accrual basis.

- General capital assets and general-long term liabilities should not be reported as assets and liabilities in governmental funds but should be reported in the governmental activities column in the government-wide statement of net position.

Assets(current assets) + Deferred outflow of resources
= Liabilities(current liabilities) + Deferred inflow of resources + Fund balance

Balance sheet					
	GF	Major-A	Major-B	Other funds	Total
Assets(current assets)					
Deferred outflows of resources					
Liabilities (current liabilities)					
Deferred inflows of resources					
Fund balance					xxx

재무제표의 구체적인 사례는 부록을 참고한다.

펀드간의 거래에서 발생한 채권 : due from other funds
펀드간의 거래에서 발생한 채무 : due to other funds

- The focus of governmental and proprietary fund financial statements is on major funds. Fund statements should present the financial information of each major fund in a separate column.

(2) Major Funds

1) Major fund reporting requirements do not apply to internal service funds

2) Non-major funds should be aggregated and displayed in a single column

3) General fund is always a major fund

4) Major fund test

다음 두 가지 조건을 모두 충족하여야 major fund로 분류된다.

① Total assets, liabilities, revenues, or expenditures of the individual governmental fund are at least 10 percent of the corresponding total for all governmental funds.

② Total assets, liabilities, revenues, or expenditures of the individual governmental fund are at least 5 percent of the corresponding total for all governmental and en-terprise funds combined.

※ Assets should be combined with deferred outflows of resources.
   Liabilities should be combined with deferred inflows of resources.

Example

Total governmental fund type assets : $200,000
Total enterprise fund assets : 300,000
Total internal service fund assets : 50,000
General fund assets : 19,000
Community special revenue fund assets : 26,000
Route 7 construction capital projet fund assets : 24,000
Route 8 construction capital projet fund assets : 131,000
How many funds should be displayed as major funds?

Major fund threshold = Max [200,000 x 10%, 500,000 x 5%] = 25,000
Major funds = GF, Community SRF, Route 8 CPF

(3) Statement of Net Position (G-wide F/S)

	Primary government (PG)			Component unit (CU)
	Governmental activities	Business-type activities	Total	
Assets				
Deferred outflows of resources				
Liabilities				
Deferred inflows of resources				
Net position	xxx			

재무제표의 구체적인 사례는 부록을 참고한다.

1) Governmental activities = governmental funds + internal service funds

2) Business-type activities = enterprise funds

3) Fiduciary funds are not reported in G-wide F/S

(4) A reconciliation between governmental fund F/S and the G-wide F/S

Governments should present a summary reconciliation at the bottom of the fund financial statements or in an accompanying schedule.

Fund balances for total governmental funds	xxx
① Capital assets used in governmental funds	+
② Long-term liabilities used in governmental funds	(−)
③ Internal service funds' net position	+
Net position for governmental activities	xxx

8 Statement of Revenues, Expenditures and Changes in Fund Balances

	GF	Major-A	Major-B	Other funds	Total
1) Revenues					
2) Expenditures					
3) Excess of revenues over expenditures					
4) OFS and OFU					
5) Special items					
6) Net change in fund balance					xxx
7) Fund balance-beginning of period					
8) Fund balance-end of period					

(1) Presentation

1) Present the financial information of each major fund in a separate column

2) Non-major funds should be aggregated and displayed in a single column

3) Revenues : by source

4) Expenditures : by character & function

5) Other financing sources : long-term debt, transfers-in

6) Other financing uses : transfers-out

7) Extraordinary items or special items

① Extraordinary items : Both unusual in nature and infrequent in occurrence

② Special items: Unusual in nature or infrequent in occurrence

(2) Statement of Activities (G-wide F/S)

	Primary government			CU
	Governmental activities	Business-type activities	Total	
1) Expenses 2) Program Revenues 3) Net(Expenses)Revenues 4) General Revenues 5) Special items 6) Net change in net position 7) Net position-beginning of period 8) Net position-end of period	xxx			

재무제표의 구체적인 사례는 부록을 참고한다.

1) Governmental activities = governmental funds + internal service funds

2) Business-type activities = enterprise funds

3) Fiduciary funds are not reported in G-wide F/S

(3) A reconciliation between governmental fund F/S and the G-wide F/S

Changes in fund balances for total governmental funds	xxx
	+
	(−)
Changes in net position for governmental activities	xxx

주요 조정사항을 요약하면 다음과 같다.

① Capital outlay less depreciation : (+)

② GOB proceeds : (-)

③ Changes in net position in internal service funds : (+)

④ A portion of property taxes or grants : (+)

⑤ Book value from sale of capital assets : (-)

Reconciliation from fund-F/S to G-wide F/S

Seoul city reported a $200,000 net increase in fund balance for governmental funds during 20X1. What amount should Seoul city report as the change in net position for governmental activities?

- Police cars (acquisition cost=$7,000, depreciation expense=$2,500)
- Disposal of park land (book value=$30,000, proceeds=$40,000)
- Increase in net position for internal service fund=$7,000
- Seoul city levied property taxes in the amount of $100,000 and 5% of the levy was not expected to be collected. At December 31, 20X1, $75,000 of the property taxes were collected, but the remainder was not expected to be collected within 60 days after the end of 20X1.

Changes in fund balances for total governmental funds	200,000
1) Police cars-acquisition cost	+7,000
2) Police cars-depreciation expense	-2,500
3) Book value of park land	-30,000
4) Increase in net position for internal service fund	+7,000
5) Property tax	+20,000
Changes in net position for governmental activities	201,500

Reconciliation from fund-F/S to G-wide F/S

Seoul city reported a $200,000 net increase in fund balance for governmental funds during 20X1. What amount should Seoul city report as the change in net position for governmental activities?

- Payment of principal on GOB = $50,000
- GOB proceeds = $80,000
- Increase in net position for enterprise fund = $7,000
- Payment of interest on GOB = $10,000
- For 20X1, the general fund of Seoul city received $50,000 grant from the state to be used for training its police force. The state recently passes legislation that requires training for all police departments in the state. The grant was received in cash on December 10, 20X1, and was used for training seminars during January 20X2.

Changes in fund balances for total governmental funds	200,000
1) Payment of principal on GOB	+50,000
2) GOB proceeds	-80,000
3) Increase in net position for enterprise fund	0
4) Payment of interest on GOB	0
5) Grant	+50,000
Changes in net position for governmental activities	220,000

9   Deferred Outflows of Resources and Deferred Inflows of Resources

(1) Revenue Recognition in Governmental Funds

When an asset is recorded in governmental fund financial statements but the revenue is not available, the government should report a deferred inflow of resources until such time as the revenue becomes available.

(2) Imposed Non-exchange Revenue Transactions

Deferred inflows of resources should be reported when resources are received or reported as a receivable before

(a) the period for which property taxes are levied or

(b) the period when resources are required to be used.

Example

For 20X1, Seoul City received an $60,000 property tax payment that was not until the subsequent fiscal year.

20X1	Cash	60,000	
	Deferred inflows of resources		60,000
20X2	Deferred inflows of resources	60,000	
	Revenue-property tax		60,000

※ 선수재산세는 수정발생주의와 발생주의 모두 deferred inflows of resources로 회계처리한다.

(3) Government-Mandated and Voluntary Non-exchange Transactions

- Resources transmitted before the eligibility requirements are met (excluding time requirements) should be reported as assets by the provider and as liabilities.

- Resources received before time requirements are met, but after all other eligibility requirements have been met, should be reported as a deferred outflow of resources by the provider and a deferred inflow of resources.

Example

For 20X1, Seoul City received $60,000 in federal education entitlements. Seoul City spent $20,000 in 20X1 and $40,000 in 20X2.

Governmental Funds	⟨20X1⟩		
	Cash	60,000	
	Revenues-grant		20,000
	Deferred inflows of resources		40,000
G-wide	⟨20X1⟩		
	Cash	60,000	
	Revenues-grant		60,000

Example

For 20X1, Seoul City received $60,000 in federal education entitlements. $20,000 can be spent in 20X1 and $40,000 cannot be spent until 20X2.

G-wide 20X1	Cash	60,000	
	Revenues-grant		20,000
	Deferred inflows of resources	40,000	
G-wide 20X2	Deferred inflows of resources	40,000	
	Revenues-grant		40,000

※ 수정발생주의도 동일하게 회계처리한다.

For 20X1, Seoul City received $60,000 in federal education grants. Eligibility requirements of $20,000 are met 20X1 and eligibility requirements of $40,000 are met in 20X2.

G-wide 20X1	Cash	60,000	
	Revenues-grant		20,000
	Grant received in advance(liability)		40,000
G-wide 20X2	Grant received in advance	40,000	
	Revenues-grant		40,000

(4) Refunding of Debt

Refunding involves the issuance of new debt whose proceeds are used to repay previously issued (old) debt.

The difference between the reacquisition price and the net carrying amount of the old debt should be reported as a deferred outflow of resources or a deferred inflow of resources and recognized as a component of interest expense in a systematic and rational manner over the remaining life of the old debt or the life of the new debt, whichever is shorter. (Accrual accounting)

06 Governmental funds excluding general fund

1 Capital project funds

(1) 의 의

정부형 자원 중에서 유형 자산의 취득 또는 건설목적으로 특정되어 있는 자원을 보고하는 펀드로서 다음과 같은 특징이 있다.

- Capital projects funds are used to account for and report financial resources that are restricted, committed, or assigned to expenditure for capital outlays, including the acquisition or construction of capital assets.
- Capital projects funds exclude those types of capital-related outflows financed by proprietary funds or fiduciary funds
- Example: city hall, municipal stadium, county courthouse, special assessment projects
- Created when project is approved and closed at the completion of projects.

(2) Financial resources inflow

1) Grants(Intergovernmental) ⇨ Revenues

2) Proceeds of GOB ⇨ Other financing sources

3) Transfers in from general fund ⇨ Other financing sources

(3) Financial resources outflow

1) Construction ⇨ Expenditures

2) Transfer out to debt service funds ⇨ Other financing uses

(4) At completion

This fund should be terminated and the excess cash left must be transferred to debt service funds

(1) Issuing general obligation bonds

- Bond par value is separately displayed as other financing sources
- Bond premiums/discounts are separately displayed as other financing sources
- Bond issuance cost are displayed as expenditures—debt service.

Seoul city issued the following bonds to build a new city hall.

- bond par value : $10,000,000
- bond premiums : $500,000
- bond issue cost : $300,000

Dr) Cash	10,200,000	
Expenditure-issuance costs	300,000	
Cr) Other financing sources-bond proceeds(par value)		10,000,000
Other financing sources-bond proceeds(premium)		500,000

※ 일반적으로 bond premium은 CPF에서 공사지출로 사용하지 않고, DFS에서 원리금상환의 자금으로 사용한다.

※ G-wide F/S

Dr) Cash	10,200,000	
Expense-insurance costs	300,000	
Cr) Bond payable		10,000,000
Premium on bond payable		500,000

Bond issuance costs should be recognized as an expense in the period incurred.

※ 기업회계에서는 채권발행비는 부채의 감소로 처리하지만, 정부회계 발생주의에서는 채권발행비는 발생즉시 비용으로 인식한다.

(2) Transfer to debt service fund

Seoul city transferred the premiums of $200,000 to debt service fund for principal payments.

⟨Capital project fund⟩		
Dr) Other financing uses-transfer out	200,000	
Cr) Cash		200,000
⟨Debt service fund⟩		
Dr) Cash	200,000	
Cr) Other financing sources-transfer in		200,000

(3) Restricted grant

Seoul city received $8 million of its grant from the state for the construction.

Dr) Cash	8,000,000	
Cr) Deferred inflows of resources		8,000,000

※ 사용이 제한된 보조금은 사용시점에서 수익으로 인식하며, 사용제한이 없는 보조금은 수령즉시 수익으로 인식한다.

(4) Construction contract

Seoul city signs several construction-related contracts for goods and service to cost $16 million

Dr) Encumbrance	16,000,000	
Cr) Budgetary Fund Balance		16,000,000

※ 건설계약시점에서 encumbrance 회계처리를 한다.

(5) Construction expenditure

Seoul city received and paid contractor invoices of $15 million for construction and related service.

Dr) Expenditures-construction	15,000,000	
Cr) Cash		15,000,000
Dr) Budgetary Fund Balance	15,000,000	
Cr) Encumbrance		15,000,000
Dr) Deferred inflows of resources	8,000,000	
Cr)Revenues-grants		8,000,000

※ 건설관련 지출은 즉시 지출로 인식하고 주정부 보조금을 수익으로 인식한다.

※ G-wide F/S

Dr) Capital assets	15,000,000
Cr) Cash	15,000,000

※ 건설관련 지출은 고정자산으로 인식하고, 주정부 보조금은 eligibility requirements 충족시점에서 수익을 인식한다.

2 Debt service funds

(1) 의 의

정부형 자원 중에서 지방채의 원금과 이자상환의 목적으로 특정되어 있는 자원을 보고하는 펀드로서 다음과 같은 특징이 있다.

- Debt service funds are used to account for and report financial resources that are restricted, committed, or assigned to expenditure for principal and interest on all general obligation debt.

- Financial resources that are being accumulated for principal and interest maturing in future years also should be reported in debt service funds.

- Debt service funds should be used to report resources if legally mandated.

- Example : Tax dedicated to servicing general obligation bonds

  ※ General Obligation Bonds(GOB) : 정부형 활동을 지원하기 위하여 발행한 채권

  Revenue Bonds(RB) : 사업형 활동을 지원하기 위하여 발행한 채권

(2) Financial resources inflow

1) Special taxes restricted to repay general obligation bond ⇨ revenue

2) Special assessment ⇨ revenue

3) Transfers in from general fund ⇨ other financing sources

(3) Financial resources outflows

1) Principal payment ⇨ expenditure

2) Interest payment ⇨ expenditure

3) Recognize expenditure when matured ⇨ year-end interest accrual (x)

(4) G-wide F/S

1) Principal payment ⇨ decrease bond payable

2) Interest payment ⇨ expenses (year-end interest accrual)

On November 1, 20X1, Seoul city issued $800,000 of 6% general obligation serial at face amount. Interest is payable each May 1 and November 1.

$80,000 of bonds mature and come due each year, beginning on November 1, 20X2.

Debt service fund			
12/31/20X1	No entry		
5/1/20X2	Dr) Expenditure-interest	24,000	
	Cr) Cash		24,000
11/1/20X2	Dr) Expenditure-interest	24,000	
	Expenditure-principal	80,000	
	Cr) Cash		104,000

G-wide F/S			
12/31/20X1	Dr) Expense-interest	8,000	
	Cr) Interest payable		8,000
5/1/20X2	Dr) Expense-interest	16,000	
	Interest payable	8,000	
	Cr) Cash		24,000
11/1/20X2	Dr) Expense-interest	24,000	
	Bond payable	80,000	
	Cr) Cash		104,000

3 Special revenue funds

(1) 의 의

정부형 자원 중에서 capital project와 debt service 목적을 제외한 목적이 특정되어 있는 자원을 보고하는 펀드로서 다음과 같은 특징이 있다.

- Special revenue funds are used to account for and report the proceeds of specific revenue sources that are restricted or committed to expenditure for specified purposes other than debt service or capital projects.

(2) Financial resource inflow

1) Gasoline tax (Motor fuel tax) : highway maintenance

2) Hotel bed tax : promote tourist

3) Restricted grants

4) Other earmarked revenue sources

(3) Reimbursement grant

후급보조금을 말하며 발생주의와 수정발생주의 모두 eligibility requirements를 충족시키는 시점에 수익을 인식한다.

> **Example**

A municipality receives a grant award on November 1, 20X1, in the amount of $30,000. The expenditure takes place on March 1, 20X2 and cash is received on April 1, 20X2.

11/1/20X1	No entry			
3/1/20X2	Dr) Expenditure	30,000	Cr) Cash	30,000
	Dr) Grant receivable	30,000	Cr) Revenue	30,000
4/1/20X2	Dr) Cash	30,000	Cr) Grant receivable	30,000

4 Permanent funds

정부형 자원 중에서 원금은 그대로 유지하고 투자수익으로만 사용이 특정되어 있는 자원을 보고하는 펀드로서 다음과 같은 특징이 있다.

- Permanent funds should be used to account for and report resources that are restricted to the extent that only earnings, and not principal, may be used for purposes that support the reporting government's programs—that is, for the benefit of the government or its citizenry.

- Permanent funds do not include private-purpose trust funds, which should be used to report situations in which the government is required to use the principal or earnings for the benefit of individuals, private organizations, or other governments.

- Example : Citizen's gifts for maintenance of city's cemetery

---

Example

⟨Case 1⟩
A local citizen was concerned about the deplorable condition of the city cemetery and contributed $5,000,000 with the stipulation that the funds be invested and held: the income is to be used for the purpose of maintaining the city cemetery.
→ permanent fund

⟨Case 2⟩
A local citizen contributed $5,000,000 with the stipulation that the funds be used for the purpose of maintaining the city cemetery.
→ special revenue fund

⟨Case 3⟩
A local citizen contributed $5,000,000 with the stipulation that the funds be invested and held: the income is to be used for the purpose of providing scholarships.
→ private purpose trust fund

5 Special assessments

(1) 의 의

재산세와는 달리 도로건설과 같은 정부의 혜택을 받은 지역주민들만이 내는 추가세금으로 재산세 부과시점에 동시에 부과된다.

A special assessment tax is a surtax levied on property owners to pay for specific local infrastructure projects such as the construction or maintenance of roads or sewer lines. The tax is charged only to the owners of property in the neighborhood that will benefit from the project. A special assessment tax is a local tax in addition to property taxes that is levied on homeowners to fund a specific project.

A special assessment bond is a type of municipal bond used to fund a development project. Interest owed to lenders is paid by taxes levied on the community benefiting from the partic-ular bond-funded project.

(2) If the city is obligated for the special assessment debt

1) The special assessment debt is accounted for in capital projects fund

2) Special assessments are accounted for in debt service fund

3) Capital assets and long-term debt are reported in G-wide F/S

(3) If the city is not obligated for the special assessment debt

1) The donation for construction is accounted for in capital project fund

2) Special assessments are accounted for in custodial fund

3) Capital assets are reported in G-wide F/S

4) Long-term debt are not reported in G-wide F/S

07 Proprietary fund

1 영리성 펀드의 특징

(1) Focus

Proprietary fund reporting focuses on the determination of operating income, changes in net position, financial position, and cash flows.

1) Accrual basis

2) Capital maintenance and economic resources

3) Budgetary/encumbrance accounting are not required.

4) Capital asset and long-term debt are reported in fund F/S and GW F/S.

(2) Fund financial statements

1) Statement of net position

2) Statement of revenues, expenses and changes in net position

3) Statement of cash flows

(3) Column

1) Proprietary fund statements should present the financial information for each major enterprise fund in a separate column.

2) Non-major enterprise funds should be aggregated and displayed in a single column, and a combined total column should be presented for all enterprise funds.

3) Major fund reporting requirements do not apply to internal service funds.

4) Major fund test

다음 2가지 조건을 모두 충족하여야 major fund로 분류된다.

① Total assets, liabilities, revenues, or expenses of the individual enterprise fund are at least 10 percent of the corresponding total for all enterprise funds.

② Total assets, liabilities, revenues, or expenses of the individual enterprise fund are at least 5 percent of the corresponding total for all governmental and enterprise funds combined.

2 Statement of net position

(1) Asset & Liability

- Assets and liabilities should be presented in a classified format to distinguish between current and long-term assets and liabilities.

- Assets + Deferred outflow of resources
  = Liabilities + Deferred inflow of resources + Net position

(2) Net position

1) Net investment in capital asset : capital asset less any related debt

2) Restricted : externally imposed by laws, contributors & creditors

3) Unrestricted

3 Statement of revenues, expenses and changes in net position

(1) Presentation

1) Operating revenues (by source)
2) Operating expenses (by nature)
3) Operating income
4) Nonoperating revenues and expenses
5) Income before capital contribution and transfers
6) Capital contributions or grant
7) Transfers
8) Increase (decrease) in net position
9) Net position—beginning of period
10) Net position—end of period

① Distinguish between operating and nonoperating revenues and expenses

② Capital contributions, special and extraordinary items, and transfers should be reported separately, after nonoperating revenues and expenses.

(2) Grant

1) Operating grant ⇨ Nonoperating revenues

2) Capital grant ⇨ Capital contributions or grant

(3) Cash inflows from general fund

1) Capital transfer ⇨ Capital contributions or grant

2) Operating transfer ⇨ Transfers

3) Quasi-external transactions ⇨ Operating revenues

(4) Quasi-external transaction (Interfund Services)

ex enterprise fund bills to other funds for utilities services performed.

General fund	Expenditure	xxx
	Due to enterprise fund	xxx
Enterprise fund	Due from general fund	xxx
	Operating revenue	xxx

(5) Special and extraordinary items

1) Extraordinary items : Both unusual in nature and infrequent in occurrence

2) Special items: Unusual in nature or infrequent in occurrence

4 Statement of cash flows

(1) Presentation using direct method

1) Cash flow from operating (CFO)	xxx
2) Cash flow from non-capital financing (CFF-NC)	xxx
3) Cash flow from capital financing (CFF-C)	xxx
4) Cash flow from investing (CFI)	xxx
5) Changes in cash flow	xxx
6) Beginning balance in cash	xxx
7) Ending balance in cash	xxx

The direct method of presenting cash flows from operating activities should be used. (including a reconciliation of operating cash flows to operating income)

(2) Cash flows from operating activities (CFO)

1) Cash inflows from operating activities

   a. Cash inflows from sales of goods or services.

   b. Cash receipts from quasi-external operating transactions with other funds.

   c. Cash receipts from other funds for reimbursement.

   d. All other cash receipts that do not result from transactions defined as capital and related financing, noncapital financing, or investing activities.

2) Cash outflows for operating activities

   a. Cash payments to acquire materials for providing services and goods.

   b. Cash payments to employees for services.

   c. Cash payments for quasi-external operating transactions with other funds.

   d. All other cash payments that do not result from transactions defined as capital and related financing, noncapital financing, or investing activities.

(3) Cash flows from noncapital financing activities (CFF–NC)

1) Cash inflows from noncapital financing activities

    a. Proceeds from borrowing not attributable to acquisition of capital assets.

    b. Cash receipts from grants except those restricted for capital purposes.

    c. Cash received from other funds except those amounts that are attributable to acquisition of capital assets, quasi-external transactions and reimbursement.

    d. Cash received from taxes collected not restricted for capital purposes.

2) Cash outflows for noncapital financing activities

    a. Repayments of borrowing for purposes other than acquiring capital assets.

    b. Interest payments on borrowing not attributable to acquisition of capital assets.

    c. Cash paid as grants to other governments or organizations

    d. Cash paid to other funds except for quasi-external operating transactions.

(4) Cash flows from capital financing activities (CFF–C)

1) Cash inflows from capital and related financing activities

    a. Proceeds from borrowing attributable to the acquisition of capital assets.

    b. Receipts from capital grants awarded to the governmental enterprise.

    c. Receipts from contributions made by other funds, other governments, and other organizations for the specific purpose of acquiring capital assets.

    d. Receipts from sales of capital assets and proceeds from insurance on capital assets that are stolen or destroyed.

2) Cash outflows for capital and related financing activities

    a. Payments to acquire capital assets.

    b. Repayments of amounts borrowed specifically to acquire capital assets.

    c. Cash payments to lenders for interest related to acquiring capital assets.

(5) Cash flows from investing activities (CFI)

1) Cash inflows from investing activities

   a. Receipts from collections of loans

   b. Receipts from sales of debt or equity investments

   c. Interest and dividends received as returns on investments.

2) Cash outflows for investing activities

   a. Disbursements for loans

   b. Payments to acquire debt or equity instruments.

(6) Cash equivalent

Highly liquid investment with a maturity of 3 months or less when purchased.

(7) Differences between GASB and FASB

1) Only direct method is acceptable

2) Reconciliation from operating income to CFO

3) Purchase and sale of capital assets : CFF-C

4) Interest and dividend revenue : CFI

5) Borrowing, repayment and interest expense of capital debt : CFF-C

6) Borrowing, repayment and interest expense of non-capital debt : CFF-NC

7) Operating grant received : CFF-NC

8) Capital grant received : CFF-C

9) Operating transfer in and transfer out: CFF-NC

10) Capital contribution received : CFF-C

11) Lease payments : CFF-C

Example

Prepare a statement of cash flows for the enterprise fund of Sample city from the following information:

Cash on hand at the beginning of the year : $122

Interest revenue from investment : 50

Wages and salaries paid : 3,400

Purchases of supplies : 1,600

Collections for services from customers : 6,500

Interest paid on capital debt : 150

Operating transfer out to other funds : 800

Purchase of fixed assets : 900

Proceeds of revenue bonds : 1,800

Purchases of investments : 400

Proceeds from sale of fixed assets : 230

Proceeds from sale of investments : 100

Operating grant received : 600

1) Cash flow from operating (CFO)

$= -3,400 - 1,600 + 6,500 = $ **+1,500**

2) Cash flow from non-capital financing (CFF-NC)

$= -800 + 600 = $ **-200**

3) Cash flow from capital financing (CFF-C)

$= -150 - 900 + 1,800 + 230 = $ **+980**

4) Cash flow from investing (CFI)

$= +50 - 400 + 100 = $ **-250**

5) Changes in cash flow

$= 1,500 - 200 + 980 - 250 = $ **+2,030**

6) Ending balance in cash

$= 122 + 2,030 = $ **$2,152**

5 Enterprise funds

(1) 의의

1) Provides goods or services to the general public

2) Financed through user charges with self-supporting

3) Example

   public utilities, airport, transit system, golf course, solid waste landfills

(2) Financial resources inflow

1) Proceeds of revenue bond ⇨ bond payable

2) Grants(Intergovernmental)

   ① Capital grant ⇨ capital contribution

   ② Operating grant ⇨ nonoperating revenues and expenses

3) Transfers from general fund

   ① Capital transfer ⇨ capital contribution

   ② Operating transfer ⇨ transfer-in

   ③ Quasi-external transaction ⇨ operating revenues

4) User charge ⇨ operating revenues

5) Interest and dividends received ⇨ nonoperating revenues and expenses

(3) Financial resources outflow

1) Construction expenditure ⇨ capital asset

2) Repayment of revenue bond ⇨ decrease bond payable

3) Operating transfer out to other funds ⇨ transfer-out

Example

Seoul city transferred $10 million from its general fund to its water utility fund to make an initial capital contribution.

⟨General fund⟩	
Dr) Other financing uses-transfer out	10,00,000
Cr) Cash	10,000,000
⟨Enterprise fund⟩	
Dr) Cash	10,000,000
Cr) Capital contribution	10,000,000

Seoul City issued $5 million in revenue bonds that are restricted for the construction of water utility. The bonds were issued at par.

Dr) Cash	5,000,000
Cr) Bond payable	5,000,000

Seoul city received $2 million of its grant from the state for the construction of water utility.

Dr) Cash	2,000,000
Cr) Capital contribution	2,000,000

Seoul city purchased the plant and equipment of water utility for 9,000,000.

Dr) Capital assets	9,00,000
Cr) Cash	9,000,000

Seoul city transferred $1 million from its general fund to its water utility fund to subsidize operating.

⟨General fund⟩		
Dr) Other financing uses-transfer out	1,000,000	
Cr) Cash		1,000,000
⟨Enterprise fund⟩		
Dr) Cash	1,000,000	
Cr) Transfer-in		1,000,000

Seoul city received $1 million of its grant from the state for the purpose of subsidizing operation of water utility.

Dr) Cash	1,000,000	
Cr) Grant revenue-nonoperating revenue		1,000,000

Seoul city billed and received $300,000 from customer households for water.

Dr) Cash	300,000	
Cr) User charge-operating revenue		300,000

Seoul city transferred $200,000 from its general fund to its water utility fund to provide water service.

⟨General fund⟩		
Dr) Expenditures	200,000	
Cr) Cash		200,000
⟨Enterprise fund⟩		
Dr) Cash	200,000	
Cr) User charge-operating revenue		200,000

6 Internal service funds

(1) 의의

1) Accounts for business-type activities of supplying goods or services to departments within the governmental unit.

2) Users of the goods should be charged on a cost reimbursement basis

3) Examples : central motor pools, central data processing, self-insurance activities

(2) Quasi-external transaction (Interfund Services)

1) Internal service fund bills to other funds for services performed.

2) Example> Motor pool services

General fund	Expenditure xxx	
	Due to internal service fund	xxx
Internal service fund	Due from general fund xxx	
	Operating revenue	xxx

(3) G-wide financial statements

1) Fund : Proprietary fund

2) G-wide : Governmental activities

7 Solid waste landfill

(1) Municipal solid waste landfill (MSWLF)

1) Enterprise funds or general funds

2) Cash inflows ⇨ when the landfill accepts the waste.

3) Cash outflows ⇨ closure and post-closure

4) Enterprise fund에서 회계처리 하는 경우 발생주의를 적용하여 미래에 예상되는 총원가의 일부를 수익이 발생하는 시점에서 인식하여야 한다.

(2) Accounting for landfill in enterprise fund

1) Revenue recognized as earned

2) Recognize expenses and liabilities on an accrual basis

(3) Total cost

추정하여야 할 총원가의 범위는 다음과 같다.

1) Cost of equipment expected to be installed. (Gas monitoring system)

2) Cost of final cover

3) Cost of monitoring and maintaining.

(4) Landfill expense

= estimated total cost × (capacity used to date / total capacity)
- expense recognized in the past

(5) Landfill liability

= estimated total cost × (capacity used to date / total capacity)
- landfill payments in the past

At the start of 20X1, Seoul city opens a landfill. During 20X1, the city uses 20,000 cubic feet of the landfill. At year-end, it estimates that total capacity will still the 100,000 cubic feet but total closure costs will be $1,800,000.

Enterprise fund	Landfill expense	$360,000	
	Landfill liability		$360,000*
	* $1,800,000 × 20% = $360,000		
General fund	No entry		

In 20X2, the city uses 25,000 cubic feet of the landfill. At year-end, it estimates that total costs have increased to $1,850,000. The city also spends 27,000 on closure-related cost (including $10,000 for equipment).

Enterprise fund	Landfill expense	$472,500	
	Landfill liability		$472,500*
	Landfill liability	$27,000	
	Cash		$27,000
	* $1,850,000 × 45% - $360,000 = 472,500		
General fund	Expenditure-landfill	$27,000	
	Cash		$27,000

☞ Landfill liability = $1,850,000 × 45% - $27,000 = $805,500

※ 수도권매립지 (Landfill)

1992년 서울특별시의 기존 쓰레기 처리장이었던 난지도가 포화상태에 이르자 정부에서는 경기도 김포군 서부의 간척지 일부를 대체 매립 예정지로 지정하였고, 이 부지를 서울특별시와 인천직할시, 경기도가 공동으로 사용하는 광역 쓰레기 매립지로 조성한 것이 수도권 매립지이다. 현재는 매립지의 대부분이 인천광역시 관할에 있지만, 조성 당시에는 아직 검단 지역이 인천에 편입되기 이전이어서 전 영역이 김포군 안에 있었기 때문에 김포 매립지라는 별칭을 갖고 있다.

08 Fiduciary fund

1 신탁형 펀드의 특징

(1) Accounting

1) Accrual basis

2) Capital maintenance

3) Economic resources

4) Budgetary/encumbrance accounting are not required.

(2) Fund financial statement

1) Statement of fiduciary net position

2) Statement of changes in fiduciary net position

(3) Fiduciary activities

The activity is a fiduciary activity if all of the following criteria are met.

1) The assets associated with the activity are controlled by the government.

2) The assets associated with the activity are not derived from the government's own-source revenues.

3) The assets associated with the activity have one or more of the following characteristics:

① The assets are administered through a trust in which the government itself is not a beneficiary (Trust)

② The assets are for the benefit of individuals and the government does not have administrative involvement with the assets (Custodial)

2 Statement of Fiduciary Net Position

(1) Column

The statement should provide a separate column for each fund type.

(2) Net position

The statement of fiduciary net position should be used to report the assets, deferred outflows of resources, liabilities, deferred inflows of resources, and fiduciary net position.

	PTF	ITF	PPTF	CF
Assets				
Cash and cash equivalent	xxx	xxx	xxx	xxx
Receivables	xxx	xxx	xxx	xxx
Investment at fair value	xxx	xxx	xxx	
Liabilities				
Accounts payable	xxx	xxx	xxx	xxx
Due to local government	xxx	xxx	xxx	xxx
Net Position				
Restricted for ~	xxx	xxx	xxx	xxx

☞ Appendix의 재무제표를 참조

3 Statement of changes in fiduciary net position

The statement of changes in fiduciary net position should be used to report additions to and deductions for each fiduciary fund type.

	PTF	ITF	PPTF	CF
Additions				
Contributions	xxx		xxx	
Investment earnings	xxx	xxx	xxx	
Sales tax collections				xxx
Deductions				
Benefit paid	xxx			
Administrative expense	xxx			
Payments of sales taxes				xxx
Others	xxx	xxx	xxx	xxx

☞ Appendix의 재무제표를 참조

4 Reporting Fiduciary Component Units

Fiduciary fund financial statements should include information about all fiduciary funds of the primary government, including fiduciary component units.

5 Pension Trust Funds

Used to report fiduciary activities for pension plans and other post-employment benefit (OPEB) plans that are administered through trusts. ⇒ Public Employees Retirement Systems (PERS)

(1) Contribution (quasi-external)

Employer contribution from general fund to pension trust fund

General fund	Expenditure	xxx	
	Cash		xxx
Pension trust fund	Cash	xxx	
	Addition-contribution		xxx

(2) Investments are reported at market value

ex appreciation of investment

| Pension trust fund | Investment | xxx | |
| | Addition-investment earnings | | xxx |

(3) Benefit paid

ex pension trust fund paid the benefits to employees

| Pension trust fund | Deduction-benefit | xxx | |
| | Cash | | xxx |

(4) Required supplementary information

1) Schedule of changes in the net pension liability and related ratios (10 years)

- Total pension liability : 기초, 증가, 감소, 기말

- Plan fiduciary net position : 기초, 증가, 감소, 기말

- Net pension liability = total pension liability − plan fiduciary net position

2) Schedule of pension contributions (10 years)

3) Schedule of the City's proportionate share of net pension liability

※ CalPERS (캘퍼스)

캘리포니아 주정부 공무원과 교육공무원, 지방 공공 기관 공무원에게 은퇴연금과 의료보장 혜택을 제공하는 미국 최대 연·기금이다. 캘리포니아 주정부 공무원들을 위한 연금으로 출발한 이래 공공 기관과 지방 정부 공무원까지 가입 대상이 확대되면서 덩치가 커졌다. 운용 자산의 절반을 국내외 주식에 쏟아 붓는 공격적인 투자 스타일로 명성이 높으며, 세계 금융시장을 주무르는 큰손 중 하나다.

6 Investment Trust Funds

Used to report fiduciary activities from the external portion of investment pools that are held in a trust.

7 Private-Purpose Trust Funds

(1) 의의

Used to report all fiduciary activities that are not required to be reported in PTF or ITF and are held in a trust.

ex A scholarship fund

(2) Contribution (donation)

	Program (O)	Program (X)
Expendable	Governmental funds or Proprietary funds	Private-purpose trust funds
Non-expendable*	Permanent fund	

*Non-expendable : The principal cannot be used

(3) Escheat Property

An escheat is the reversion of property to a governmental entity in the absence of legal claimants or heirs. Escheat property generally should be reported in either an private-purpose trust funds or the fund to which the property ultimately escheat.

8 Custodial Funds

(1) 의의

Used to report fiduciary activities that are not required to be reported in PTF, ITF, or PPTF.

☞ replace an agency fund with a custodial fund (2019)

(2) Examples

1) Tax billed and collected on behalf of other government

2) Special assessments when the municipality is not obligated

3) Cash-conduit arrangements : Pass-through grant

4) The external portion of investment pools that are not held in a trust.

An example of a custodial fund addition description is property taxes collected for other governments. An example of a custodial fund deduction description is property taxes distributed to other governments.

09 Interfund activity

1 Reciprocal interfund activity

This is the internal counterpart to exchange and exchange-like transactions.

(1) Interfund loans

Amounts provided with a requirement for repayment

Borrower funds	Cash	xxx	
	Due to other funds		xxx
Lender funds	Due from other funds	xxx	
	Cash		xxx

☞ 펀드 손익계산서에 영향을 주지 않는 거래이다.

(2) Interfund services provided and used

1) Sales and purchases of goods and services between funds for a price

Seller funds	Cash	xxx	
	Operating revenue		xxx
Purchaser funds	Expenditure (or expense)	xxx	
	Cash		xxx

⇒ Unpaid amounts should be reported as interfund receivables and payables

2) Examples

① Water provided from enterprise fund to general fund

② Motor pool service provided from internal service fund to general fund

③ Pension service provided from pension trust fund to general fund

2 Non-reciprocal interfund activity

This is the internal counterpart to nonexchange transactions.

(1) Interfund transfers

1) Flows of assets without equivalent flows of assets in return and without a requirement for repayment.

2) In governmental funds, transfers should be reported as other financing uses in the funds making transfers and as other financing sources in the funds receiving transfers.

3) In proprietary funds, transfers should be reported after nonoperating revenues and expenses.

4) Examples

① Operating transfer from general fund to capital project fund

② Operating transfer from general fund to debt service fund

③ Operating transfer from capital project fund to debt service fund

④ Operating transfer from general fund to enterprise fund

⑤ Capital contribution from general fund to enterprise fund

(2) Interfund reimbursements

1) Repayments from the funds responsible for particular expenditures or expenses to the funds that initially paid for them.

2) Example

General fund and special revenue fund personnel attend a conference together, for which the total cost is $10,000. The entire bill is paid by general fund but $3,000 was for special revenue fund.

GF	Cash	xxx
	Expenditure	xxx

10   Government-wide financial statements

1   Reporting entity

(1) Reporting entity

The reporting entity consists of the primary government and component units (organizations for which the primary government is financially accountable)

(2) Primary government

1) State government or general purpose government (municipality or county)

2) Special-purpose government that meets all of the following criteria:

(a school district or a park district)

> A primary government is also a
> a. It has a separately elected governing body.
> b. It is legally separate.
> c. It is fiscally independent of other state and local governments.

A special-purpose government is fiscally independent if it has the authority to do all three of the following:

> a. Determine its budget without another government's having the authority to approve and modify that budget.
> b. Levy taxes or set rates without approval by another government.
> c. Issue bond without approval by another government.

(3) Component units

1) Component units are legally separate organizations for which the elected officials of the primary government are financially accountable.

2) Component units can be other organizations for which the nature and significance of their relationship with a primary government are such that exclusion would cause the financial statements to be misleading.

3) The primary government is financially accountable if it appoints a voting majority of the organization's governing body and it is able to impose its will on that organization.

4) The primary government may be financially accountable if an organization is fiscally dependent on the primary government.

(4) Reporting components units in G-wide F/S

1) Discrete Presentation of Component Units

Most component units should be discretely presented. Discrete presentation entails reporting component unit financial data in a column separate from the financial data of the primary government.

2) Blending Component Units

Because of the closeness of their relationships with the primary government, some component units should be blended as though they are part of the primary government.

(5) Criteria for Blending Component Units

A component unit should be included in the primary government financial statements using the blending method in any of these circumstances:

1) The component unit's governing body is substantively the same as the governing body of the primary government and a) or b)
   a) there is a financial benefit or burden relationship between the primary government and the component unit
   b) management of the primary government has operational responsibility for the component unit.
2) The component unit provides services entirely to the primary government or exclusively benefits the primary government.
3) The component unit's total debt outstanding is expected to be repaid entirely or almost entirely with resources of the primary government.

2 Government-wide F/S

(1) Accountability

1) Fund F/S ⇒ Fiscal accountability (적법성)

2) G-wide F/S ⇒ Operational accountability (운영의 효율성)

(2) Separate rows and columns

1) Separate rows and columns should be used to distinguish between the total primary government and its discretely presented component units.

2) A total column should be presented for the primary government.

3) A total column for the entity as a whole may be presented but is not required and prior-year data may be presented but also are not required.

4) Separate rows and columns also should be used to distinguish between the governmental and business-type activities of the primary government.

   ※ Governmental activities = governmental funds + internal service fund

   ※ Business-type activities = enterprise fund

(3) Special purpose government as primary government

4가지 유형으로 구분하여 필수 재무제표를 달리한다.

① Governmental activities

② Business-type activities

③ Fiduciary activities

④ Governmental activities & Business-type activities

※ ② Business-type activities special purpose government and ③ Fiduciary activities special purpose government are not required for G-wide F/S

3 Statement of net position

(1) Accounting basis

1) Accrual basis of accounting

2) Economic resources

(2) Net position

1) Net investment in capital assets

capital assets net of accumulated depreciation - the outstanding balances of borrowings that are attributable to the acquisition of those assets

2) Restricted net position

when constraints placed on net position use are either

a) Externally imposed by creditors, grantors or contributors

b) Imposed by law through constitutional provisions or enabling legislation

3) Unrestricted net position

total net position - (net investment in capital assets + restricted)

(3) Internal balances

1) Intra-activity

Interfund receivables & payables should be eliminated in the governmental and business-type activities.

ex General fund ⇨ Capital project fund

General fund ⇨ Internal service funds

2) Inter-activity

Interfund receivables & payables between governmental and business-type activities should be presented as internal balances.

ex Enterprise fund ⇨ Internal service funds

General fund ⇨ Enterprise fund

3) Amounts reported in the funds as receivable from or payable to fiduciary funds should be included in the statement of net assets as receivable from and payable to external parties, rather than as internal balances.

4) All internal balances should be eliminated in the total primary government column.

(4) Capital assets that are not being depreciated

① Land

② Infrastructure assets reported using the modified approach

③ Collections or individual items that are inexhaustible.

(5) Infrastructure assets

1) Examples of infrastructure assets :

roads, bridges, tunnels, water systems, dams, and lighting systems

2) A government may choose to use a modified approach for infrastructure

3) Modified approach

① Infrastructure assets are not depreciated.

② All expenditures except for additions and improvements should be expensed in the period incurred.

⇨ Additions or improvements increase the capacity or efficiency of infrastructure assets rather than preserve the useful life of the assets.

4) Two requirements to adopt modified approach

a) the government must manage the eligible infrastructure assets

b) the government must document the condition level prescribed

5) Required supplementary information

Information related to infrastructure assets using the modified approach

4 Statement of activities

(1) Accrual accounting

(2) Presentation

1) Expenses (by function)
2) Program revenues
3) Net (expenses) revenue
4) General revenues
5) Special items
6) Transfers
7) Increase (decrease) in net position
8) Net position—beginning of period
9) Net position—end of period

The operations of the reporting government should be presented in a format that reports the net (expense) revenue of its individual functions. Governments should report all expenses by function.

General revenues, special and extraordinary items, and transfers should be reported separately after the total net expenses of the government's functions.

(3) Program revenues

① Charges for service
② Operating grant and contribution restricted for program
③ Capital grant and contribution restricted for program

(4) General revenues

1) All revenues are general revenues unless they are required to be reported as program revenues.

2) All taxes, even those that are levied for a specific purpose, are general revenues.

3) All other nontax revenues (including interest, grants, and contributions) that do not meet the criteria to be reported as program revenues should also be reported as general revenues.

4) General revenues should be reported after total net expense of the government's functions.

(5) Special items

① Special items: Unusual in nature or infrequent in occurrence

　　ex gain on sale of park land

② Extraordinary items : Both unusual in nature and infrequent in occurrence

(6) Transfer

1) Intra-activity

Interfund transfers should be eliminated in the governmental and business-type activities.

　　ex General fund ⇨ Capital project fund

　　General fund ⇨ Internal service funds

2) Inter-activity

Interfund transfers between governmental and business-type activities should be presented as transfers.

　　ex Enterprise fund ⇨ Internal service funds

　　General fund ⇨ Enterprise fund

3) Interfund services provided and used should not be eliminated in the statement of activities.

During the year ended December 31, 20X1, Seoul City had the following selected transactions :

- The water utility enterprise fund billed the general fund $25,000 for water usage.
- The general fund transferred $30,000 to a debt service fund to pay interest on general obligation bonds.
- The general fund made a permanent transfer of $100,000 to an enterprise fund. The enterprise fund used the amount transferred to acquire capital assets.
- The general fund transferred $200,000 to a capital projects fund for the town's portion of the cost for the renovation of the town hall.
- The general fund transferred $7,000 to the pension trust fund. The amount represented the employer's contribution.

Q1) On the statement of revenues, expenditures and changes in fund balances for governmental fund for the ended December 31, 20X1, what amount should be reported for transfer out in the general fund column?

Q2) On the statement of revenues, expenditures and changes in fund balances for governmental fund for the ended December 31, 20X1, what amount should be reported for expenditures in the general fund column?

Q3) On the government-wide statement of activities for the ended December 31, 20X1, what amount should be reported for transfers in the governmental activities column?

Q4) On the government-wide statement of activities for the ended December 31, 20X1, what amount should be reported for expenses in the governmental activities column?

정답

Q1) 30,000 + 100,000 + 200,000 = $330,000
Q2) 25,000 + 7,000 = $32,000
Q3) $100,000
Q4) $32,000

Example

During the year ended December 31, 20X1, Seoul City had the following interfund receivables and payables :
- between general fund and enterprise fund : $3,000
- between general fund and capital project fund : $4,000
- between general fund and internal service fund : $2,000
- between internal service fund and enterprise fund : $1,000

Q1) On the government-wide statement of net position at December 31, 20X1, what amount should be reported for internal balances in the governmental activities column?

Q2) On the government-wide statement of net position at December 31, 20X1, what amount should be reported for internal balances in the business-type activities column?

Q3) On the government-wide statement of net position at December 31, 20X1, what amount should be reported for internal balances in the total primary government column?

정답

Q1) 3,000 + 1,000 = $4,000
Q2) $4,000
Q3) $0

As of December 31, 20X1, Seoul City had the following selected items :
- Cost of capital assets financed with general obligation bond and tax : $100,000
- Accumulated depreciation on the capital assets : 25,000
- Outstanding debt related to the capital assets : 20,000

Q1) On the government-wide statement of net position at December 31, 20X1, what amount should be reported for capital assets in the governmental activities column?

Q2) On the government-wide statement of net position at December 31, 20X1, what amount should be reported for capital assets in the business-type activities column?

Q3) On the government-wide statement of net position at December 31, 20X1, what amount should be reported for net investment in capital assets under the net position section in the governmental activities column?

정답

Q1) 100,000 − 25,000 = $75,000
Q2) $0
Q3) 75,000 − 20,000 = $55,000

11   Special Issues

1   Intangible Assets (GASBS 51)

(1) Recognition

An intangible asset should be recognized in the statement of net position only if it is identifiable. All intangible assets should be classified as capital assets. An intangible asset is considered identifiable when either of the following conditions is met:

a) The asset is separable

b) The asset arises from contractual or other legal rights.

(2) Amortization

Intangible assets with indefinite useful lives should not be amortized. The useful life of an intangible asset that arises from contractual or other legal rights should not exceed the period to which the service capacity of the asset is limited by contractual or legal provisions.

2   Land and Other Real Estate Held as Investments by Endowments (GASBS 52)

Land and other real estate held as investments by endowments should be reported at fair value at the reporting date. Changes in fair value during the period should be reported as investment income.

3   Derivative Instruments (GASBS 53)

(1) Recognition

Derivative instruments should be reported on the statement of net position. The classification of derivative instruments depends on whether they represent assets or liabilities.

(2) Measurement

1) Derivative instruments should be measured at fair value.

2) Changes in fair values of investment derivative instruments, including derivative instruments that are determined to be ineffective, should be reported within the investment revenue classification on the flow of resources statement.

3) Changes in fair values of hedging derivative instruments are reported as either deferred inflows or deferred outflows in the statement of net position.

(3) Methods of Evaluating Effectiveness

1) If a potential hedging derivative instrument is first evaluated using the consistent critical terms method and does not meet the criteria for effectiveness of that method, at least one quantitative method also should be applied.

2) The consistent critical terms method evaluates effectiveness by qualitative consideration of the critical terms of the hedgeable item and the potential hedging derivative instrument

3) Three quantitative methods have been identified to evaluate effectiveness.

① the synthetic instrument method

② the dollar-offset method

③ the regression analysis method

4 Fair Value Measurement and Application (GASBS 72)

(1) Definition of Fair Value

Fair value is the price that would be received to sell an asset or paid to transfer a liability in an orderly transaction between market participants at the measurement date.

(2) Valuation Approaches

1) Market Approach

The market approach to measuring fair value uses prices and other relevant information generated by market transactions involving identical or similar assets or liabilities.

2) Cost Approach

The cost approach to measuring fair value reflects the amount that would be required currently to replace the present service capacity of an asset.

3) Income Approach

The income approach to measuring fair value converts future amounts to a single current amount (such as would be determined by using the discounted present value technique).

(3) Fair Value Hierarchy

The fair value hierarchy categorizes the inputs to valuation techniques used to measure fair value into three levels.

1) Level 1 inputs

are quoted prices (unadjusted) for identical assets or liabilities in active markets that a government can access at the measurement date.

2) Level 2 inputs

are inputs—other than quoted prices included within Level 1—that are observable for an asset or liability, either directly or indirectly.

3) Level 3 inputs

are unobservable inputs for an asset or liability

5 Asset Retirement Obligations (GASBS 83)

An ARO is a legally enforceable liability associated with the retirement of a tangible capital asset.

A government should recognize an ARO when the liability is incurred and reasonably estimable. When an ARO is recognized, a government also should recognize a corresponding deferred outflow of resources.

Subsequent to initial measurement, a government should at least annually adjust the current value of its ARO for the effects of general inflation or deflation. For a liability that increases or decreases before the time of retirement of the tangible capital asset, a government should adjust the corresponding deferred outflow of resources.

6 Majority Equity Interests (GASBS 90)

An investment is a security that (a) a government holds primarily for the purpose of income or profit and (b) has a present service capacity based solely on its ability to generate cash or to be sold to generate cash.

A majority equity interest that meets the definition of an investment should be measured using the equity method, unless it is held by a special-purpose government engaged only in fiduciary activities. Those governments and funds should measure the majority equity interest at fair value.

If a government's holding of a majority equity interest in a legally separate organization does not meet the definition of an investment, the government should report the legally separate organization as a component unit.

7 Interest Cost Incurred before the End of a Construction Period (GASBS 89)

Effective Date: December 15, 2019

Interest cost incurred before the end of a construction period should be recognized as an expense in the period in which the cost is incurred for financial statements prepared using the economic resources measurement focus.

As a result, interest cost incurred before the end of a construction period will not be included in the historical cost of a capital asset reported in a business-type activity or enterprise fund.

12 Comprehensive Annual Financial Report (CAFR)

1 Comprehensive Annual Financial Report (CAFR)

I. Introduction section

(1) Letter of transmittal
(2) Organization chart
(3) List of principal officials

II. Financial section

(1) Auditor's report
(2) Management's discussion and analysis (MD&A)
(3) Government-wide F/S→ 2개
(4) Fund F/S→ 7개
(5) Notes
(6) Required supplementary information(RSI)
(7) Other supplementary information not required by GAAP

※ (2)와 (6)은 재무보고서의 필수사항이지만 재무제표는 아니다.

III. Statistical section

(1) Financial trends information
(2) Revenue capacity information
(3) Debt capacity Information
(4) Demographic and economic information
(5) Operating information

※ presenting ten year trends

2 Management's discussion and analysis (MD&A)

Governments are required to present MD&A before the basic financial statements. At a minimum, MD&A should include

(1) A brief discussion of the F/S

(2) Condensed financial information derived from government-wide financial statements comparing the current year to the prior year.

(3) An analysis of the government's overall financial position and results of operations.

(4) An analysis of balances and transactions of individual funds.

(5) An analysis of significant variation between the original budget, final budget and actual results for the year

(6) A description of significant capital asset and long-term debt for the year

(7) A discussion by governments that use the modified approach to report infrastructure assets

(8) A description of any known facts, decisions or conditions that would have a significant effect on the government's financial position

3 Government-wide financial statements

(1) Statement of Net Position

(2) Statement of Activities

4 Fund financial statements

(1) Governmental funds

1) Balance Sheet

2) Statement of Revenue, Expenditures and Changes in Fund Balances

(2) Proprietary funds

1) Statement of Net Position

2) Statement of Revenue, Expenses and Changes in Net Position

3) Statement of Cash Flow

(3) Fiduciary funds

1) Statement of Fiduciary Net Position

2) Statement of Changes in Fiduciary Net Position

5 Notes to the financial statements

The notes to the financial statements are an integral part of the basic financial statements.

(1) Summary of significant accounting policies

1) Reporting entity

2) Basis of presentation

3) Measurement focus and basis of accounting.

4) Encumbrances

5) Assets, liabilities, deferred inflows, deferred outflows, and net position.

(2) Reconciliation of government-wide and fund financial statements

(3) Stewardship, compliance and accountability

(4) Detailed notes

Deposits, investments, capital assets, leases, long-term liabilities, interfund receivables, payables and transfers

(5) Subsequent events

(6) Commitments and contingencies

(7) Pension funds and other post-employment benefits

6 Required supplementary information other than MD&A

(1) Schedule of changes in the net pension liability and related ratios (10 years)

(2) Schedule of contributions for pension plans (10 years)

(3) Budgetary comparison schedule

(4) Information related to infrastructure assets using the modified approach

7 Other supplementary information not required by GAAP

(1) Combining financial statements

(2) Individual fund financial statements

8 Reporting by special-purpose governments engaged only in business-type activities

Governments engaged only in business-type activities should present only the financial statements required for enterprise funds.

(1) MD&A

(2) Enterprise fund financial statements

　1) Statement of net position

　2) Statement of revenues, expenses, and changes in net position

　3) Statement of cash flows

(3) Notes to financial statements

(4) RSI other than MD&A

13 Tasked-Based Simulation

[Q 10-1]

For each of the following events or transaction, identify the fund of the funds that will be affected.

1. Account for resources that are legally restricted to the extent that only earnings, an not principal, may be used to support government programs.
2. Account for resources that are the external portion of the government investment pools that are belonging to others.
3. Motor-fuel tax
4. The transfer of title of property or an estate to the state when an individual dies without a will and legal heirs.
5. Special assessment if city is not obligated
6. Accounts for ordinary operations of a governmental unit which are financed from taxes
7. Account for resources used for the construction of city hall
8. Account for resources used for the construction of water utility
9. Account for the accumulation of resources of interest and principal for GOB
10. Account for the accumulation of resources of interest and principal for revenue bond
11. All transactions not accounted for in some other fund are accounted for in this fund
12. Public Employee Retirement System
13. Self-insurance funds
14. Accounts for revenues from specific (earmarked) sources
15. A cost reimbursement fee basis
16. Hotel tax used to promote tourist
17. Motor pools
18. Property tax collections for other cities
19. Account for the operation of governmental facilities and services that are intended to be primarily from user charges
20. Account for services provided to other departments within governmental unit.

21. Special assessment if city is obligated

22. Account for resources that are legally restricted to the extent that only earnings, an not principal, may be used to support activities other than government programs.

23. A governmental unit operates a municipal pool. Costs are intended to be recovered primarily from user charges.

24. A bond offering was issued to subsidize the construction of a new convention center.

25. A town received a donation of cash that must be used for the benefit of a local bird sanctuary.

26. A central computing center was established to handle the data processing needs of a municipality.

27. A local municipality provides water and sewer services to residents for a fee.

28. A village receives a grant from the state government. The funds are to be used solely for preserving wetlands.

29. A county government serves as a tax collection agency for all towns and cities located within the county.

30. A county government offers to pool the cash available for investment from cities located within its boundaries.

31. A wealthy citizen donates $10,000,000 for city park maintenance. The principal cannot be spent.

32. A wealthy citizen donates $10,000,000 for city park maintenance. The principal may be spent as needed.

33. A village collects cigarette taxes from vendors. The tax funds must be remitted to the state.

[Q 10-2]

General fund entered into a number of transactions for the current fiscal year.

1. Borrowed $75,000 by issuing six-month tax anticipation notes.
2. Ordered equipment with an estimated cost of $33,000.
3. Received the equipment along with an invoice for its actual cost, $33,250.
4. Transferred $200,000 of general fund resources to a debt service fund.
5. On January 1, the township levied property taxes of $1,000,000. The township expects to collect all except $100,000 by the end of the fiscal year or within not more than 60 days thereafter. Of the remaining $100,000, half is expected to prove uncollectible.
6. The township received a $100,000 restricted grant for certain library programs from another unit of government. The grant will be accounted for in the general fund.
7. The township incurred $75,000 of expenditures for the programs covered by the library grant.
8. Borrowed $600,000 by issuing bonds at par. The bonds mature in 10 years.
9. Sold equipment at the end of its expected useful life. The equipment had no expected residual value when acquired (at a cost of $13,000), but it sold for $1,200.
10. Determined that it is probable that a lawsuit involving a claim against a department will result in a settlement of at least $50,000. However, it is not expected that any payments will be required for two years or more.

• Instructions •

Prepare the journal entry in the general fund.

[Q 10-3]

Seoul City entered into a number of transactions for the current fiscal year.

1. The City issued $10 million of general obligation bonds at par to finance construction of a new county office building.
2. The City purchased a truck for a general governmental department. The cost of the truck, $22,000, was paid in cash.
3. The City-owned and -operated electric utility billed residents and businesses $500,000 for electricity sales.
4. The City paid $2 million to High Rise Construction Company during 2008 for work completed during the year.
5. The City paid general governmental employee salaries of $4,500. Another $500 of salaries accrued but has not been paid.
6. The City borrowed $7,500 on a six-month note to finance general operating costs of the government.
7. The City sold general fixed assets with an original cost of $300,000 for $30,000 at the end of their useful life. The use of the resources received is not restricted.
8. "Profits" of $500,000 from the airport enterprise fund were transferred to the general fund of the city to subsidize general fund operations.
9. Interest income collected on the city's general fund investments totaled $70,000 for the year.
10. A wealthy citizen donates $10,000,000 for city park maintenance. The principal cannot be spent.
11. Automobiles and vans for general governmental use are purchased for $375,000.

• Instructions •

Identify the fund or funds affected by each transaction and determine how each transaction will affect the accounting equation of the particular fund.

[Q 10-4]

The preclosing account balances of the general fund of the City of Seoul on June 30, 20X2, were as follows:

Debits

Cash	$ 80,000
Taxes receivable-delinquent	160,000
Due from capital project fund	18,000
Estimated revenues	1,000,000
Expenditures	940,000
Operating transfers out	10,000
Encumbrances	20,000
	$2,228,000

Credits

Allowance for uncollectible taxes-delinquent	$ 30,000
Vouchers payable	58,000
Notes payable	60,000
Budgetary fund balance	60,000
Fund balance—unassigned	80,000
Revenues	980,000
Appropriations	960,000
	$2,228,000

The fund balance-unassigned at the beginning of the year was $80,000, and there were no carryover encumbrances at the beginning of the fiscal year. The end of year encumbrances are a result of enabling legislation.

• Instructions •

1. Prepare a statement of revenues, expenditures, and changes in total fund balance for the year ended June 30, 20X2.
2. Prepare a general fund balance sheet at June 30, 20X2.

[Q 10-5]

The following data are available from the City of Seoul's financial records on December 31, 20X1:

1. The net change in fund balance—total governmental funds for the city is $1,408,950.
2. The city purchased general fixed assets at a historical cost of $225,000 during the year. Depreciation of $35,000 is recorded in the year of purchase.
3. Grants receivable in the amount of $165,000 are recorded as deferred inflows of resources in the fund statements but would be recognized as revenue under accrual accounting.
4. A capital lease payable in the amount of $75,000 has been recorded as an expenditure in the general fund. The related long-term debt at year-end is $55,000.
5. General long-term debt in the amount of $350,000 has been issued and recorded in the general fund.
6. During 20X1, the general fund transferred $200,000 to the capital projects fund.
7. During 20X1, the general fund transferred $60,000 to the enterprise fund.

• Instructions •

Determine the city's change in net position of governmental activities that will appear in the government—wide statements.

[Q 10-6]

The City of Seoul authorized construction of a $600,000 addition to the municipal building in September 20X1. The addition will be financed by $200,000 from the general fund and a $400,000 serial bond issue to be sold in April 20X2.

1. On October 1, 20X1, the general fund transferred $200,000 to the capital projects fund.
2. On November 1, 20X1, a contract for the addition was awarded to Crooked Construction for $580,000.
3. On April 15, 20X2, the $400,000, 7% bonds were sold for $401,000 and the premium was transferred to the debt service fund.
4. On May 2, 20X2, construction was completed and Crooked Construction submitted a bill for $580,000.
5. On May 12, 20X2, the bill to Crooked Construction was paid in full. The capital project fund was closed, and the remaining cash was transferred to the general fund.

• Instructions •

Prepare journal entries for the capital projects fund and any other fund involved to the extent of requiring journal entries to record the transactions described.

[Q 10-7]

Seoul County had a beginning cash balance in its enterprise fund of $122. During the year, the following transactions affecting cash flows occurred:

Interest from investment	$45
Wages and salaries paid	3,470
Operating grant received	1,200
Collections for services from customers	6,380
Interest paid on long-term debt	150
Capital grant received	880
Purchase of fixed assets	900
Proceeds of revenue bonds	800
Purchases of investments	440
Proceeds from sale of fixed assets	23
Proceeds from sale of investments	33
Operating transfers from other funds	600

• Instructions •

Prepare a statement of cash flows for the Seoul County enterprise fund.

[Q 10-8]

For the year ended December 31, 20X1, the general fund levied property taxes of $250,000 and the following information pertains to the 20X1 property taxes .

Collections during 20X1	$130,000
Expected collections by March 1, 20X2	60,000
Expected collections during the remainder of 20X2	??
Estimated to be uncollectible	4%
Total levy	$250,000

For the year ended December 31, 20X2, the general fund levied property taxes of $300,000 and the following information pertains to the 20X2 property taxes.

Collections during 20X2	$190,000
Expected collections by March 1, 20X3	30,000
Expected collections during the remainder of 20X3	??
Estimated to be uncollectible	5%
Total levy	$300,000

• Instructions •

1. Prepare journal entries for the general fund during 20X1.

2. Prepare journal entries for the general fund during 20X2.

[Q 10-9]

The following data are available from the governmental funds' financial records on for the ended December 31, 20X1:

1. General obligation bonds with a par value of $750,000 are issued at $769,000 to finance construction of a government office building.
2. Ordered equipment with an estimated cost of $33,000.
3. Received the equipment along with an invoice for its actual cost, $33,250.
4. Transferred $200,000 of general fund resources to a debt service fund.
5. On January 1, the township levied property taxes of $1,000,000. The township expects to collect all except $100,000 by the end of the fiscal year or within not more than 60 days thereafter. Of the remaining $100,000, half is expected to prove uncollectible.
6. The township received a $100,000 restricted grant for certain library programs from another unit of government. The grant will be accounted for in the general fund.
7. The township incurred $75,000 of expenditures for the programs covered by the library grant.
8. Sold equipment at the end of its expected useful life. The equipment had expected residual value of $1,000 when acquired (at a cost of $13,000), but it sold for $1,200.

• Instructions •

Prepare the following conversion worksheet from fund financial statement balances to government–wide financial statement balances.

Accounts	Fund financial statement balances		Adjustments/ Eliminations		Government-wide statement balances	
	DR	CR	DR	CR	DR	CR

[Multiple Choice Questions]

01. Which of the following terms refers to an actual cost rather than an estimate?

a. Expenditure

b. Appropriation

c. Budget

d. Encumbrance

02. If a credit was made to the budgetary fund balance account in the process of recording a budget, it can be assumed that?

a. Estimated revenue exceed appropriations

b. Appropriations exceed actual revenues

c. Actual expenses exceed appropriations

d. Appropriations exceed estimated revenue

03. Which of the following accounts of a governmental unit is credited to close it out at the end of the fiscal year?

a. Appropriations

b. Revenue

c. Assigned fund balance for encumbrance

d. Encumbrances

04. What type of account is used to earmark the fund balance to liquidate the contingent obligations of goods ordered but not yet received?

a. Appropriations

b. Obligations

c. Assigned fund balance for encumbrance

d. Encumbrances

05. The following balances are included in the records of K-city at December 31, 20X1:

Appropriations-supplies	$7,500
Expenditures-supplies	4,500
Encumbrances-supply orders	750

How much does the city have available for additional purchases of supplies?

a. 2,250

b. 3,000

c. 3,750

d. 6,750

06. Interest expenditures on bonds payable should be recorded in a Debt Service Fund

a. at the end of the fiscal periods

b. when bonds are issued

c. when legally payable

d. when paid

07. Lacking sufficient cash for operation, a city borrows money from a bank, using as collateral the expected receipts from levied property taxes. Upon receipt of cash from the bank, the general fund would credit?

a. Revenue

b. Tax anticipation note payable

c. Other financing sources

d. Taxes receivable

08. Grants that are to be transferred to secondary recipients by a local government should be accounted for in which funds if the government is merely a cash conduit?

a. Investment trust fund

b. Special revenue fund

c. Custodial fund

d. Enterprise fund

09. According to GASB 34, a summary reconciliation of the government-wide and fund F/S

a. Must be presented at the bottom of the fund statement or in an accompany schedules

b. Must be presented as required supplementary schedules

c. Must be presented in the notes

d. In recommended but not required.

10. In what fund type should the proceeds from special assessment bonds issued to finance construction of sidewalks be reported?

a. Custodial fund   b. Special revenue fund

c. Debt service funds   d. Capital project fund

11. GASB 34 requires that a statement of revenue, expenditures and changes in fund balances be reported for governmental funds. In that statement

a. Debt refunding are treated as extraordinary items

b. Revenues are classified by function

c. Proceeds of long-term debt should be reported as other financing sources classification.

d. Expenditures are classified by major expenditure source

12. City issued bond anticipation notes and recorded the proceeds in the capital project fund. The City subsequently took the necessary legal steps to refinance the notes. Accordingly, the notes should be reported as a liability in the

a. Government-wide F/S but not the fund F/S

b. General fund

c. Debt service funds

d. Capital project fund

13. According to GASB 34, fiduciary fund F/S report

a. Information by major fund

b. Three components of net position

c. A separate column for each fund type.

d. No separate schedules for pension plan.

14. GASB 34 requires that a statement of revenue, expenses and changes in net position be reported for enterprise funds. In that statement

a. Combine special items in subtotal presented before non-operating revenues.

b. Expense are classified by function

c. Distinguish between operating and non-operating revenues and expense.

d. Must define operating items in the same way as in the statement of cash flow

15. In a statement of net position for enterprise fund, GASB 34 requires that

a. Net position be reported in the two components: restricted and unrestricted

b. Capital contribution be reported in a separate component of net position.

c. Designations be shown on the face of the statement

d. Assets and liabilities be classified as current or non-current.

16. An unrestricted grant received from another government to support enterprise fund operations should be reported as

a. Contributed capital.

b. Non-operating revenues.

c. Operating revenues.

d. Revenues and expenditures.

17. A City acquired police cars for $60,000 in January 20X1. The cars had an estimated four-year useful life and a zero salvage value. The City used the straight-line method to depreciate all of its capital assets. The City sold the cars for $40,000 in December 31, 20X2. On the statement of revenues, expenditures, and changes in fund balances prepared for the governmental funds for the year ended December 31, 20X2, what amount should be reported in the City's general fund related to the disposal of police cars ?

a. As other financing sources for $ 40,000

b. As revenue for $ 10,000

c. As special items for $ 40,000

d. As special items for $ 10,000

18. On 1/1/20X1, County issued $100 million of 10%, 20 year bonds at 102. Interest is payable semiannually. The proceeds were restricted for the construction of a new county water plant for its Water Enterprise Fund. The bond issuance should be reflected in the Statement of Revenue, Expense and Changes in Net position as ?

a. Revenue of $102 million

b. Other financing sources of $102 million

c. Other financing sources of $100 million

d. None of the above

19. A city issues a 60-day tax anticipation note to fund operation. What recording should be made?

a. In the government-wide financial statement, the liability should be reported whereas in the fund-based financial statement, an other financing source should be shown.

b. In the government-wide F/S and in the fund-based F/S, the liability should be reported.

c. In the government-wide F/S and in the fund-based F/S , the other financing source should be reported.

d. None of the above

20. A city issues a five-year bonds payable to finance construction of city hall. What recording should be made?

    a. In the government-wide financial statement, the liability should be reported whereas in the fund-based financial statement, an other financing source should be shown.

    b. In the government-wide F/S and in the fund-based F/S, the liability should be reported.

    c. In the government-wide F/S and in the fund-based F/S , the other financing source should be reported.

    d. None of the above

21. Cash of $60,000 is transferred from general fund to a debt service fund. On the financial statement, what is reported?

    a. No reporting is made

    b. Other financing sources increase by $60,000 while Other financing uses increase by $60,000.

    c. Revenues increase by $60,000 while Expenditures increase by $60,000.

    d. Revenues increase by $60,000 while Expenses increase by $60,000

22. Cash of $60,000 is transferred from general fund to an enterprise fund. On the financial statement, what is reported?

    a. No reporting is made

    b. Transfers in increase by $60,000 while Transfers out increase by $60,000.

    c. Revenues increase by $60,000 while Expenditures increase by $60,000.

    d. Revenues increase by $60,000 while Expenses increase by $60,000

23. A citizen of the K-city gives the city a gift of $100,000 in investments. The citizen requires that the investments be held but any resulting income must be used to maintain the city's cemetery. In which fund should this asset be maintained?

a. Permanent fund

b. Special revenue fund

c. Debt service funds

d. Capital project fund

24. A city constructs a special assessment projects (a sidewalk) for which it is secondarily liable. Bonds of $90,000 are issued. Another $10,000 is authorized and transferred out of general fund. The sidewalk is built for $100,000. The citizens are billed for $90,000. They pay this amount and the debt is paid off. Where is the $100,000 expenditure recorded?

a. Custodial fund

b. Special revenue fund

c. Debt service funds

d. Capital project fund

25. Which of the following is not necessary for special purpose local government to be viewed as a primary government?

a. It must have a separate elected governing body

b. It must have specifically defined geographic boundaries.

c. It must be fiscally independent.

d. It must have corporate powers to prove that it is legally independent.

26. Which of the following is not necessary for being deemed fiscally independent?

    a. It can hold property in its own name.

    b. It can issue bonded debt without outside approval.

    c. It can pass its own budget without outside approval.

    d. It can set taxes without outside approval.

27. Which of the following characteristics would require a component unit to be presented on a blended rather than discretely presented basis?

    a. The primary government and the component unit are located at the same physical location.

    b. Substantially all of the debt of the component unit is expected to be repaid by the primary government.

    c. The chairman of the component's governing board is appointed by the governing board of the primary government.

    d. The component unit provides services to the citizens of the primary government.

28. For which of the following fund balance classifications is the intent of the governing board to use funds for a specific purpose a critical factor?

    a. Committed.   b. Restricted.

    c. Assigned.   d. Nonspendable.

29. Which of the following is not an example of a deferred inflow of resources?

    a. Grant received in advance of meeting timing requirements.

    b. Grant received in advance of meeting the eligibility requirements.

    c. Resources are received before the period for which property taxes are levied.

    d. Gain from refunding of debt.

30. Which of the following is an example of a deferred outflow of resources?

    a. Interest cost incurred before the end of a construction period.

    b. Changes in fair values of hedging derivative instruments.

    c. Debt issuance costs

    d. Lessee at the commencement of the lease

Accounting and **R**eporting **F**or the **US CPA E**xam

Volume
1

Accounting and Reporting

부록

Appendix

STATE OF CALIFORNIA

ANNUAL COMPREHENSIVE FINANCIAL REPORT

For the Fiscal Year Ended
June 30, 2021

Prepared by the office of

MALIA M. COHEN
California State Controller

Contents

REQUIRED SUPPLEMENTARY INFORMATION

COMBINING FINANCIAL STATEMENTS AND SCHEDULES – NONMAJOR AND OTHER FUNDS

Principal Officials of the State of California

Executive Branch

Gavin Newsom
Governor

Eleni Kounalakis
Lieutenant Governor

Betty T. Yee
State Controller

Xavier Becerra
Attorney General

Fiona Ma, CPA
State Treasurer

Alex Padilla
Secretary of State

Tony Thurmond
Superintendent of Public Instruction

Ricardo Lara
Insurance Commissioner

Board of Equalization
Ted Gaines, Member, First District
Malia Cohen, Member, Second District
Antonio Vazquez, Member, Third District
Mike Schaefer, Member, Fourth District

Legislative Branch

Toni G. Atkins
President pro Tempore, Senate

Anthony Rendon
Speaker of the Assembly

Judicial Branch

Tani G. Cantil-Sakauye
Chief Justice, State Supreme Court

Organization Chart of the State of California

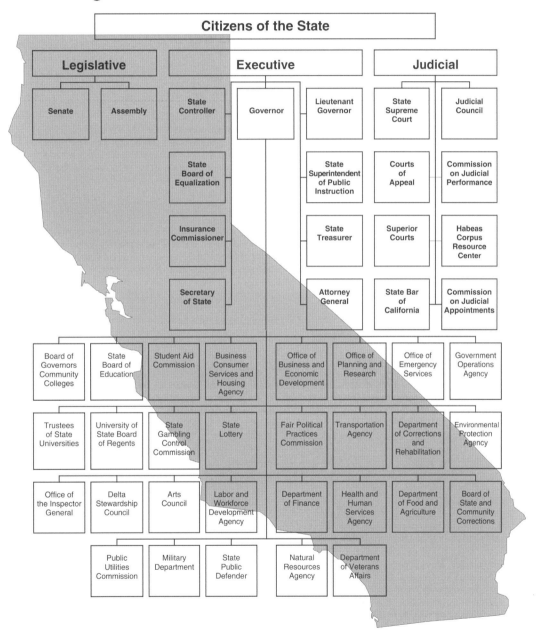

Elaine M. Howle *State Auditor*

Independent Auditor's Report

THE GOVERNOR AND THE LEGISLATURE OF THE
STATE OF CALIFORNIA

Report on the Financial Statements

We have audited the accompanying financial statements of the governmental activities, the business-type activities, the aggregate discretely presented component units, each major fund, and the aggregate remaining fund information of the State of California, as of and for the year ended June 30, 2018, and the related notes to the financial statements, which collectively comprise the State of California's basic financial statements as listed in the table of contents.

Management's Responsibility for the Financial Statements

Management is responsible for the preparation and fair presentation of these financial statements in accordance with accounting principles generally accepted in the United States of America; this includes the design, implementation, and maintenance of internal control relevant to the preparation and fair presentation of financial statements that are free from material misstatement, whether due to fraud or error.

Auditor's Responsibility

Our responsibility is to express opinions on these financial statements based on our audit. We did not audit the financial statements of the following:

Government-wide Financial Statements

- Certain governmental funds that, in the aggregate, represent one percent of the assets and deferred outflows, and less than one percent of the revenues of the governmental activities.

- Certain enterprise funds that, in the aggregate, represent 75 percent of the assets and deferred outflows, and 54 percent of the revenues of the business-type activities.

- The University of California and the California Housing Finance Agency that represent 92 percent of the assets and deferred outflows, and 94 percent of the revenues of the discretely presented component units.

Fund Financial Statements

- The following major enterprise funds: Electric Power fund, Water Resources fund, State Lottery fund, and California State University fund.

- The Golden State Tobacco Securitization Corporation, the Public Building Construction, the Public Employees' Retirement, the State Teachers' Retirement, the State Water Pollution Control Revolving, the Safe Drinking Water State Revolving, and the 1943 Veterans Farm and Home Building funds, that represent 85 percent of the assets and deferred outflows, and 53 percent of the additions, revenues and other financing sources of the aggregate remaining fund information.

- The discretely presented component units noted above.

Management's Discussion and Analysis

The following Management's Discussion and Analysis is required supplementary information to the State of California's financial statements. It describes and analyzes the financial position of the State, providing an overview of the State's activities for the fiscal year ended June 30, 2018. We encourage readers to consider the information that we present here in conjunction with the information presented in the Controller's transmittal letter at the front of this report and in the State's financial statements and notes, which follow this section.

Financial Highlights – Primary Government

Government-wide Highlights

California's economy continued to expand during fiscal year 2017-18, resulting in a longer-than-average recovery period for the State. Amid signs that growth is beginning to slow, the administration has focused on paying down liabilities and continuing to build reserves. For the fiscal year ended June 30, 2018, the State's general revenues increased by $14.4 billion (9.7%) over the prior year—even more than the 5.7% growth experienced in fiscal year 2016-17. Expenses and transfers for the State's governmental activities increased by $12.0 billion (4.6%) and were less than total revenues received, resulting in an $11.0 billion increase in the governmental activities' net position, as restated. Total revenues and transfers for the State's business-type activities also surpassed expenses by $3.5 billion in fiscal year 2017-18.

Net Position – Although current year activity reflects a combined $14.5 billion increase in the primary government's net position, net position at the beginning of the year was restated as a result of the recognition of net other postemployment benefits (OPEB) liabilities associated with the implementation of GASB Statement No. 75, *Accounting and Financial Reporting for Postemployment Benefits Other Than Pensions*, (see Note 1 for further detail). The impact on the primary government's beginning net position as a result of this implementation was a decrease of $62.2 billion—$47.8 billion for governmental activities and $14.4 billion for business-type activities. The primary government's beginning net position was also decreased by a $1.5 billion restatement for previously unreported trial courts' net pension liability.

The primary government ended fiscal year 2017-18 with a net deficit position of $70.6 billion, an improvement of $14.5 billion (17.1%) over the previous year. The total net deficit position is reduced by $112.1 billion for net investment in capital assets and by $47.1 billion for restricted net position, yielding a negative unrestricted net position of $229.8 billion. Restricted net position is dedicated for specified uses and is not available to fund current activities. More than 83.2%, or $191.2 billion, of the negative $229.8 billion consists of unfunded, employee-related, long-term liabilities (net pension liability, net OPEB liability, and compensated absences) that are recognized as soon as an obligation occurs, even though payment will occur over many future periods . In addition, the State's outstanding bonded debt consists of $65.6 billion to build capital assets of school districts and other local governmental entities. Bonded debt reduces the State's unrestricted net position; however, local governments, not the State, own the capital assets that would normally offset this reduction.

Fund Highlights

Governmental Funds – As of June 30, 2018, the primary government's governmental funds reported a combined ending fund balance of $45.2 billion, an increase of $9.0 billion over the prior fiscal year. The

Government-wide
Financial Statements

Statement of Net Position

June 30, 2018
(amounts in thousands)

	Primary Government			Component
	Governmental Activities	Business-type Activities	Total	Units
ASSETS				
Current assets:				
Cash and pooled investments	$ 47,470,591	$ 6,501,147	$ 53,971,738	$ 2,905,037
Amount on deposit with U.S. Treasury	—	2,970,373	2,970,373	—
Investments	494,505	2,750,013	3,244,518	7,458,829
Restricted assets:				
Cash and pooled investments	440,303	1,295,898	1,736,201	347,283
Investments	—	—	—	49,102
Due from other governments	—	155,541	155,541	—
Net investment in direct financing leases	23,589	11,384	34,973	—
Receivables (net)	21,673,854	2,072,187	23,746,041	4,834,661
Internal balances	(309,029)	309,029	—	—
Due from primary government	—	—	—	237,372
Due from other governments	21,853,537	279,633	22,133,170	133,472
Prepaid items	233,767	66,169	299,936	4,445
Inventories	72,489	16,038	88,527	244,706
Recoverable power costs (net)	—	109,000	109,000	—
Other current assets	29,219	7,248	36,467	440,413
Total current assets	91,982,825	16,543,660	108,526,485	16,655,320
Noncurrent assets:				
Restricted assets:				
Cash and pooled investments	176,851	729,400	906,251	39,908
Investments	—	352,066	352,066	67,679
Loans receivable	—	2,054,876	2,054,876	—
Investments	—	1,961,682	1,961,682	33,799,835
Net investment in direct financing leases	265,937	218,229	484,166	—
Receivables (net)	2,046,378	448,140	2,494,518	2,398,005
Loans receivable	3,468,095	4,727,643	8,195,738	3,087,842
Recoverable power costs (net)	—	1,631,000	1,631,000	—
Long-term prepaid charges	1,370	1,860,013	1,861,383	142
Capital assets:				
Land	20,208,641	271,240	20,479,881	1,347,708
State highway infrastructure	77,067,674	—	77,067,674	—
Collections – nondepreciable	22,627	24,604	47,231	544,051
Buildings and other depreciable property	31,700,263	14,696,314	46,396,577	53,850,588
Intangible assets – amortizable	2,222,889	431,102	2,653,991	1,607,137
Less: accumulated depreciation/amortization	(15,220,711)	(6,089,314)	(21,310,025)	(26,811,356)
Construction/development in progress	16,289,087	2,474,761	18,763,848	3,004,984
Intangible assets – nonamortizable	417,669	118,412	536,081	5,411
Other noncurrent assets	—	25,612	25,612	377,142
Total noncurrent assets	138,666,770	25,935,780	164,602,550	73,319,076
Total assets	**230,649,595**	**42,479,440**	**273,129,035**	**89,974,396**
DEFERRED OUTFLOWS OF RESOURCES	32,295,813	4,471,312	36,767,125	4,763,120
Total assets and deferred outflows of resources	**$ 262,945,408**	**$ 46,950,752**	**$ 309,896,160**	**$ 94,737,516**

| | Primary Government | | | |
	Governmental Activities	Business-type Activities	Total	Component Units
LIABILITIES				
Current liabilities:				
Accounts payable	$ 28,077,598	$ 529,802	$ 28,607,400	$ 3,137,105
Due to component units	237,372	—	237,372	—
Due to other governments	9,438,510	154,151	9,592,661	—
Revenues received in advance	2,043,266	366,580	2,409,846	1,512,088
Tax overpayments	6,240,122	—	6,240,122	—
Deposits	442,450	—	442,450	1,107,909
Contracts and notes payable	3,633	—	3,633	13,353
Unclaimed property liability	985,801	—	985,801	—
Interest payable	1,221,406	64,459	1,285,865	28,017
Securities lending obligations	—	—	—	1,209,769
Benefits payable	—	508,722	508,722	—
Current portion of long-term obligations	5,466,955	2,051,597	7,518,552	4,104,731
Other current liabilities	705,162	554,573	1,259,735	1,418,517
Total current liabilities	54,862,275	4,229,884	59,092,159	12,531,489
Noncurrent liabilities:				
Loans payable	248,542	—	248,542	1,037
Lottery prizes and annuities	—	712,236	712,236	—
Compensated absences payable	3,593,097	191,000	3,784,097	333,772
Workers' compensation benefits payable	3,874,233	4,147	3,878,380	487,528
Commercial paper and other borrowings	859,695	742,748	1,602,443	2,926
Capital lease obligations	412,444	290,145	702,589	405,977
General obligation bonds payable	76,062,632	668,125	76,730,757	—
Revenue bonds payable	15,558,641	13,164,196	28,722,837	22,634,129
Mandated cost claims payable	1,911,013	—	1,911,013	—
Net other postemployment benefits liability	73,717,443	15,618,786	89,336,229	19,169,577
Net pension liability	88,027,149	10,066,991	98,094,140	10,085,998
Other noncurrent liabilities	1,515,366	249,830	1,765,196	2,355,691
Total noncurrent liabilities	265,780,255	41,708,204	307,488,459	55,476,635
Total liabilities	**320,642,530**	**45,938,088**	366,580,618	**68,008,124**
DEFERRED INFLOWS OF RESOURCES	10,951,388	2,922,069	13,873,457	6,929,318
Total liabilities and deferred inflows of resources	$ **331,593,918**	$ **48,860,157**	$ 380,454,075	$ **74,937,442**

(continued)

Statement of Net Position (continued)

June 30, 2018

(amounts in thousands)

	Primary Government			Component Units
	Governmental Activities	Business-type Activities	Total	
NET POSITION				
Net investment in capital assets	$ 109,614,321	$ 2,469,723	$ 112,084,044	$ 14,156,347
Restricted:				
Nonexpendable – endowments	—	1,708	1,708	6,888,846
Expendable:				
Endowments and gifts	—	—	—	12,384,775
General government	3,819,332	149,678	3,969,010	—
Education	638,621	103,463	742,084	1,911,126
Health and human services	2,876,923	1,963,389	4,840,312	—
Natural resources and environmental protection	5,187,743	2,800,511	7,988,254	—
Business, consumer services, and housing	4,006,045	22,356	4,028,401	—
Transportation	9,090,734	6,866	9,097,600	—
Corrections and rehabilitation	28,382	65,877	94,259	—
Unemployment programs	—	6,971,597	6,971,597	—
Indenture	—	—	—	620,505
Statute	—	—	—	1,751,828
Other purposes	9,405,422	—	9,405,422	16,888
Total expendable	35,053,202	12,083,737	47,136,939	16,685,122
Unrestricted	(213,316,033)	(16,464,573)	(229,780,606)	(17,930,241)
Total net position (deficit)	**(68,648,510)**	**(1,909,405)**	**(70,557,915)**	**19,800,074**
Total liabilities, deferred inflows of resources, and net position	**$ 262,945,408**	**$ 46,950,752**	**$ 309,896,160**	**$ 94,737,516**

(concluded)

Statement of Activities

Year Ended June 30, 2018
(amounts in thousands)

FUNCTIONS/PROGRAMS	Expenses	Charges for Services	Program Revenues Operating Grants and Contributions	Capital Grants and Contributions
Primary government				
Governmental activities:				
General government	$ 18,378,216	$ 5,726,900	$ 1,586,619	$ —
Education	70,280,444	37,147	7,422,025	—
Health and human services	137,828,737	12,968,379	75,321,724	—
Natural resources and environmental protection	8,304,162	6,319,879	362,249	—
Business, consumer services, and housing	1,258,104	957,885	43,944	—
Transportation	14,259,461	6,053,140	3,008,504	1,882,595
Corrections and rehabilitation	14,921,295	39,887	67,562	—
Interest on long-term debt	4,154,485	—	—	—
Total governmental activities	269,384,904	32,103,217	87,812,627	1,882,595
Business-type activities:				
Electric Power	952,000	952,000	—	—
Water Resources	1,221,866	1,221,866	—	—
State Lottery	7,006,591	6,975,168	—	—
Unemployment Programs	12,133,531	15,594,045	—	—
California State University	9,806,114	3,387,420	2,006,533	—
State Water Pollution Control Revolving	32,335	86,789	46,304	—
Safe Drinking Water State Revolving	21,994	22,675	79,828	—
Housing Loan	57,088	52,735	—	—
Other enterprise programs	96,078	86,911	—	—
Total business-type activities	31,327,597	28,379,609	2,132,665	—
Total primary government	**$ 300,712,501**	**$ 60,482,826**	**$ 89,945,292**	**$ 1,882,595**
Component Units				
University of California	35,229,304	23,321,094	9,972,697	144,998
California Housing Finance Agency	130,742	81,924	—	—
Nonmajor component units	2,211,654	1,074,325	685,361	14,578
Total component units	**$ 37,571,700**	**$ 24,477,343**	**$ 10,658,058**	**$ 159,576**

General revenues:
Personal income taxes
Sales and use taxes
Corporation taxes
Motor vehicle excise tax
Insurance taxes
Managed care organization enrollment tax
Other taxes
Investment and interest income (loss)
Escheat
Other
Transfers
Total general revenues and transfers
Change in net position
Net position (deficit) – beginning, restated
Net position (deficit) – ending

Net (Expenses) Revenues and Changes in Net Position

	Primary Government			
Governmental Activities	Business-type Activities	Total		Component Units
$ (11,064,697)		$ (11,064,697)		
(62,821,272)		(62,821,272)		
(49,538,634)		(49,538,634)		
(1,622,034)		(1,622,034)		
(256,275)		(256,275)		
(3,315,222)		(3,315,222)		
(14,813,846)		(14,813,846)		
(4,154,485)		(4,154,485)		
(147,586,465)		(147,586,465)		
	$ —			
	—	—		
	(31,423)	(31,423)		
	3,460,514	3,460,514		
	(4,412,161)	(4,412,161)		
	100,758	100,758		
	80,509	80,509		
	(4,353)	(4,353)		
	(9,167)	(9,167)		
	(815,323)	(815,323)		
$ (147,586,465)	$ (815,323)	$ (148,401,788)		
				$ (1,790,515)
				(48,818)
				(437,390)
				$ (2,276,723)
$ 94,460,551	$ —	$ 94,460,551		$ —
39,784,494	—	39,784,494		—
12,608,756	—	12,608,756		—
6,680,858	—	6,680,858		—
2,754,056	—	2,754,056		—
2,397,531	—	2,397,531		—
3,573,848	—	3,573,848		—
297,782	—	297,782		2,500,161
378,180	—	378,180		—
—	—	—		3,326,055
(4,339,995)	4,339,995	—		—
158,596,061	4,339,995	162,936,056		5,826,216
11,009,596	3,524,672	14,534,268		3,549,493
(79,658,106)	(5,434,077)	(85,092,183)		16,250,581
$ (68,648,510)	$ (1,909,405)	$ (70,557,915)		$ 19,800,074

Fund Financial
Statements

Reconciliation of the Governmental Funds Balance Sheet to the Statement of Net Position

(amounts in thousands)

Total fund balances – governmental funds		$ 45,232,028

Amounts reported for governmental activities in the Statement of Net Position are different from those in the Governmental Funds Balance Sheet because:

- The following capital assets used in governmental activities are not financial resources and, therefore, are not reported in the funds:

Land	20,206,561	
State highway infrastructure	77,067,674	
Collections – nondepreciable	22,627	
Buildings and other depreciable property	31,063,376	
Intangible assets – amortizable	2,151,760	
Less: accumulated depreciation/amortization	(14,712,382)	
Construction/development in progress	15,305,452	
Intangible assets – nonamortizable	417,669	
		131,522,737

- State revenues that are earned and measurable, but not available within 12 months of the end of the reporting period, are reported as deferred inflows of resources in the funds.   1,980,949

- Internal service funds are used by management to charge the costs of certain activities, such as building construction and architectural services, procurement, and technology services, to individual funds. The assets and liabilities of the internal service funds are included in governmental activities in the Statement of Net Position, excluding amounts for activity between the internal service funds and governmental funds.   (10,598,967)

- Bond premiums/discounts and prepaid insurance charges are amortized over the life of the bonds and are included in the governmental activities in the Statement of Net Position.   (5,874,364)

- Deferred inflows and outflows of resources related to pension and OPEB transactions are not reported in the funds.   20,484,703

- Deferred inflows and outflows of resources resulting from bond refunding gains and losses, respectively, are amortized over the life of the bonds and are not reported in the funds.   438,081

- General obligation bonds and related accrued interest totaling $75,216,385, revenue bonds totaling $6,522,482, and commercial paper totaling $859,695 are not due and payable in the current period and are not reported in the funds.   (82,598,562)

- The following liabilities are not due and payable in the current period and are not reported in the funds:

Compensated absences	(3,456,370)	
Capital leases	(481,261)	
Net pension liability	(86,608,104)	
Net other postemployment benefits liability	(71,369,628)	
Mandated cost claims	(1,911,013)	
Workers' compensation	(3,829,948)	
Proposition 98 funding guarantee	(340,003)	
Pollution remediation obligations	(1,141,189)	
Other noncurrent liabilities	(97,599)	
		(169,235,115)

Net position of governmental activities		$ (68,648,510)

Balance Sheet

Governmental Funds

June 30, 2018

(amounts in thousands)

	General		Federal	
ASSETS				
Cash and pooled investments	$	16,898,352	$	286,580
Investments		—		—
Receivables (net)		16,930,904		81,870
Due from other funds		3,429,655		—
Due from other governments		1,346,744		19,457,729
Interfund receivables		552,739		
Loans receivable		35,697		225,717
Other assets		3,707		—
Total assets	**$**	**39,197,798**	**$**	**20,051,896**
LIABILITIES				
Accounts payable	$	1,913,451	$	686,325
Due to other funds		5,944,148		16,598,568
Due to component units		124,954		—
Due to other governments		2,869,939		2,424,808
Interfund payables		6,231,963		
Revenues received in advance		650,871		61,749
Tax overpayments		6,240,122		
Deposits		3,102		—
Unclaimed property liability		985,801		—
Other liabilities		389,684		34,525
Total liabilities		**25,354,035**		**19,805,975**
DEFERRED INFLOWS OF RESOURCES		1,656,859		17,267
Total liabilities and deferred inflows of resources		**27,010,894**		**19,823,242**
FUND BALANCES				
Nonspendable		559,644		—
Restricted		9,807,729		228,654
Committed		171,020		—
Assigned		—		—
Unassigned		1,648,511		—
Total fund balances		**12,186,904**		**228,654**
Total liabilities, deferred inflows of resources, and fund balances	**$**	**39,197,798**	**$**	**20,051,896**

	Transportation	Environmental and Natural Resources	Health Care Related Programs	Nonmajor Governmental	Total
$	6,669,276	$ 9,295,371	$ 2,337,846	$ 10,265,117	$ 45,752,542
	—	—		494,505	494,505
	1,434,462	463,831	3,371,114	1,284,990	23,567,171
	1,743,556	121,974	24,486	1,125,975	6,445,646
	2,680	6,139	927,968	95,200	21,836,460
	1,755,668	2,236,995	550,200	1,458,343	6,553,945
	—	231,335	23,000	2,735,536	3,251,285
	13,391	—	—	12,120	29,218
$	11,619,033	$ 12,355,645	$ 7,234,614	$ 17,471,786	$ 107,930,772
$	539,315	$ 249,035	$ 29,542	$ 517,351	$ 3,935,019
	381,669	23,069	6,451,325	605,336	30,004,115
	6,754	—	—	105,664	237,372
	379,732	196,063	16,196	3,942,644	9,829,382
	315,348	126,665	—	135,963	6,809,939
	17,895	197,597	5,511	150,723	1,084,346
	—	—	—	—	6,240,122
	2,872	927	—	433,594	440,495
	—	—	—	—	985,801
	574,176	9,645	1,964	141,210	1,151,204
	2,217,761	803,001	6,504,538	6,032,485	60,717,795
	57,080	37,770	—	211,973	1,980,949
	2,274,841	840,771	6,504,538	6,244,458	62,698,744
	—	—	—	69,868	629,512
	9,294,367	5,112,157	627,108	9,789,262	34,859,277
	49,825	6,402,717	102,968	1,341,852	8,068,382
	—	—	—	26,346	26,346
	—	—	—		1,648,511
	9,344,192	11,514,874	730,076	11,227,328	45,232,028
$	11,619,033	$ 12,355,645	$ 7,234,614	$ 17,471,786	$ 107,930,772

Statement of Revenues, Expenditures, and Changes in Fund Balances

Governmental Funds

Year Ended June 30, 2018

(amounts in thousands)

	General	Federal
REVENUES		
Personal income taxes	$ 92,808,996	$ —
Sales and use taxes	25,090,956	—
Corporation taxes	12,597,928	—
Motor vehicle excise taxes	101,307	—
Insurance taxes	2,563,904	—
Managed care organization enrollment tax	—	—
Other taxes	614,421	—
Intergovernmental	—	89,697,344
Licenses and permits	6,193	—
Charges for services	389,297	—
Fees	44,302	—
Penalties	248,828	97
Investment and interest	264,675	—
Escheat	378,177	—
Other	516,036	—
Total revenues	**135,625,020**	**89,697,441**
EXPENDITURES		
Current:		
General government	5,669,626	1,571,618
Education	61,331,083	7,424,246
Health and human services	36,130,003	74,847,506
Natural resources and environmental protection	2,338,402	369,165
Business, consumer services, and housing	68,550	39,297
Transportation	144,046	4,879,706
Corrections and rehabilitation	12,960,903	67,562
Capital outlay	405,930	—
Debt service:		
Bond and commercial paper retirement	2,467,541	9,830
Interest and fiscal charges	2,723,232	1,563
Total expenditures	**124,239,316**	**89,210,493**
Excess (deficiency) of revenues over (under) expenditures	11,385,704	486,948
OTHER FINANCING SOURCES (USES)		
General obligation bonds and commercial paper issued		
Refunding debt issued	—	—
Payment to refund long-term debt	—	—
Premium on bonds issued	169,262	—
Remarketing bonds issued	—	—
Payment to remarket long-term debt	—	—
Capital leases	405,930	—
Transfers in	660,597	—
Transfers out	(6,244,975)	(486,173)
Total other financing sources (uses)	**(5,009,186)**	**(486,173)**
Net change in fund balances	6,376,518	775
Fund balances (deficit) – beginning	**5,810,386**	**227,879**
Fund balances – ending	**$ 12,186,904**	**$ 228,654**

* Restated

Transportation	Environmental and Natural Resources	Health Care Related Programs	Nonmajor Governmental	Total
$ —	$ —	$ —	$ 1,675,447	$ 94,484,443
712,895	—	—	13,973,218	39,777,069
—	—	—	—	12,597,928
6,406,668	58,742	—	114,141	6,680,858
—	—	190,152	—	2,754,056
—	—	2,397,531	—	2,397,531
—	173,944	—	2,759,817	3,548,182
—	—	2,394,468	812,657	92,904,469
4,881,585	507,182	—	3,366,660	8,761,620
150,978	130,560	36	304,443	975,314
956,451	2,586,480	5,708,896	3,191,017	12,487,146
8,177	200,272	7,038	596,913	1,061,325
74,768	118,178	32,158	117,639	607,418
—	—	—	4,616	382,793
117,109	3,216,894	354,140	1,114,560	5,318,739
13,308,631	**6,992,252**	**11,084,419**	**28,031,128**	284,738,891
565,613	128,545	3,868	11,039,119	18,978,389
12,699	5,846	280,400	848,353	69,902,627
2,450	89,920	11,259,371	15,689,025	138,018,275
257,762	4,766,332	193	256,024	7,987,878
122,957	108,489	—	850,072	1,189,365
11,946,227	187,226	—	11,835	17,169,040
—	—	—	1,637,059	14,665,524
—	147,131	—	59,708	612,769
412,436	870,053	331,080	4,507,916	8,598,856
14,624	9,948	289	1,212,048	3,961,704
13,334,768	**6,313,490**	**11,875,201**	**36,111,159**	281,084,427
(26,137)	678,762	(790,782)	(8,080,031)	3,654,464
1,738,610	1,616,985	628,855	1,298,915	5,283,365
1,062,740	838,695	—	4,355,420	6,256,855
(1,017,036)	(716,219)	—	(1,567,949)	(3,301,204)
146,473	161,501	514	558,570	1,036,320
325,000	—	—	100,000	425,000
(325,000)	—	—	(100,000)	(425,000)
—	—	—	—	405,930
8,401	45,787	181,720	3,370,091	4,266,596
(1,657,123)	(49,481)	(10,048)	(107,794)	(8,555,594)
282,065	**1,897,268**	**801,041**	**7,907,253**	5,392,268
255,928	2,576,030	10,259	(172,778)	9,046,732
9,088,264	**8,938,844**	**719,817**	**11,400,106** *	36,185,296
$ **9,344,192**	$ **11,514,874**	$ **730,076**	$ **11,227,328**	$ 45,232,028

Reconciliation of the Statement of Revenues, Expenditures, and Changes in Fund Balances of Governmental Funds to the Statement of Activities

(amounts in thousands)

Net change in fund balances – total governmental funds	$ **9,046,732**

Amounts reported for governmental activities in the Statement of Activities are different from those in the Statement of Revenues, Expenditures, and Changes in Fund Balances of Governmental Funds because:

- Governmental funds report capital outlays as expenditures. However, in the Statement of Activities, the cost of those assets is allocated over their estimated useful lives as depreciation expense. In the current year, these amounts are:

Purchase of assets	5,951,091	
Disposal of assets	(2,508,158)	
Depreciation expense, net of asset disposal	(986,944)	
		2,455,989

- Some revenues in the Statement of Activities do not provide current financial resources and, therefore, are unavailable in governmental funds. — (34,724)

- Internal service funds are used by management to charge the costs of certain activities, such as building construction and architectural services, procurement, and technology services, to individual funds. The net revenue (expense) of the internal service funds is reported with governmental activities. — (54,687)

- The issuance of long-term debt instruments provides current financial resources to governmental funds, while the repayment of the principal of long-term debt is an expenditure of governmental funds. Neither transaction, however, has any effect on the Statement of Activities. Also, governmental funds report the effect of premiums, discounts, and similar items when debt is first issued, whereas these amounts are deferred and amortized in the Statement of Activities. The following shows the effect of these differences in the treatment of long-term debt and related items:

	General Obligation Bonds	Revenue Bonds	Commercial Paper	Total	
Debt issued	(8,869,045)	(1,785,190)	(1,310,985)	(11,965,220)	
Premium on debt issued	(942,938)	(93,383)	—	(1,036,321)	
Accreted interest	—	(45,928)	—	(45,928)	
Principal repayments	4,904,299	2,085,186	1,609,370	8,598,855	
Payments to refund long-term debt	3,726,204	—	—	3,726,204	
Related expenses not reported in governmental funds:					
Premium/discount amortization	271,186	72,899	—	344,085	
Deferred gain/loss on refunding	(11,595)	(56,095)	—	(67,690)	
Prepaid insurance	—	(245)	—	(245)	
Accrued interest	(15,417)	8,146	—	(7,271)	
	(937,306)	185,390	298,385		(453,531)

(continued)

- The following expenses reported in the Statement of Activities do not require the use of current financial resources and, therefore, are not recognized as expenditures in governmental funds. Once the use of current financial resources is required, expenditures are recognized in governmental funds but are eliminated from the Statement of Activities. In the current period, the net adjustment consists of:

Compensated absences	(82,052)
Capital leases	(64,793)
Net pension liability	2,546,822
Net other postemployment benefits liability	(2,502,899)
Mandated cost claims	542,026
Workers' compensation	(229,292)
Proposition 98 funding guarantee	100,000
Pollution remediation obligations	(171,796)
Other noncurrent liabilities	(88,199)
	49,817

Change in net position of governmental activities $ **11,009,596**

(concluded)

Statement of Net Position

Proprietary Funds

June 30, 2018

(amounts in thousands)

	Electric Power	Water Resources
ASSETS		
Current assets:		
Cash and pooled investments...	$ —	$ 731,382
Amount on deposit with U.S. Treasury..	—	—
Investments	—	—
Restricted assets:		
Cash and pooled investments	658,000	—
Due from other governments..	—	—
Net investment in direct financing leases	—	—
Receivables (net)..	—	97,140
Due from other funds	8,000	4,229
Due from other governments	—	53,636
Prepaid items...	—	—
Inventories..	—	5,437
Recoverable power costs (net)	109,000	—
Other current assets	—	—
Total current assets	775,000	891,824
Noncurrent assets:		
Restricted assets:		
Cash and pooled investments	582,000	147,297
Investments..	302,000	50,066
Loans receivable..	—	—
Investments	—	—
Net investment in direct financing leases	—	—
Receivables (net)..	—	—
Interfund receivables..	—	95,129
Loans receivable	—	10,924
Recoverable power costs (net)	1,631,000	—
Long-term prepaid charges	—	1,858,668
Capital assets:		
Land...	—	162,457
Collections – nondepreciable	—	—
Buildings and other depreciable property...	—	5,185,367
Intangible assets – amortizable...	—	39,483
Less: accumulated depreciation/amortization	—	(2,185,494)
Construction/development in progress..	—	1,396,750
Intangible assets – nonamortizable...	—	111,439
Other noncurrent assets..	—	—
Total noncurrent assets	2,515,000	6,872,086
Total assets...	**3,290,000**	**7,763,910**
DEFERRED OUTFLOWS OF RESOURCES..	99,000	401,026
Total assets and deferred outflows of resources...	$ **3,389,000**	$ **8,164,936**

| Business-type Activities – Enterprise Funds | | | | | Governmental Activities |
State Lottery	Unemployment Programs	California State University	Nonmajor Enterprise	Total	Internal Service Funds
$ 428,696	$ 3,304,229	$ 814,235	$ 1,222,605	$ 6,501,147	$ 1,718,049
—	2,970,373	—	—	2,970,373	—
48,234	—	2,701,779	—	2,750,013	—
—	—	—	637,898	1,295,898	440,303
—	—	—	155,541	155,541	—
—	—	11,384	—	11,384	493,644
550,014	1,191,096	192,753	41,184	2,072,187	87,632
4,034	25,050	4,950	14,866	61,129	841,909
—	36,823	—	189,174	279,633	17,077
—	—	66,078	91	66,169	233,767
7,292	—	—	3,309	16,038	72,489
—	—	—	—	109,000	—
7,248	—	—	—	7,248	—
1,045,518	7,527,571	3,791,179	2,264,668	16,295,760	3,904,870
—	—	103	—	729,400	176,851
—	—	—	—	352,066	—
—	—	—	2,054,876	2,054,876	—
738,736	—	1,204,731	18,215	1,961,682	—
—	—	218,229	—	218,229	7,996,250
—	79,766	368,374	—	448,140	—
—	1,052,664	—	17,517	1,165,310	32,576
—	—	70,647	4,646,072	4,727,643	216,810
—	—	—	—	1,631,000	—
1,345	—	—	—	1,860,013	719
18,798	—	88,713	1,272	271,240	2,080
—	—	24,604	—	24,604	—
291,312	28,572	9,171,853	19,210	14,696,314	636,887
—	244,118	145,820	1,681	431,102	71,129
(112,804)	(53,564)	(3,718,982)	(18,470)	(6,089,314)	(508,329)
—	—	1,077,824	187	2,474,761	983,635
—	—	6,973	—	118,412	—
—	—	20,476	5,136	25,612	—
937,387	1,351,556	8,679,365	6,745,696	27,101,090	9,608,608
1,982,905	8,879,127	12,470,544	9,010,364	43,396,850	13,513,478
62,049	133,337	3,752,587	23,313	4,471,312	733,002
$ 2,044,954	$ 9,012,464	$ 16,223,131	$ 9,033,677	$ 47,868,162	$ 14,246,480

(continued)

Statement of Net Position (continued)

Proprietary Funds
June 30, 2018
(amounts in thousands)

		Electric Power		Water Resources
LIABILITIES				
Current liabilities:				
Accounts payable	$	2,000	$	184,962
Due to other funds		—		53,216
Due to other governments		—		118,940
Revenues received in advance		—		—
Deposits		—		—
Contracts and notes payable		—		—
Interest payable		23,000		10,685
Benefits payable		—		—
Current portion of long-term obligations		806,000		179,334
Other current liabilities		—		—
Total current liabilities		831,000		547,137
Noncurrent liabilities:				
Interfund payables		628		60,910
Lottery prizes and annuities		—		—
Compensated absences payable		—		26,926
Workers' compensation benefits payable		—		—
Commercial paper and other borrowings		—		580,672
Capital lease obligations		—		—
General obligation bonds payable		—		28,090
Revenue bonds payable		2,542,000		2,739,607
Net other postemployment benefits liability		8,000		912,912
Net pension liability		5,372		630,912
Revenues received in advance		—		—
Other noncurrent liabilities		—		97,316
Total noncurrent liabilities		2,556,000		5,077,345
Total liabilities		**3,387,000**		**5,624,482**
DEFERRED INFLOWS OF RESOURCES		2,000		1,335,026
Total liabilities and deferred inflows of resources		**3,389,000**		**6,959,508**
NET POSITION				
Net investment in capital assets		—		826,871
Restricted:				
Nonexpendable – endowments		—		—
Expendable:				
Construction		—		—
Debt service		—		378,557
Security for revenue bonds		—		—
Lottery		—		—
Unemployment programs		—		—
Other purposes		—		—
Total expendable		—		378,557
Unrestricted		—		—
Total net position (deficit)		**—**		**1,205,428**
Total liabilities, deferred inflows of resources, and net position	$	**3,389,000**	$	**8,164,936**

Business-type Activities – Enterprise Funds					Governmental Activities
State Lottery	Unemployment Programs	California State University	Nonmajor Enterprise	Total	Internal Service Funds
$ 66,116	$ —	$ 271,560	$ 5,119	$ 529,757	$ 540,458
385,956	217,269	136	12,255	668,832	277,903
—	34,614	—	597	154,151	12,141
2,177	37,105	327,235	63	366,580	958,920
—	—	—	—	—	1,955
—	—	—	—	—	22,575
—	—	—	30,774	64,459	148,490
—	508,722	—	—	508,722	
668,401	—	301,797	96,065	2,051,597	612,382
241	56,814	497,363	155	554,573	17,966
1,122,891	854,524	1,398,091	145,028	4,898,671	2,592,790
13,798	—	156,283	17,004	248,623	941,810
712,236	—	—	—	712,236	
—	55,177	99,898	8,999	191,000	145,414
2,458	—	—	1,689	4,147	44,285
—	—	162,076	—	742,748	—
—	—	290,145	—	290,145	—
—	—	—	640,035	668,125	—
—	—	6,134,207	1,748,382	13,164,196	8,880,040
218,073	517,915	13,918,525	43,361	15,618,786	2,347,815
140,043	343,505	8,899,962	47,197	10,066,991	1,419,045
—	—	10,149	—	10,149	
—	—	110,664	31,701	239,681	27,948
1,086,608	916,597	29,781,909	2,538,368	41,956,827	13,806,357
2,209,499	1,771,121	31,180,000	2,683,396	46,855,498	16,399,147
24,868	50,619	1,504,986	4,570	2,922,069	245,932
2,234,367	1,821,740	32,684,986	2,687,966	49,777,567	16,645,079
197,306	219,127	1,225,523	896	2,469,723	509,253
—	—	1,708	—	1,708	—
—	—	18,348	—	18,348	193,925
—	—	27,974	211,650	618,181	—
—	—	—	2,210,416	2,210,416	—
55,950	—	—	—	55,950	—
—	6,971,597	—	—	6,971,597	—
—	—	57,141	2,152,104	2,209,245	—
55,950	6,971,597	103,463	4,574,170	12,083,737	193,925
(442,669)	—	(17,792,549)	1,770,645	(16,464,573)	(3,101,777)
(189,413)	7,190,724	(16,461,855)	6,345,711	(1,909,405)	(2,398,599)
$ 2,044,954	$ 9,012,464	$ 16,223,131	$ 9,033,677	$ 47,868,162	$ 14,246,480

(concluded)

Statement of Revenues, Expenses, and Changes in Fund Net Position

Proprietary Funds
Year Ended June 30, 2018
(amounts in thousands)

	Electric Power	Water Resources
OPERATING REVENUES		
Unemployment and disability insurance	$ —	$ —
Lottery ticket sales	—	—
Power sales	—	88,148
Student tuition and fees	—	—
Services and sales	—	1,118,365
Investment and interest	—	—
Rent	—	—
Grants and contracts	—	—
Other	—	—
Total operating revenues	—	1,206,513
OPERATING EXPENSES		
Lottery prizes	—	—
Power purchases (net of recoverable power costs)	(8,000)	342,115
Personal services	—	374,955
Supplies	—	—
Services and charges	8,000	103,093
Depreciation	—	80,101
Scholarships and fellowships	—	—
Distributions to beneficiaries	—	—
Interest expense	—	—
Amortization of long-term prepaid charges	—	—
Other	—	—
Total operating expenses	—	900,264
Operating income (loss)	—	306,249
NONOPERATING REVENUES (EXPENSES)		
Donations and grants	—	—
Private gifts	—	—
Investment and interest income (loss)	952,000	15,353
Interest expense and fiscal charges	(952,000)	(105,429)
Lottery payments for education	—	—
Other	—	(216,173)
Total nonoperating revenues (expenses)	—	(306,249)
Income (loss) before capital contributions and transfers	—	—
Transfers in	—	—
Transfers out	—	—
Change in net position	—	—
Total net position (deficit) – beginning	—	1,205,428
Total net position (deficit) – ending	$ —	$ 1,205,428

* Restated

| Business-type Activities – Enterprise Funds | | | | | Governmental Activities |
State Lottery	Unemployment Programs	California State University	Nonmajor Enterprise	Total	Internal Service Funds
$ —	$ 15,535,487	$ —	$ —	$ 15,535,487	$ —
6,965,792	—	—	—	6,965,792	—
—	—	—	—	88,148	—
—	—	2,220,797	—	2,220,797	—
—	—	575,908	94,442	1,788,715	3,335,466
—	—	—	134,270	134,270	14,683
—	—	—	—	—	426,219
—	—	77,792	—	77,792	—
—	—	229,550	1,744	231,294	—
6,965,792	**15,535,487**	**3,104,047**	**230,456**	27,042,295	**3,776,368**
4,476,580	—	—	—	4,476,580	—
—	—	—	—	334,115	—
101,055	247,796	6,801,999	52,141	7,577,946	1,137,783
12,658	—	1,532,795	42,364	1,587,817	24,510
701,133	70,859	—	43,260	926,345	2,147,934
18,311	10,567	355,263	390	464,632	52,390
—	—	891,148	—	891,148	—
—	11,804,309	—	—	11,804,309	—
—	—	—	31,056	31,056	416,069
—	—	—	—	—	179
—	—	—	9,536	9,536	—
5,309,737	**12,133,531**	**9,581,205**	**178,747**	28,103,484	**3,778,865**
1,656,055	3,401,956	(6,477,158)	51,709	(1,061,189)	(2,497)
—	—	2,006,533	126,132	2,132,665	—
—	—	61,386	—	61,386	—
9,252	58,558	67,351	18,399	1,120,913	4,241
(31,967)	—	(224,909)	(28,748)	(1,343,053)	(37)
(1,664,887)	—	—	—	(1,664,887)	—
124	—	154,636	255	(61,158)	(5,397)
(1,687,478)	**58,558**	**2,064,997**	**116,038**	245,866	**(1,193)**
(31,423)	3,460,514	(4,412,161)	167,747	(815,323)	(3,690)
—	—	4,338,333	1,662	4,339,995	8,945
—	—	—	—	—	(59,942)
(31,423)	3,460,514	(73,828)	169,409	3,524,672	(54,687)
(157,990)*	3,730,210 *	(16,388,027)*	6,176,302 *	(5,434,077)	(2,343,912)*
$ **(189,413)**	$ **7,190,724**	$ **(16,461,855)**	$ **6,345,711**	$ (1,909,405)	$ **(2,398,599)**

Statement of Cash Flows

Proprietary Funds

Year Ended June 30, 2018

(amounts in thousands)

	Electric Power	Water Resources
CASH FLOWS FROM OPERATING ACTIVITIES		
Receipts from customers/employers	$ 8,000	$ 1,222,810
Receipts from interfund services provided	—	—
Payments to suppliers	(4,000)	(421,068)
Payments to employees	(14,000)	(374,955)
Payments for interfund services used	—	—
Payments for Lottery prizes	—	—
Claims paid to other than employees	—	—
Other receipts (payments)	23,000	59,083
Net cash provided by (used in) operating activities	**13,000**	**485,870**
CASH FLOWS FROM NONCAPITAL FINANCING ACTIVITIES		
Changes in notes receivable and capital leases receivable	—	—
Changes in interfund receivables	—	—
Changes in interfund payables and loans payable	—	—
Receipt of bond charges	918,000	—
Proceeds from general obligation bonds	(719,000)	—
Retirement of general obligation bonds	—	—
Proceeds from revenue bonds	—	—
Retirement of revenue bonds	—	—
Interest received	—	—
Interest paid	(176,000)	—
Transfers in	—	—
Transfers out	—	—
Grants received	—	—
Lottery payments for education	—	—
Net cash provided by (used in) noncapital financing activities	**23,000**	**—**
CASH FLOWS FROM CAPITAL AND RELATED FINANCING ACTIVITIES		
Acquisition of capital assets	—	(716,441)
Proceeds from sale of capital assets	—	—
Proceeds from notes payable and commercial paper	—	500,484
Principal paid on notes payable and commercial paper	—	(66,976)
Proceeds from capital leases	—	—
Payment on capital leases	—	—
Retirement of general obligation bonds	—	(34,235)
Proceeds from revenue bonds	—	(39,760)
Retirement of revenue bonds	—	(138,570)
Interest paid	—	(79,462)
Grants received	—	—
Net cash provided by (used in) capital and related financing activities	**—**	**(574,960)**
CASH FLOWS FROM INVESTING ACTIVITIES		
Purchase of investments	—	(202,547)
Proceeds from maturity and sale of investments	—	211,911
Change in loans receivable	—	1,010
Earnings on investments	32,000	14,650
Net cash provided by (used in) investing activities	**32,000**	**25,024**
Net increase (decrease) in cash and pooled investments	68,000	(64,066)
Cash and pooled investments – beginning	**1,172,000**	**942,745**
Cash and pooled investments – ending	**$ 1,240,000**	**$ 878,679**

* Restated

	Business-type Activities – Enterprise Funds					Governmental Activities
	State Lottery	Unemployment Programs	California State University	Nonmajor Enterprise	Total	Internal Service Funds
$	6,939,646	$ 15,511,212	$ 2,796,368	$ 357,355	$ 26,835,391	$ 16,577
	—	1,037	—	3,826	4,863	4,407,261
	(234,403)	(70,889)	(1,524,764)	(61,058)	(2,316,182)	(1,532,921)
	(63,997)	(245,174)	(5,176,140)	(56,732)	(5,930,998)	(1,089,764)
	(26,033)	(18,131)	—	(907)	(45,071)	(7,319)
	(4,713,465)	—	—	—	(4,713,465)	—
	(480,513)	(11,752,892)	—	—	(12,233,405)	(506,839)
	50	38,621	(630,296)	(806,385)	(1,315,927)	(448,350)
	1,421,285	**3,463,784**	**(4,534,832)**	**(563,901)**	285,206	**838,645**
	—	—	(30,844)	—	(30,844)	—
	—	(818,663)	—	(17,517)	(836,180)	(457,602)
	—	(385,137)	(155,908)	15,000	(526,045)	783,380
	—	—	—	—	918,000	—
	—	—	—	110,257	(608,743)	—
	—	—	—	(85,660)	(85,660)	—
	—	—	—	527,000	527,000	—
	—	—	(15,149)	(41,350)	(56,499)	—
	—	—	27,644	—	27,644	—
	—	—	(20,953)	(43,386)	(240,339)	(37)
	—	—	3,303,623	1,662	3,305,285	8,945
	—	—	—	—	—	(59,942)
	—	—	2,146,698	119,554	2,266,252	—
	(1,701,168)	—	—	—	(1,701,168)	—
	(1,701,168)	**(1,203,800)**	**5,255,111**	**585,560**	2,958,703	**274,744**
	(29,923)	(1,833)	(890,328)	(335)	(1,638,860)	(894,845)
	108	—	5,159	2	5,269	3,438
	—	—	—	—	500,484	—
	—	—	—	—	(66,976)	—
	—	—	19,054	—	19,054	—
	—	—	(413,793)	—	(413,793)	—
	—	—	—	—	(34,235)	—
	—	—	168,039	—	128,279	615,418
	—	—	—	—	(138,570)	(806,025)
	—	—	—	—	(79,462)	—
	—	—	60,773	—	60,773	—
	(29,815)	**(1,833)**	**(1,051,096)**	**(333)**	(1,658,037)	**(1,082,014)**
	(42,539)	—	(9,359,378)	(6,055)	(9,610,519)	—
	55,267	(2,958,643)	9,130,461	5,804	6,444,800	—
	—	—	—	—	1,010	—
	22,560	58,558	67,757	16,278	211,803	4,241
	35,288	**(2,900,085)**	**(161,160)**	**16,027**	(2,952,906)	**4,241**
	(274,410)	(641,934)	(491,977)	37,353	(1,367,034)	35,616
	703,106	3,946,163	1,306,315	1,823,150 *	9,893,479	2,299,587
$	**428,696**	$ **3,304,229**	$ **814,338**	$ **1,860,503**	$ 8,526,445	$ **2,335,203**

(continued)

Statement of Cash Flows (continued)

Proprietary Funds

Year Ended June 30, 2018

(amounts in thousands)

	Electric Power	Water Resources
RECONCILIATION OF OPERATING INCOME (LOSS) TO NET CASH PROVIDED BY (USED IN) OPERATING ACTIVITIES		
Operating income (loss)	$ —	$ 306,249
Adjustments to reconcile operating income (loss) to net cash provided by (used in) operating activities:		
Depreciation	—	80,101
Provisions and allowances	—	—
Amortization of premiums and discounts	—	—
Amortization of long-term prepaid charges and credits	—	(890,707)
Other	—	59,083
Change in account balances:		
Receivables	—	9,535
Due from other funds	—	—
Due from other governments	—	(18,383)
Prepaid items	—	—
Inventories	—	(427)
Net investment in direct financing leases	—	—
Recoverable power costs (net)	19,000	—
Other current assets	—	—
Loans receivable	—	—
Deferred outflow of resources	(7,000)	—
Accounts payable	—	712,174
Due to other funds	—	(14,233)
Due to component units	—	23,590
Due to other governments	—	—
Deposits	—	—
Contracts and notes payable	—	—
Interest payable	—	—
Revenues received in advance	—	—
Other current liabilities	—	—
Benefits payable	—	—
Lottery prizes and annuities	—	—
Compensated absences payable	—	—
Other noncurrent liabilities	1,000	218,888
Deferred inflow of resources	—	—
Total adjustments	13,000	179,621
Net cash provided by (used in) operating activities	**$ 13,000**	**$ 485,870**
Noncash investing, capital, and financing activities:		
State's contribution for pension benefits and OPEB	$ —	$ —
Long-term debt retirement from bond issuance	—	531,255
Amortization/defeasance of bond premium and discount	61,000	50,505
Issuance of notes receivable through proceeds from long-term debt	—	—
Amortization of deferred loss on refundings	30,000	10,151
Unclaimed lottery prizes directly allocated to another entity	—	—
Interest accreted on annuitized prizes	—	—
Unrealized loss on investments	—	—
Interest accreted on zero coupon bonds	—	—
Contributed capital assets	—	—
Change in accrued capital asset purchases	—	—
Acquisition of capital assets through long-term debt	—	—
Other miscellaneous noncash transactions	—	—

| Business-type Activities – Enterprise Funds | | | | | Governmental Activities |
State Lottery	Unemployment Programs	California State University	Nonmajor Enterprise	Total	Internal Service Funds
$ 1,656,055	$ 3,401,956	$ (6,477,158)	$ 51,709	$ (1,061,189)	$ (2,497)
18,311	10,567	355,263	390	464,632	52,390
12,847	—	—	768	13,615	—
—	—	—	(300)	(300)	(95,734)
—	—	—	—	(890,707)	179
33	—	(55,144)	(11,786)	(7,814)	12,618
(60,276)	(6,070)	(15,543)	(733)	(73,087)	(64,543)
(1,426)	(23,672)	15,143	(581)	(10,536)	(30,324)
—	2,082	—	(2,207)	(18,508)	(5,526)
3,532	—	(7,915)	(79)	(4,462)	(15,757)
1,497	—	—	(437)	633	7,312
—	—	—	—	—	497,726
(649)	—	—	(2,022)	(2,671)	—
—	—	—	(604,081)	(604,081)	—
—	(55,419)	(404,597)	(6,069)	(473,085)	(238,476)
11,388	(1)	2,364	2,362	728,287	121,398
(22,886)	34,560	—	7,849	5,290	134,418
—	—	—	—	23,590	—
—	(2,052)	—	573	(1,479)	745
—	—	344	—	344	393
—	—	—	—	—	3,557
—	—	—	426	426	47,295
(549)	(18,205)	9,608	8	(9,138)	132,288
186	10,609	12,828	661	24,284	(2,654)
—	51,417	18,954	(6,391)	63,980	—
(236,884)	—	—	—	(236,884)	—
—	5,498	(33,995)	(305)	(28,802)	2,574
40,106	2,611	557,425	(1,664)	818,366	46,503
—	49,903	1,487,591	8,008	1,545,502	234,760
(234,770)	61,828	1,942,326	(615,610)	1,346,395	841,142
$ 1,421,285	$ 3,463,784	$ (4,534,832)	$ (563,901)	$ 285,206	$ 838,645

(concluded)

State Lottery	Unemployment Programs	California State University	Nonmajor Enterprise	Total	Internal Service Funds
$ —	$ —	$ 1,034,710	$ —	$ 1,034,710	$ —
—	—	—	—	531,255	—
—	—	30,100	—	141,605	—
—	—	48,706	—	48,706	—
—	—	6,198	—	46,349	—
36,049	—	—	—	36,049	—
31,967	—	—	—	31,967	—
29,851	—	—	—	29,851	—
15,991	—	—	—	15,991	—
—	—	15,580	—	15,580	—
—	—	14,133	—	14,133	—
—	—	8,055	—	8,055	—
—	—	3,846	1,678	5,524	—

Statement of Fiduciary Net Position

Fiduciary Funds and Similar Component Units
June 30, 2021
(amounts in thousands)

	Pension and Other Employee Benefit Trust	Private Purpose Trust	Investment Trust Local Agency Investment	Custodial
ASSETS				
Cash and pooled investments	$ 3,705,613	$ 51,865	$ 37,049,805	$ 2,692,549
Investments, at fair value:				
Short-term	40,055,776	—	—	—
Equity securities	414,072,794	6,392,548	—	—
Debt securities	182,097,183	3,535,204	—	—
Real estate	86,232,491	322,281	—	—
Securities lending collateral	27,256,282	—	—	—
Other	118,318,399	2,424,831		—
Total investments	868,032,925	12,674,864	—	—
Receivables (net)	11,363,470	8,411	46,155	1,958,064
Due from other funds	747,212	75,859	—	—
Due from other governments	—	—	—	23
Interfund receivable	—	—	—	46,062
Loans receivable	3,701,331	—	—	21,974
Other assets	734,282	307,988	—	15
Total assets	**888,284,833**	**13,118,987**	**37,095,960**	**4,718,687**
DEFERRED OUTFLOWS OF RESOURCES	156,309	—	—	1
Total assets and deferred outflows of resources	**888,441,142**	**13,118,987**	**37,095,960**	**4,718,688**
LIABILITIES				
Accounts payable	9,719,880	35,515	78	249,994
Due to other governments	3	6,194	29,275	2,803,064
Tax overpayments	—	—	—	(177)
Benefits payable	4,113,997	—	—	—
Revenues received in advance	—	16,853	—	675
Deposits	—	307,967	—	930,751
Securities lending obligations	27,133,696	—	—	—
Loans payable	3,702,701	—	—	—
Other liabilities	13,120,873	—	—	22,437
Total liabilities	**57,791,150**	**366,529**	**29,353**	**4,006,744**
DEFERRED INFLOWS OF RESOURCES	380,333	—	—	118
Total liabilities and deferred inflows of resources	**58,171,483**	**366,529**	**29,353**	**4,006,862**
NET POSITION				
Restricted:				
Pension and other postemployment benefits	806,025,328	—	—	—
Deferred compensation participants	24,236,563	—	—	—
Pool participants	—	—	37,066,607	—
Individuals, organizations, or other governments	7,768	12,752,458	—	711,826
Total net position	**$ 830,269,659**	**$ 12,752,458**	**$ 37,066,607**	**$ 711,826**

Statement of Changes in Fiduciary Net Position

Fiduciary Funds and Similar Component Units

Year Ended June 30, 2021

(amounts in thousands)

	Pension and Other Employee Benefit Trust	Private Purpose Trust	Investment Trust Local Agency Investment	Custodial
ADDITIONS				
Contributions:				
Employer	$ 30,256,975	$ —	$ —	$ 35,594
Plan member	9,568,619	—	—	—
Non-employer	3,730,902	—	—	—
Total contributions	43,556,496	—	—	35,594
Investment income:				
Net appreciation (depreciation) in fair value of investments	152,224,913	6,754	—	—
Interest, dividends, and other investment income	13,292,160	2,148,626	188,145	720
Less: investment expense	(1,516,609)	(2,950)	—	—
Net investment income	164,000,464	2,152,430	188,145	720
Receipts from depositors	—	3,159,841	27,343,632	78,116
Other	134,327	—	—	176,797
Total additions	**207,691,287**	**5,312,271**	**27,531,777**	**291,227**
DEDUCTIONS				
Distributions paid and payable to participants	47,695,661	—	186,239	35,594
Refunds of contributions	396,099	—	—	—
Administrative expense	928,165	106	1,907	1,113
Interest expense	89,604	—	—	—
Payments to and for depositors	382,162	2,666,000	22,350,197	105,979
Total deductions	**49,491,691**	**2,666,106**	**22,538,343**	**142,686**
Change in net position	158,199,596	2,646,165	4,993,434	148,541
Net position – beginning	**672,070,063** *	**10,106,293**	**32,073,173**	**563,285**
Net position – ending	**$ 830,269,659**	**$ 12,752,458**	**$ 37,066,607**	**$ 711,826**

* Restated

Schedule of Changes in Net Pension Liability and Related Ratios

For the Past Four Fiscal Years[1]

(amounts in thousands)

PUBLIC EMPLOYEES' RETIREMENT FUND PLANS

STATE MISCELLANEOUS[2]

	2014[3]	2015[3]
Total pension liability		
Service cost	$ 1,477,762	$ 1,576,695
Interest on total pension liability	6,670,928	6,970,837
Differences between expected and actual experience	—	693,639
Changes of assumptions	—	—
Benefit payments, including refunds of employee contributions	(4,844,631)	(5,098,222)
Net change in total pension liability	3,304,059	4,142,949
Total pension liability – beginning	**88,885,115**	**92,189,174**
Total pension liability – ending (a)	**$ 92,189,174**	**$ 96,332,123**
Plan fiduciary net position		
Contributions – employer	$ 2,156,312	$ 2,608,785
Contributions – employee	766,896	771,046
Net investment income	10,370,838	1,505,042
Benefit payments, including refunds of employee contributions	(4,844,631)	(5,098,222)
Net plan to plan resource movement	—	(354)
Administrative expense	(86,473)	(76,678)
Net change in plan fiduciary net position	8,362,942	(290,381)
Plan fiduciary net position – beginning	**60,017,620**	**68,380,562**
Plan fiduciary net position – ending (b)	**$ 68,380,562**	**$ 68,090,181**
State's net pension liability – ending (a) – (b)	**$ 23,808,612**	**$ 28,241,942**
Plan fiduciary net position as a percentage of the total pension liability	74.17%	70.68%
Covered payroll	$ 10,019,739	$ 10,640,884
State's net pension liability as a percentage of covered payroll	237.62%	265.41%

[1] This schedule will be built prospectively until it contains ten years of data.

[2] This schedule includes amounts attributable to related organizations, fiduciary component units, and discretely presented component units, which are not part of the primary government.

[3] The date in the column heading represents the end of the measurement period of the net pension liability, which is one year prior to the reporting period.

Schedule of State Pension Contributions

For the Past Four Fiscal Years[1]

(amounts in thousands)

		2015		2016
PUBLIC EMPLOYEES' RETIREMENT FUND PLANS				
STATE MISCELLANEOUS[2]				
Actuarially determined contribution	$	2,421,157	$	2,718,895
Contributions in relation to the actuarially determined contribution		(2,583,400)		(2,814,126)
Contribution deficiency (excess)	**$**	**(162,243)**	**$**	**(95,231)**
Covered payroll	$	10,655,117	$	11,197,607
Contributions as a percentage of covered payroll		24.25%		25.13%
STATE INDUSTRIAL[2]				
Actuarially determined contribution	$	92,024	$	103,293
Contributions in relation to the actuarially determined contribution		(104,769)		(116,594)
Contribution deficiency (excess)	**$**	**(12,745)**	**$**	**(13,301)**
Covered payroll	$	577,713	$	625,220
Contributions as a percentage of covered payroll		18.14%		18.65%
STATE SAFETY[2]				
Actuarially determined contribution	$	341,509	$	368,444
Contributions in relation to the actuarially determined contribution		(387,508)		(404,595)
Contribution deficiency (excess)	**$**	**(45,999)**	**$**	**(36,151)**
Covered payroll	$	2,003,716	$	2,100,289
Contributions as a percentage of covered payroll		19.34%		19.26%
STATE PEACE OFFICERS AND FIREFIGHTERS[2]				
Actuarially determined contribution	$	1,086,102	$	1,197,160
Contributions in relation to the actuarially determined contribution		(1,148,597)		(1,263,436)
Contribution deficiency (excess)	**$**	**(62,495)**	**$**	**(66,276)**
Covered payroll	$	3,115,364	$	3,241,763
Contributions as a percentage of covered payroll		36.87%		38.97%

[1] This schedule will be built prospectively until it contains ten years of data.

[2] This schedule includes amounts attributable to related organizations, fiduciary component units, and discretely presented component units, which are not part of the primary government.

Budgetary Comparison Schedule

General Fund and Major Special Revenue Funds

Year Ended June 30, 2018

(amounts in thousands)

	General			
	Budgeted Amounts		Actual	Variance with
	Original	Final	Amounts	Final Budget
REVENUES				
Corporation tax	$ 10,655,743	$ 11,246,000	$ 12,260,663	$ 1,014,663
Intergovernmental	—	—	—	—
Cigarette and tobacco taxes	64,903	67,000	65,248	(1,752)
Insurance gross premiums tax	2,438,099	2,514,000	2,569,271	55,271
Vehicle license fees	26,218	26,218	28,903	2,685
Motor vehicle fuel tax	—	—	—	—
Personal income tax	89,403,019	91,971,000	94,263,065	2,292,065
Retail sales and use taxes	25,164,877	25,384,000	25,127,131	(256,869)
Other major taxes and licenses	376,595	371,000	377,129	6,129
Other revenues	1,159,890	1,247,782	1,506,189	258,407
Total revenues	**129,289,344**	**132,827,000**	**136,197,599**	**3,370,599**
EXPENDITURES				
Business, consumer services, and housing	59,077	61,122	60,788	(334)
Transportation	5,252	5,252	5,252	—
Natural resources and environmental protection	2,225,818	2,650,784	2,231,544	(419,240)
Health and human services	35,011,303	35,980,524	34,809,447	(1,171,077)
Corrections and rehabilitation	11,241,406	11,719,123	11,614,818	(104,305)
Education	65,067,299	64,956,753	64,840,149	(116,604)
General government:				
Tax relief	420,424	425,424	411,750	(13,674)
Debt service	4,779,168	4,779,438	4,764,484	(14,954)
Other general government	7,183,581	7,075,348	5,997,603	(1,077,745)
Total expenditures	**125,993,328**	**127,653,768**	**124,735,835**	**(2,917,933)**
OTHER FINANCING SOURCES (USES)				
Transfers from other funds	—	—	414,296	—
Transfers to other funds	—	—	(4,261,838)	—
Other additions (deductions)	—	—	447,535	—
Total other financing sources (uses)	**—**	**—**	**(3,400,007)**	**—**
Excess (deficiency) of revenues and other sources over (under) expenditures and other uses	—	—	8,061,757	—
Fund balances – beginning	—	—	5,930,654	—
Fund balances – ending	$ —	$ —	$ 13,992,411	$ —

* Restated

	Federal				Transportation			
	Budgeted Amounts		Actual	Variance with	Budgeted Amounts		Actual	Variance with
	Original	Final	Amounts	Final Budget	Original	Final	Amounts	Final Budget
$	—	$ —	$ —	$ —	$ —	$ —	$ —	$ —
	81,368,222	81,368,222	81,368,222	—	—	—	—	—
	—	—	—	—	—	—	—	—
	—	—	—	—	—	—	—	—
	—	—	—	—	—	—	—	—
	—	—	—	—	5,113,278	6,832,602	6,641,508	(191,094)
	—	—	—	—	—	—	—	—
	—	—	—	—	5,746,624	5,446,622	5,637,538	190,916
	96	96	96	—	396,435	414,826	448,136	33,310
	81,368,318	**81,368,318**	**81,368,318**	**—**	**11,256,337**	**12,694,050**	**12,727,182**	**33,132**
	38,981	38,981	38,981	—	111,668	114,544	112,000	(2,544)
	4,575,673	4,575,673	4,575,673	—	13,601,269	13,897,414	10,646,171	(3,251,243)
	365,831	365,831	365,831	—	115,835	169,592	167,955	(1,637)
	66,375,441	66,375,441	66,375,441	—	8,252	8,352	2,295	(6,057)
	67,546	67,546	67,546	—	—	—	—	—
	7,396,252	7,396,252	7,396,252	—	9,262	9,262	9,262	—
	—	—	—	—	—	—	—	—
	—	—	—	—	1,996	1,950	1,349	(601)
	1,396,169	1,396,169	1,396,169	—	293,218	301,849	295,283	(6,566)
	80,215,893	**80,215,893**	**80,215,893**	**—**	**14,141,500**	**14,502,963**	**11,234,315**	**(3,268,648)**
	—	—	5,331,592	—	—	—	17,530,673	—
	—	—	(6,482,865)	—	—	—	(18,232,280)	—
	—	—	(5,024)	—	—	—	844,163	—
	—	**—**	**(1,156,297)**	**—**	**—**	**—**	**142,556**	**—**
	—	—	(3,872)	—	—	—	1,635,423	—
	—	—	**6,229**	—	—	—	**4,979,675** *	—
$	—	$ —	$ **2,357**	$ —	$ —	$ —	$ **6,615,098**	$ —

(continued)

Reconciliation of Budgetary Basis Fund Balances of the General Fund and Major Special Revenue Funds to GAAP Basis Fund Balances

June 30, 2018

(amounts in thousands)

	General	Federal	Transportation	Environmental and Natural Resources	Health Care Related Programs
			Major Special Revenue Funds		
Budgetary fund balance reclassified into GAAP statement fund structure	$ 13,992,411	$ 2,357	$ 6,615,098	$ 11,326,453	$ 2,907,760
Basis difference:					
Interfund receivables	549,739	—	1,755,668	335,000	—
Loans receivable	35,697	225,717	—	231,335	23,000
Interfund payables	(6,266,808)	—	(1,070,797)	(360,359)	(8,113)
Escheat property	(1,077,358)	—	—	—	—
Tax revenues	(756,200)	—	—	—	—
Fund classification changes	9,941,491	2,942	—	—	—
Other	53,371	—	2,616,708	82,798	—
Timing difference:					
Liabilities budgeted in subsequent years	(4,285,439)	(2,362)	(572,485)	(100,353)	(2,192,571)
GAAP fund balance – ending	$ 12,186,904	$ 228,654	$ 9,344,192	$ 11,514,874	$ 730,076

Notes to the Required Supplementary Information

Budgetary Comparison Schedule

The State annually reports its financial condition based on a Generally Accepted Accounting Principles (GAAP) basis and on the State's budgetary provisions (budgetary basis). The Budgetary Comparison Schedule for the General Fund and Major Special Revenue Funds reports the original budget, the final budget, the actual expenditures, and the variance between the final budget and the actual expenditures, using the budgetary basis of accounting.

On the budgetary basis, individual appropriations are charged as expenditures when commitments for goods and services are incurred. However, for financial reporting purposes, the State reports expenditures based on the year in which goods and services are received. The Budgetary Comparison Schedule includes all of the current year expenditures for the General Fund and major special revenue funds as well as related appropriations that typically are legislatively authorized annually, continually, or by project. While the encumbrances relate to all programs' expenditures on a budgetary basis, adjustments for encumbrances are made under "other general government," except for Environmental and Natural Resources where adjustments for encumbrances are made under each program's expenditures.

The Budgetary Comparison Schedule is not presented in this document at the legal level of budgetary control because such a presentation would be extremely lengthy and cumbersome. The State of California prepares a separate report, the Comprehensive Annual Financial Report Supplement, which includes statements that demonstrate compliance with the legal level of budgetary control in accordance with

Infrastructure Assets Using the Modified Approach

Pursuant to Governmental Accounting Standards Board (GASB) Statement No. 34, the State uses the modified approach to report the cost of its infrastructure assets (state bridges, roadways, and high-speed rail). Under the modified approach, the State does not report depreciation expense for infrastructure assets but capitalizes all costs that add to the capacity and efficiency of state-owned bridges, roads, and the high-speed rail system. All maintenance and preservation costs are expensed and not capitalized.

A. Infrastructure Asset Reporting Categories

The infrastructure assets reported in the State's financial statements for the fiscal year ending June 30, 2018, are in the following categories and amounts: state highway infrastructure, consisting of completed highway projects totaling $77.1 billion, land purchased for highway projects totaling $14.5 billion, and infrastructure construction-in-progress (uncompleted highway projects) totaling $10.4 billion; and high-speed rail system infrastructure, consisting of construction-in-progress (uncompleted rail construction projects) totaling $2.3 billion, purchased land totaling $916 million, and land use rights totaling $3 million.

Donation and Relinquishment: Donation and relinquishment activity affects the inventory of statewide lane miles, land, and/or bridges as adjustments to the infrastructure assets and/or land balance in the State's financial statements. For the fiscal year ending June 30, 2018, there were no donations of infrastructure land, and relinquishments were $40 million of state highway infrastructure (completed highway projects) and $8 million of infrastructure land.

B. Condition Baselines and Assessments

1. Bridges

The federal Fixing America's Surface Transportation (FAST) Act required all states to adopt national asset management performance measures to establish nationwide consistency for condition reporting of highway assets.

Previously, the State used the Bridge Health Index (BHI)—a numerical rating scale from 0 to 100 that used element-level inspection data—to determine the aggregate condition of its bridges. Under the FAST Act, the national performance measure for bridges is total deck area of the structures in good, fair, or poor condition. The inspection data is based on the American Association of State Highway Transportation Officials' *Guide Manual for Bridge Element Inspection* and the *Caltrans Bridge Element Inspection Manual*.

The following table shows the State's established condition baseline and actual BHI for fiscal year 2015-16:

Fiscal Year Ended June 30	Established BHI Baseline[1]	Actual BHI
2016	80.0	94.5

[1] The actual statewide BHI should not be lower than the minimum BHI established by the State.

Combining Balance Sheet
Nonmajor Governmental Funds
June 30, 2018
(amounts in thousands)

	Special Revenue		
	Business and Professions Regulatory and Licensing	Financing for Local Governments and the Public	Cigarette, Tobacco, and Cannabis Tax
ASSETS			
Cash and pooled investments	$ 1,244,111	$ 1,094,401	$ 1,097,849
Investments	—	—	—
Receivables (net)	88,870	3,656	414,073
Due from other funds	60,090	303,973	1,855
Due from other governments	6,532	1,149	—
Interfund receivables	171,626	279,776	88,585
Loans receivable	100,038	2,577,678	—
Other assets	—	—	—
Total assets	$ 1,671,267	$ 4,260,633	$ 1,602,362
LIABILITIES			
Accounts payable	$ 12,194	$ 11,687	$ 78,297
Due to other funds	48,556	3,526	44,547
Due to component units	—	—	98,097
Due to other governments	678	264,961	138,168
Interfund payables	130,184	—	—
Revenues received in advance	60,015	2,510	—
Deposits	—	—	—
Other liabilities	33,966	837	—
Total liabilities	285,593	283,521	359,109
DEFERRED INFLOWS OF RESOURCES	—	—	211,973
Total liabilities and deferred inflows of resources	285,593	283,521	571,082
FUND BALANCES			
Nonspendable	—	—	—
Restricted	709,764	3,731,506	1,031,280
Committed	675,910	245,606	—
Assigned	—	—	—
Total fund balances	1,385,674	3,977,112	1,031,280
Total liabilities, deferred inflows of resources, and fund balances	$ 1,671,267	$ 4,260,633	$ 1,602,362

	Special Revenue			
Local Revenue and Public Safety	Trial Courts	Golden State Tobacco Securitization Corporation	Other Special Revenue Programs	Total Nonmajor Special Revenue
$ 2,883,932	$ 1,048,541	$ 392,417	$ 1,875,108	$ 9,636,359
—	344,618	149,887	—	494,505
98,347	264,299	189,117	226,466	1,284,828
38,810	—	—	441,012	845,740
—	34,616	—	52,096	94,393
119,851	257,163	—	537,585	1,454,586
—	—	—	56,028	2,733,744
—	12,120	—	—	12,120
$ 3,140,940	$ 1,961,357	$ 731,421	$ 3,188,295	$ 16,556,275
$ —	$ 209,066	$ 1,379	$ 201,289	$ 513,912
39,339	55,905	—	84,733	276,606
—	—	—	7,567	105,664
3,020,717	114,943	—	390,502	3,929,969
—	—	—	4,971	135,155
—	22,548	—	65,650	150,723
—	408,326	—	25,268	433,594
—	86,252	—	19,970	141,025
3,060,056	897,040	1,379	799,950	5,686,648
				211,973
3,060,056	897,040	1,379	799,950	5,898,621
—	69,868	—	—	69,868
19,712	901,195	730,042	2,131,536	9,255,035
61,172	66,908	—	256,809	1,306,405
—	26,346	—	—	26,346
80,884	1,064,317	730,042	2,388,345	10,657,654
$ 3,140,940	$ 1,961,357	$ 731,421	$ 3,188,295	$ 16,556,275

(continued)

Schedule of Net Position by Component

For the Past Ten Fiscal Years

(accrual basis of accounting, amounts in thousands)

	2009	2010	2011 [2]	2012
Governmental activities				
Net investment in capital assets	$ 83,285,184	$ 84,085,632	$ 85,460,957	$ 80,768,527
Restricted – Expendable..	8,391,814	14,987,867	27,865,821	24,871,510
Unrestricted [1]..	(86,302,434)	(103,272,097)	(123,783,314)	(123,897,753)
Total governmental activities net position (deficit)......	**$ 5,374,564**	**$ (4,198,598)**	**$ (10,456,536)**	**$ (18,257,716)**
Business-type activities				
Net investment in capital assets	$ (130,634)	$ 89,334	$ 1,382,957	$ 1,561,258
Restricted – Nonexpendable	—	—	21,812	21,584
Restricted – Expendable..	3,855,051	3,404,682	3,615,945	4,571,036
Unrestricted...	717,740	(4,250,609)	(4,214,494)	(3,346,849)
Total business-type activities net position (deficit)......	**$ 4,442,157**	**$ (756,593)**	**$ 806,220**	**$ 2,807,029**
Primary government				
Net investment in capital assets	$ 83,154,550	$ 84,174,966	$ 86,843,914	$ 82,329,785
Restricted – Nonexpendable	—	—	21,812	21,584
Restricted – Expendable..	12,246,865	18,392,549	31,481,766	29,442,546
Unrestricted...	(85,584,694)	(107,522,706)	(127,997,808)	(127,244,602)
Total primary government net position (deficit)..........	**$ 9,816,721**	**$ (4,955,191)**	**$ (9,650,316)**	**$ (15,450,687)**

[1] Governmental activities' unrestricted net position reflects a negative balance because of outstanding bonded debt issued to build capital assets for school districts and other local governmental entities and unfunded employee-related obligations—net pension liability, net other postemployment benefits (OPEB) liability and compensated absences.

[2] In fiscal year 2011, the net position of governmental activities and business-type activities changed primarily as a result of the reclassification of the $1.2 billion beginning net position of the California State University Fund from a governmental fund to an enterprise fund.

[3] In fiscal year 2014, the net position of governmental activities and business-type activities changed primarily as a result of the reclassification of the $380 million beginning net position of the Public Buildings Construction Fund from an enterprise fund to an internal service fund.

[4] In fiscal year 2015, the net position of governmental activities and business-type activities significantly decreased as a result of implementing GASB Statements No. 68 and No. 71 requiring the recognition of net pension liability and related pension expense and deferred outflows and inflows of resources.

[5] In fiscal year 2018, the net position of governmental activities and business-type activities significantly decreased as a result of implementing GASB Statement No. 75 requiring the recognition of net OPEB liability and related OPEB expense and deferred outflows and inflows of resources.

	2013	2014 [3]	2015 [4]	2016	2017	2018 [5]
	$ 84,931,030	$ 94,001,659	$ 100,694,652	$ 104,596,917	$ 107,042,274	$ 109,614,321
	24,315,913	24,950,740	26,632,502	29,060,971	33,832,232	35,053,202
	(117,383,903)	(116,948,128)	(169,744,967)	(168,542,861)	(169,499,683)	(213,316,033)
	$ **(8,136,960)**	$ **2,004,271**	$ **(42,417,813)**	$ **(34,884,973)**	$ **(28,625,177)**	$ **(68,648,510)**
	$ 1,718,648	$ 2,065,550	$ 2,278,252	$ 2,520,621	$ 2,295,270	$ 2,469,723
	20,627	16,219	13,448	8,653	1,746	1,708
	5,151,915	4,897,314	4,523,496	5,750,634	6,307,218	12,083,737
	(2,824,738)	(1,661,692)	(5,360,817)	(3,707,406)	(1,321,132)	(16,464,573)
	$ **4,066,452**	$ **5,317,391**	$ **1,454,379**	$ **4,572,502**	$ **7,283,102**	$ **(1,909,405)**
	$ 86,649,678	$ 96,067,209	$ 102,972,904	$ 107,117,538	$ 109,337,544	$ 112,084,044
	20,627	16,219	13,448	8,653	1,746	1,708
	29,467,828	29,848,054	31,155,998	34,811,605	40,139,450	47,136,939
	(120,208,641)	(118,609,820)	(175,105,784)	(172,250,267)	(170,820,815)	(229,780,606)
	$ **(4,070,508)**	$ **7,321,662**	$ **(40,963,434)**	$ **(30,312,471)**	$ **(21,342,075)**	$ **(70,557,915)**

Schedule of Revenue Base

For the Past Ten Calendar Years
(amounts in thousands)

	2008	2009	2010	2011
Personal Income by Industry				
(items restated as footnoted) [1]				
Farm earnings	$ 11,106,106	$ 12,353,918	$ 13,158,193	$ 15,198,140
Forestry, fishing, and other natural resources	5,846,897	5,843,512	6,400,497	6,693,485
Mining	7,161,014	4,407,806	4,620,076	5,251,493
Construction and utilities	73,677,307	63,527,010	64,196,131	62,972,017
Manufacturing	122,746,904	113,311,993	115,565,437	119,852,946
Wholesale trade	56,664,424	51,178,861	52,651,124	56,488,847
Retail trade	70,141,490	66,566,961	69,564,024	72,732,632
Transportation and warehousing	33,195,174	31,539,745	33,579,755	36,376,555
Information, finance, and insurance	118,514,884	119,984,148	130,737,220	135,321,324
Real estate and rental and leasing	31,513,132	33,474,649	36,963,992	47,395,981
Services	433,280,763	417,996,629	439,206,312	467,337,237
Federal, civilian	22,294,322	23,413,156	25,736,809	26,083,443
Military	14,559,860	15,579,596	16,264,215	16,062,725
State and local government	179,150,537	177,405,543	177,461,935	181,063,132
Other [2]	426,911,691	417,646,137	441,733,296	489,583,154
Total personal income	**$ 1,606,764,505**	**$ 1,554,229,664**	**$ 1,627,839,016**	**$ 1,738,413,111**
Average effective rate [3]	5.7%	5.2%	4.7%	5.3%

Source: Bureau of Economic Analysis, U.S. Department of Commerce

[1] Prior years were updated based on more current information.

[2] Other personal income includes dividends, interest, rental income, residence adjustment, government transfers for individuals, and deductions for social insurance.

[3] The total direct rate for personal income is not available. The average effective rate equals personal income tax revenue divided by adjusted gross income.

2012	2013	2014	2015	2016	2017
$ 17,356,593	$ 20,049,107	$ 22,059,308	$ 21,372,154	$ 18,530,925	$ 22,523,816
7,504,590	7,928,931	8,377,804	9,306,866	9,839,986	10,174,653
6,041,129	6,522,865	6,767,639	5,039,127	3,837,717	3,026,435
67,862,415	75,578,567	81,245,751	89,612,217	94,829,175	102,994,717
124,666,659	126,302,825	133,264,173	139,817,905	145,764,299	154,388,705
59,067,338	61,598,279	66,001,226	70,528,366	70,466,840	73,976,742
77,323,055	79,202,104	82,466,141	86,378,279	86,199,023	89,451,738
37,949,820	39,849,739	42,798,845	46,656,349	49,806,143	53,857,784
144,204,507	157,149,112	160,946,504	175,499,613	191,586,390	209,566,441
55,245,202	52,971,172	50,451,414	52,958,405	55,357,883	59,699,575
506,565,209	515,553,620	553,295,287	590,143,886	611,756,625	642,486,823
26,157,961	25,771,225	26,498,641	27,663,625	28,560,772	29,370,219
15,933,633	15,353,761	15,043,948	14,905,222	15,395,195	15,031,600
179,834,589	190,303,808	200,325,665	212,335,637	221,798,464	230,772,194
527,754,528	511,537,315	572,097,688	631,082,019	655,684,428	666,807,962
$ 1,853,467,228	$ 1,885,672,430	$ 2,021,640,034	$ 2,173,299,670	$ 2,259,413,865	$ 2,364,129,404
5.0%	6.1%	5.6%	6.1%	6.0%	5.9%

(continued)

Schedule of Ratios of Outstanding Debt by Type

For the Past Ten Fiscal Years
(amounts in thousands, except per capita)

	2009	2010	2011	2012
Governmental activities				
General obligation bonds [1]	$ 68,653,507	$ 77,745,789	$ 79,469,085	$ 81,060,111
Revenue bonds [2]	7,767,855	7,611,939	7,511,092	7,421,198
Certificates of participation and commercial paper [3]	1,407,908	1,342,119	1,335,340	46,098
Capital lease obligations [4]	4,456,039	4,967,290	4,882,233	5,176,341
Total governmental activities	**82,285,309**	**91,667,137**	**93,197,750**	**93,703,748**
Business-type activities				
General obligation bonds [1]	1,702,377	1,477,663	1,218,639	1,118,634
Revenue bonds [2]	23,053,114	24,538,094	23,290,315	24,790,918
Commercial paper	51,307	64,518	139,974	67,325
Capital lease obligations	—	—	791,489	817,687
Total business-type activities	**24,806,798**	**26,080,275**	**25,440,417**	**26,794,564**
Total primary government	**$ 107,092,107**	**$ 117,747,412**	**$ 118,638,167**	**$ 120,498,312**
Debt as a percentage of personal income [5,7]	6.7%	7.6%	7.3%	6.9%
Amount of debt per capita [6,7]	$ 2,926	$ 3,186	$ 3,178	$ 3,199

Note: Details regarding the State's outstanding debt can be found in Notes 9, 12, 13, 15, and 16 of the financial statements.

[1] Beginning in fiscal year 2013, refunding gains/losses are no longer included in bonds payable, but are shown as deferred inflows and deferred outflows of resources.

[2] Prior to fiscal year 2014, the Public Buildings Construction Fund was included in business-type activities.

[3] All certificates of participation were retired in fiscal year 2016.

[4] Prior to fiscal year 2014, governmental activities reported a capital lease obligation to the Public Buildings Construction Fund. In fiscal year 2014, the fund was reclassified from an enterprise fund to an internal service fund and the governmental activities' obligation and the fund's net investment in direct financing leases were netted against each other within governmental activities.

[5] Ratio calculated using personal income data shown on pages 324 and 325 for the prior calendar year.

[6] Amount calculated using population data shown on pages 324 and 325 for the prior calendar year.

[7] Some prior years were updated based on more current information.

	2013	2014	2015	2016	2017	2018
	$ 82,346,211	$ 83,276,347	$ 80,509,802	$ 79,043,295	$ 79,503,871	$ 79,663,028
	7,735,053	18,917,443	18,409,971	17,210,499	16,879,900	16,364,255
	538,593	598,094	493,770	771,215	1,158,080	859,695
	5,319,487	260,088	274,760	370,182	416,468	481,261
	95,939,344	103,051,972	99,688,303	97,395,191	97,958,319	97,368,239
	887,053	674,394	650,133	794,369	703,754	694,100
	25,558,129	12,991,827	12,670,619	13,928,374	14,955,858	14,319,372
	77,560	204,647	237,186	47,416	147,765	749,877
	909,871	1,250,274	1,210,409	389,385	353,453	309,928
	27,432,613	15,121,142	14,768,347	15,159,544	16,160,830	16,073,277
	$ 123,371,957	$ 118,173,114	$ 114,456,650	$ 112,554,735	$ 114,119,149	$ 113,441,516
	6.7%	6.3%	5.7%	5.2%	5.1%	4.8%
	$ 3,245	$ 3,082	$ 2,957	$ 2,884	$ 2,904	$ 2,869

Schedule of Demographic and Economic Indicators

For the Past Ten Calendar Years

	2008	2009	2010	2011
Population (in thousands) [1]				
California	36,604	36,961	37,328	37,673
% Change	1.0%	1.0%	1.0%	0.9%
United States	304,094	306,772	309,338	311,644
% Change	1.0%	0.9%	0.8%	0.7%
Total personal income (in millions) [1]				
California	$ 1,606,765	$ 1,554,230	$ 1,627,839	$ 1,738,413
% Change	1.5%	-3.3%	4.7%	6.8%
United States	$ 12,438,527	$ 12,051,307	$ 12,541,995	$ 13,315,478
% Change	3.6%	-3.1%	4.1%	6.2%
Per capita personal income [1,2]				
California	$ 43,895	$ 42,050	$ 43,609	$ 46,145
% Change	0.5%	-4.2%	3.7%	5.8%
United States	$ 40,904	$ 39,284	$ 40,545	$ 42,727
% Change	2.7%	-4.0%	3.2%	5.4%
Labor force and employment (in thousands)				
California				
Civilian labor force	18,203	18,208	18,316	18,385
Employed	16,890	16,145	16,052	16,227
Unemployed	1,313	2,064	2,265	2,158
Unemployment rate	7.2%	11.3%	12.4%	11.7%
United States employment rate	5.8%	9.3%	9.6%	8.9%

Sources: Economic Research Unit, California Department of Finance; Bureau of Economic Analysis, U.S. Department of Commerce; Labor Market Information Division, California Employment Development Department; and Bureau of Labor Statistics, U.S. Department of Labor.

Note: This schedule presents data available as of January 2019.

[1] Some prior years were updated based on more current information.

[2] Calculated by dividing total personal income by population.

	2012		2013		2014		2015		2016		2017
	38,019		38,347		38,701		39,032		39,296		39,537
	0.9%		0.9%		0.9%		0.9%		0.7%		0.6%
	313,993		316,235		318,623		321,040		323,406		325,719
	0.8%		0.7%		0.8%		0.8%		0.7%		0.7%
$	1,853,467	$	1,885,672	$	2,021,640	$	2,173,300	$	2,259,414	$	2,364,129
	6.6%		1.7%		7.2%		7.5%		4.0%		4.6%
$	13,998,383	$	14,175,503	$	14,983,140	$	15,711,634	$	16,115,630	$	16,820,250
	5.1%		1.3%		5.7%		4.9%		2.6%		4.4%
$	48,751	$	49,173	$	52,237	$	55,679	$	57,497	$	59,796
	5.6%		0.9%		6.2%		6.6%		3.3%		4.0%
$	44,582	$	44,826	$	47,025	$	48,940	$	49,831	$	51,640
	4.3%		0.5%		4.9%		4.1%		1.8%		3.6%
	18,511		18,573		18,941		18,996		19,099		19,319
	16,740		17,044		17,600		17,894		18,141		18,515
	1,771		1,530		1,341		1,102		957		804
	9.6%		8.2%		7.1%		5.8%		5.0%		4.2%
	8.1%		7.4%		6.2%		5.3%		4.9%		4.4%

Schedule of Capital Asset Statistics by Function

For the Past Ten Fiscal Years

	2009	2010	2011	2012
General Government				
Department of Food and Agriculture				
Vehicles and mobile equipment	803	746	809	804
Square footage of structures (in thousands)	466	466	466	466
Department of Justice				
Vehicles and mobile equipment	870	816	677	531
Department of Military				
Vehicles and mobile equipment	182	208	249	233
Square footage of structures (in thousands)	3,383	3,154	3,530	3,511
Department of Veterans Affairs				
Veterans homes	5	6	6	6
Vehicles and mobile equipment	120	113	132	143
Square footage of structures (in thousands)	1,683	1,600	2,086	2,086
Education				
California State University [1]				
Vehicles and mobile equipment	4,015	4,338	4,415	4,326
Campuses	23	23	23	23
Square footage of structures (in thousands)	66,686	69,049	71,287	73,785
Health and Human Services				
Department of Developmental Services				
Vehicles and mobile equipment	701	569	818	789
Developmental centers	7	5	5	5
Square footage of structures (in thousands)	5,187	5,185	5,294	5,294
Department of State Hospitals [2]				
Vehicles and mobile equipment	658	665	709	718
State hospitals	5	5	5	5
Square footage of structures (in thousands)	6,348	6,331	6,331	6,336

Source: California Department of General Services (DGS)

Note: This schedule presents data available as of February 2019.

[1] Some prior years were updated based on more current information provided by California State University.

[2] In fiscal year 2012, portions of the Department of Mental Health became the Department of State Hospitals.

2013	2014	2015	2016	2017	2018
792	747	747	752	677	823
455	455	455	455	462	384
527	520	520	484	511	509
211	211	211	217	218	261
3,623	4,019	3,977	3,965	3,954	3,770
8	8	8	8	8	8
267	285	285	235	280	292
2,488	2,543	2,541	2,541	2,552	2,552
4,467	4,555	4,619	4,945	4,838	5,216
23	23	23	23	23	23
73,866	73,316	73,988	75,292	75,786	76,227
632	424	571	640	559	616
4	4	3	3	3	3
5,279	5,308	4,699	3,664	3,664	3,595
699	886	752	678	674	728
7	7	7	8	5	5
6,457	6,460	6,445	6,445	5,944	5,944

(continued)

UNITED STATES
SECURITIES AND EXCHANGE COMMISSION
Washington, DC 20549

FORM 10-K

☑ Annual report pursuant to Section 13 or 15(d) of the Securities Exchange Act of 1934
For the fiscal year ended December 31, 2022

or

☐ Transition report pursuant to Section 13 or 15(d) of the Securities Exchange Act of 1934
For the transition period from _____ to _____
Commission file number 1-3950

Ford Motor Company

(Exact name of Registrant as specified in its charter)

Delaware	38-0549190
(State of incorporation)	*(I.R.S. Employer Identification No.)*

One American Road	
Dearborn, Michigan	48126
(Address of principal executive offices)	*(Zip Code)*

313-322-3000
(Registrant's telephone number, including area code)

Securities registered pursuant to Section 12(b) of the Act:

Title of each class	Trading symbols	Name of each exchange on which registered
Common Stock, par value $.01 per share	F	New York Stock Exchange
6.200% Notes due June 1, 2059	FPRB	New York Stock Exchange
6.000% Notes due December 1, 2059	FPRC	New York Stock Exchange
6.500% Notes due August 15, 2062	FPRD	New York Stock Exchange

Securities registered pursuant to Section 12(g) of the Act: None.

Indicate by check mark if the registrant is a well-known seasoned issuer, as defined in Rule 405 of the Securities Act. Yes ☑ No ☐

Indicate by check mark if the registrant is not required to file reports pursuant to Section 13 or Section 15(d) of the Act. Yes ☐ No ☑

Indicate by check mark whether the registrant (1) has filed all reports required to be filed by Section 13 or 15(d) of the Securities Exchange Act of 1934 during the preceding 12 months (or for such shorter period that the registrant was required to file such reports), and (2) has been subject to such filing requirements for the past 90 days. Yes ☑ No ☐

Indicate by check mark whether the registrant has submitted electronically every Interactive Data File required to be submitted pursuant to Rule 405 of Regulation S-T (§ 232.405 of this chapter) during the preceding 12 months (or for such shorter period that the registrant was required to submit such files). Yes ☑ No ☐

FORD MOTOR COMPANY AND SUBSIDIARIES
CONSOLIDATED BALANCE SHEETS
(in millions)

	December 31, 2021	December 31, 2022
ASSETS		
Cash and cash equivalents (Note 9)	$ 20,540	$ 25,134
Marketable securities (Note 9)	29,053	18,936
Ford Credit finance receivables, net of allowance for credit losses of $282 and $255 (Note 10)	32,543	38,720
Trade and other receivables, less allowances of $48 and $105	11,370	15,729
Inventories (Note 11)	12,065	14,080
Assets held for sale (Note 22)	9	97
Other assets	3,416	3,780
Total current assets	108,996	116,476
Ford Credit finance receivables, net of allowance for credit losses of $643 and $590 (Note 10)	51,256	49,903
Net investment in operating leases (Note 12)	26,361	22,772
Net property (Note 13)	37,139	37,265
Equity in net assets of affiliated companies (Note 14)	4,545	2,798
Deferred income taxes (Note 7)	13,796	15,552
Other assets	14,942	11,118
Total assets	$ 257,035	$ 255,884
LIABILITIES		
Payables	$ 22,349	$ 25,605
Other liabilities and deferred revenue (Note 16 and Note 25)	18,686	21,097
Debt payable within one year (Note 19)		
Company excluding Ford Credit	3,175	730
Ford Credit	46,517	49,434
Total current liabilities	90,727	96,866
Other liabilities and deferred revenue (Note 16 and Note 25)	27,705	25,497
Long-term debt (Note 19)		
Company excluding Ford Credit	17,200	19,200
Ford Credit	71,200	69,605
Deferred income taxes (Note 7)	1,581	1,549
Total liabilities	208,413	212,717
EQUITY		
Common Stock, par value $0.01 per share (4,068 million shares issued of 6 billion authorized)	40	41
Class B Stock, par value $0.01 per share (71 million shares issued of 530 million authorized)	1	1
Capital in excess of par value of stock	22,611	22,832
Retained earnings	35,769	31,754
Accumulated other comprehensive income/(loss) (Note 23)	(8,339)	(9,339)
Treasury stock	(1,563)	(2,047)
Total equity attributable to Ford Motor Company	48,519	43,242
Equity attributable to noncontrolling interests	103	(75)
Total equity	48,622	43,167
Total liabilities and equity	$ 257,035	$ 255,884

The following table includes assets to be used to settle liabilities of the consolidated variable interest entities ("VIEs"). These assets and liabilities are included in the consolidated balance sheets above. See Note 24 for additional information on our VIEs.

	December 31, 2021	December 31, 2022
ASSETS		
Cash and cash equivalents	$ 3,407	$ 2,274
Ford Credit finance receivables, net	43,001	49,142
Net investment in operating leases	7,540	12,545
Other assets	39	264
LIABILITIES		
Other liabilities and deferred revenue	$ 6	$ 2
Debt	38,274	45,451

FORD MOTOR COMPANY AND SUBSIDIARIES
CONSOLIDATED INCOME STATEMENTS
(in millions, except per share amounts)

	For the years ended December 31,		
	2020	2021	2022
Revenues			
Automotive	$ 115,894	$ 126,150	$ 148,980
Ford Credit	11,203	10,073	8,978
Mobility	47	118	99
Total revenues (Note 4)	127,144	136,341	158,057
Costs and expenses			
Cost of sales	112,752	114,651	134,397
Selling, administrative, and other expenses	10,193	11,915	10,888
Ford Credit interest, operating, and other expenses	8,607	5,252	6,496
Total costs and expenses	131,552	131,818	151,781
Operating income/(loss)	(4,408)	4,523	6,276
Interest expense on Company debt excluding Ford Credit	1,649	1,803	1,259
Other income/(loss), net (Note 5)	4,899	14,733	(5,150)
Equity in net income/(loss) of affiliated companies (Note 14)	42	327	(2,883)
Income/(Loss) before income taxes	(1,116)	17,780	(3,016)
Provision for/(Benefit from) income taxes (Note 7)	160	(130)	(864)
Net income/(loss)	(1,276)	17,910	(2,152)
Less: Income/(Loss) attributable to noncontrolling interests	3	(27)	(171)
Net income/(loss) attributable to Ford Motor Company	$ (1,279)	$ 17,937	$ (1,981)
EARNINGS/(LOSS) PER SHARE ATTRIBUTABLE TO FORD MOTOR COMPANY COMMON AND CLASS B STOCK (Note 8)			
Basic income/(loss)	$ (0.32)	$ 4.49	$ (0.49)
Diluted income/(loss)	(0.32)	4.45	(0.49)
Weighted-average shares used in computation of earnings/(loss) per share			
Basic shares	3,973	3,991	4,014
Diluted shares	3,973	4,034	4,014

CONSOLIDATED STATEMENTS OF COMPREHENSIVE INCOME
(in millions)

	For the years ended December 31,		
	2020	2021	2022
Net income/(loss)	$ (1,276)	$ 17,910	$ (2,152)
Other comprehensive income/(loss), net of tax (Note 23)			
Foreign currency translation	(901)	43	(933)
Marketable securities	85	(175)	(423)
Derivative instruments	222	73	322
Pension and other postretirement benefits	27	18	30
Total other comprehensive income/(loss), net of tax	(567)	(41)	(1,004)
Comprehensive income/(loss)	(1,843)	17,869	(3,156)
Less: Comprehensive income/(loss) attributable to noncontrolling interests	2	(23)	(175)
Comprehensive income/(loss) attributable to Ford Motor Company	$ (1,845)	$ 17,892	$ (2,981)

FORD MOTOR COMPANY AND SUBSIDIARIES
CONSOLIDATED STATEMENTS OF EQUITY
(in millions)

	Capital Stock	Cap. in Excess of Par Value of Stock	Retained Earnings/ (Accumulated Deficit)	Accumulated Other Comprehensive Income/(Loss) (Note 23)	Treasury Stock	Total	Equity Attributable to Non-controlling Interests	Total Equity
			Equity Attributable to Ford Motor Company					
Balance at December 31, 2019	$ 41	$ 22,165	$ 20,320	$ (7,728)	$ (1,613)	$ 33,185	$ 45	$ 33,230
Adoption of accounting standards	—	—	(202)	—	—	(202)	—	(202)
Net income/(loss)	—	—	(1,279)	—	—	(1,279)	3	(1,276)
Other comprehensive income/(loss), net of tax	—	—	—	(566)	—	(566)	(1)	(567)
Common stock issued (a)	—	125	—	—	—	125	—	125
Treasury stock/other	—	—	—	—	23	23	86	109
Dividend and dividend equivalents declared (b)	—	—	(596)	—	—	(596)	(12)	(608)
Balance at December 31, 2020	$ 41	$ 22,290	$ 18,243	$ (8,294)	$ (1,590)	$ 30,690	$ 121	$ 30,811
Balance at December 31, 2020	$ 41	$ 22,290	$ 18,243	$ (8,294)	$ (1,590)	$ 30,690	$ 121	$ 30,811
Net income/(loss)	—	—	17,937	—	—	17,937	(27)	17,910
Other comprehensive income/(loss), net of tax	—	—	—	(45)	—	(45)	4	(41)
Common stock issued (a)	—	321	—	—	—	321	—	321
Treasury stock/other	—	—	—	—	27	27	5	32
Dividend and dividend equivalents declared (b)	—	—	(411)	—	—	(411)	—	(411)
Balance at December 31, 2021	$ 41	$ 22,611	$ 35,769	$ (8,339)	$ (1,563)	$ 48,519	$ 103	$ 48,622
Balance at December 31, 2021	$ 41	$ 22,611	$ 35,769	$ (8,339)	$ (1,563)	$ 48,519	$ 103	$ 48,622
Net income/(loss)	—	—	(1,981)	—	—	(1,981)	(171)	(2,152)
Other comprehensive income/(loss), net of tax	—	—	—	(1,000)	—	(1,000)	(4)	(1,004)
Common stock issued (a)	1	221	—	—	—	222	—	222
Treasury stock/other	—	—	—	—	(484)	(484)	7	(477)
Dividend and dividend equivalents declared (b)	—	—	(2,034)	—	—	(2,034)	(10)	(2,044)
Balance at December 31, 2022	$ 42	$ 22,832	$ 31,754	$ (9,339)	$ (2,047)	$ 43,242	$ (75)	$ 43,167

(a) Includes impacts of share-based compensation.
(b) We declared dividends per share of Common and Class B Stock of $0.15 and $0.10 in 2020 and 2021, respectively, and in 2022, $0.10 per share in the first and second quarter and $0.15 per share in the third and fourth quarter. On February 2, 2023, we declared a regular dividend of $0.15 per share and a supplemental dividend of $0.65 per share.

FORD MOTOR COMPANY AND SUBSIDIARIES
CONSOLIDATED STATEMENTS OF CASH FLOWS
(in millions)

	For the years ended December 31,		
	2020	2021	2022
Cash flows from operating activities			
Net income/(loss)	$ (1,276)	$ 17,910	$ (2,152)
Depreciation and tooling amortization (Note 12 and Note 13)	8,751	7,318	7,642
Other amortization	(1,294)	(1,358)	(1,149)
Held-for-sale impairment charges (Note 22)	23	—	32
Brazil manufacturing exit non-cash charges (excluding accelerated depreciation of $145, $322, and $17) (Note 21)	1,159	48	(82)
(Gains)/Losses on extinguishment of debt (Note 5 and Note 19)	1	1,702	121
Provision for/(Benefit from) credit and insurance losses	929	(298)	46
Pension and other postretirement employee benefits ("OPEB") expense/(income) (Note 17)	1,027	(4,865)	(378)
Equity method investment dividends received in excess of (earnings)/losses and impairments	130	116	3,324
Foreign currency adjustments	(420)	532	(27)
Net realized and unrealized (gains)/losses on cash equivalents, marketable securities, and other investments (Note 5)	(315)	(9,159)	7,518
Net (gain)/loss on changes in investments in affiliates (Note 5)	(3,446)	(368)	147
Stock compensation (Note 6)	199	305	336
Provision for deferred income taxes	(269)	(563)	(1,910)
Decrease/(Increase) in finance receivables (wholesale and other)	12,104	7,656	(10,560)
Decrease/(Increase) in accounts receivable and other assets	(63)	(1,141)	(1,183)
Decrease/(Increase) in inventory	148	(1,778)	(2,576)
Increase/(Decrease) in accounts payable and accrued and other liabilities	6,809	(36)	7,268
Other	72	(234)	436
Net cash provided by/(used in) operating activities	24,269	15,787	6,853
Cash flows from investing activities			
Capital spending	(5,742)	(6,227)	(6,866)
Acquisitions of finance receivables and operating leases	(55,901)	(48,379)	(45,533)
Collections of finance receivables and operating leases	48,746	52,094	46,276
Proceeds from sale of business (Note 22)	1,340	145	449
Purchases of marketable securities and other investments	(39,624)	(27,491)	(17,458)
Sales and maturities of marketable securities and other investments	32,395	33,229	19,117
Settlements of derivatives	(323)	(272)	94
Capital contributions to equity method investments (Note 24)	(4)	(57)	(738)
Other	498	(297)	312
Net cash provided by/(used in) investing activities	(18,615)	2,745	(4,347)
Cash flows from financing activities			
Cash payments for dividends and dividend equivalents	(596)	(403)	(2,009)
Purchases of common stock	—	—	(484)
Net changes in short-term debt	(2,291)	3,273	5,460
Proceeds from issuance of long-term debt	65,900	27,901	45,470
Payments of long-term debt	(60,514)	(54,164)	(45,655)
Other	(184)	(105)	(271)
Net cash provided by/(used in) financing activities	2,315	(23,498)	2,511
Effect of exchange rate changes on cash, cash equivalents, and restricted cash	225	(232)	(414)
Net increase/(decrease) in cash, cash equivalents, and restricted cash	$ 8,194	$ (5,198)	$ 4,603
Cash, cash equivalents, and restricted cash at beginning of period (Note 9)	$ 17,741	$ 25,935	$ 20,737
Net increase/(decrease) in cash, cash equivalents, and restricted cash	8,194	(5,198)	4,603
Cash, cash equivalents, and restricted cash at end of period (Note 9)	$ 25,935	$ 20,737	$ 25,340

For the US CPA

UNITED STATES
SECURITIES AND EXCHANGE COMMISSION
Washington, DC 20549

FORM 10-Q

☑ Quarterly report pursuant to Section 13 or 15(d) of the Securities Exchange Act of 1934
For the quarterly period ended June 30, 2023

or

☐ Transition report pursuant to Section 13 or 15(d) of the Securities Exchange Act of 1934
For the transition period from _____ to _____
Commission file number 1-3950

Ford Motor Company
(Exact name of Registrant as specified in its charter)

Delaware	**38-0549190**
(State of incorporation)	*(I.R.S. Employer Identification No.)*

One American Road	
Dearborn, Michigan	**48126**
(Address of principal executive offices)	*(Zip code)*

313-322-3000
(Registrant's telephone number, including area code)

Securities registered pursuant to Section 12(b) of the Act:

Title of each class	Trading symbols	Name of each exchange on which registered
Common Stock, par value $.01 per share	F	New York Stock Exchange
6.200% Notes due June 1, 2059	FPRB	New York Stock Exchange
6.000% Notes due December 1, 2059	FPRC	New York Stock Exchange
6.500% Notes due August 15, 2062	FPRD	New York Stock Exchange

Indicate by check mark if the registrant (1) has filed all reports required to be filed by Section 13 or 15(d) of the Securities Exchange Act of 1934 during the preceding 12 months (or for such shorter period that the registrant was required to file such reports), and (2) has been subject to such filing requirements for the past 90 days. Yes ☑ No ☐

Indicate by check mark whether the registrant has submitted electronically every Interactive Data File required to be submitted pursuant to Rule 405 of Regulation S-T (§232.405 of this chapter) during the preceding 12 months (or for such shorter period that the registrant was required to submit such files). Yes ☑ No ☐

Indicate by check mark whether the registrant is a large accelerated filer, an accelerated filer, a non-accelerated filer, a smaller reporting company, or an emerging growth company. See definitions of "large accelerated filer," "accelerated filer," "smaller reporting company," and "emerging growth company" in Rule 12b-2 of the Exchange Act.

Large Accelerated Filer ☑   Accelerated filer ☐   Non-accelerated filer ☐   Smaller reporting company ☐
Emerging growth company ☐

If an emerging growth company, indicate by check mark if the registrant has elected not to use the extended transition period for complying with any new or revised financial accounting standards provided pursuant to Section 13(a) of the Exchange Act. ☐

Indicate by check mark whether the registrant is a shell company (as defined in Rule 12b-2 of the Exchange Act). Yes ☐ No ☑

As of July 24, 2023, Ford had outstanding 3,931,373,526 shares of Common Stock and 70,852,076 shares of Class B Stock.

부록-59

FORD MOTOR COMPANY AND SUBSIDIARIES
CONSOLIDATED BALANCE SHEETS
(in millions)

	December 31, 2022	June 30, 2023
		(unaudited)
ASSETS		
Cash and cash equivalents (Note 7)	$ 25,134	$ 26,406
Marketable securities (Note 7)	18,936	16,415
Ford Credit finance receivables, net of allowance for credit losses of $255 and $260 (Note 8)	38,720	42,557
Trade and other receivables, less allowances of $105 and $101	15,729	14,482
Inventories (Note 9)	14,080	17,703
Other assets	3,877	4,149
Total current assets	116,476	121,712
Ford Credit finance receivables, net of allowance for credit losses of $590 and $613 (Note 8)	49,903	52,567
Net investment in operating leases	22,772	21,662
Net property	37,265	38,503
Equity in net assets of affiliated companies	2,798	3,578
Deferred income taxes	15,552	15,860
Other assets	11,118	12,109
Total assets	$ 255,884	$ 265,991
LIABILITIES		
Payables	$ 25,605	$ 27,749
Other liabilities and deferred revenue (Note 12 and Note 20)	21,097	23,925
Debt payable within one year (Note 14)		
Company excluding Ford Credit	730	410
Ford Credit	49,434	48,931
Total current liabilities	96,866	101,015
Other liabilities and deferred revenue (Note 12 and Note 20)	25,497	25,754
Long-term debt (Note 14)		
Company excluding Ford Credit	19,200	19,169
Ford Credit	69,605	74,726
Deferred income taxes	1,549	1,721
Total liabilities	212,717	222,385
EQUITY		
Common Stock, par value $0.01 per share (4,084 million shares issued of 6 billion authorized)	41	41
Class B Stock, par value $0.01 per share (71 million shares issued of 530 million authorized)	1	1
Capital in excess of par value of stock	22,832	23,029
Retained earnings	31,754	31,577
Accumulated other comprehensive income/(loss) (Note 18)	(9,339)	(8,924)
Treasury stock	(2,047)	(2,047)
Total equity attributable to Ford Motor Company	43,242	43,677
Equity attributable to noncontrolling interests	(75)	(71)
Total equity	43,167	43,606
Total liabilities and equity	$ 255,884	$ 265,991

The following table includes assets to be used to settle liabilities of the consolidated variable interest entities ("VIEs"). These assets and liabilities are included in the consolidated balance sheets above.

	December 31, 2022	June 30, 2023
		(unaudited)
ASSETS		
Cash and cash equivalents	$ 2,274	$ 2,421
Ford Credit finance receivables, net	49,142	52,504
Net investment in operating leases	12,545	8,929
Other assets	264	279
LIABILITIES		
Other liabilities and deferred revenue	$ 2	$ —
Debt	45,451	47,891

FORD MOTOR COMPANY AND SUBSIDIARIES
CONSOLIDATED INCOME STATEMENTS
(in millions, except per share amounts)

	For the periods ended June 30,			
	2022	2023	2022	2023
	Second Quarter		First Half	
	(unaudited)			
Revenues				
Company excluding Ford Credit	$ 37,934	$ 42,427	$ 70,129	$ 81,512
Ford Credit	2,256	2,527	4,537	4,916
Total revenues (Note 3)	40,190	44,954	74,666	86,428
Costs and expenses				
Cost of sales	33,191	37,471	62,227	72,140
Selling, administrative, and other expenses	2,759	2,750	5,499	5,256
Ford Credit interest, operating, and other expenses	1,372	2,272	2,729	4,458
Total costs and expenses	37,322	42,493	70,455	81,854
Operating income/(loss)	2,868	2,461	4,211	4,574
Interest expense on Company debt excluding Ford Credit	312	304	620	612
Other income/(loss), net (Note 4)	(1,823)	255	(6,673)	479
Equity in net income/(loss) of affiliated companies	58	(124)	25	6
Income/(Loss) before income taxes	791	2,288	(3,057)	4,447
Provision for/(Benefit from) income taxes	153	272	(576)	768
Net income/(loss)	638	2,016	(2,481)	3,679
Less: Income/(Loss) attributable to noncontrolling interests	(29)	99	(38)	5
Net income/(loss) attributable to Ford Motor Company	$ 667	$ 1,917	$ (2,443)	$ 3,674
EARNINGS/(LOSS) PER SHARE ATTRIBUTABLE TO FORD MOTOR COMPANY COMMON AND CLASS B STOCK (Note 6)				
Basic income/(loss)	$ 0.17	$ 0.48	$ (0.61)	$ 0.92
Diluted income/(loss)	0.16	0.47	(0.61)	0.91
Weighted-average shares used in computation of earnings/(loss) per share				
Basic shares	4,021	4,003	4,014	3,996
Diluted shares	4,052	4,041	4,014	4,035

CONSOLIDATED STATEMENTS OF COMPREHENSIVE INCOME
(in millions)

	For the periods ended June 30,			
	2022	2023	2022	2023
	Second Quarter		First Half	
	(unaudited)			
Net income/(loss)	$ 638	$ 2,016	$ (2,481)	$ 3,679
Other comprehensive income/(loss), net of tax (Note 18)				
Foreign currency translation	(1,018)	278	(872)	771
Marketable securities	(83)	(44)	(336)	66
Derivative instruments	(94)	(369)	50	(424)
Pension and other postretirement benefits	12	3	20	6
Total other comprehensive income/(loss), net of tax	(1,183)	(132)	(1,138)	419
Comprehensive income/(loss)	(545)	1,884	(3,619)	4,098
Less: Comprehensive income/(loss) attributable to noncontrolling interests	(33)	103	(42)	9
Comprehensive income/(loss) attributable to Ford Motor Company	$ (512)	$ 1,781	$ (3,577)	$ 4,089

FORD MOTOR COMPANY AND SUBSIDIARIES
CONSOLIDATED STATEMENTS OF EQUITY
(in millions, unaudited)

	Capital Stock	Cap. in Excess of Par Value of Stock	Retained Earnings	Accumulated Other Comprehensive Income/(Loss) (Note 18)	Treasury Stock	Total	Equity Attributable to Non-controlling Interests	Total Equity
				Equity Attributable to Ford Motor Company				
Balance at December 31, 2021	$ 41	$ 22,611	$ 35,769	$ (8,339)	$ (1,563)	$ 48,519	$ 103	$ 48,622
Net income/(loss)	—	—	(3,110)	—	—	(3,110)	(9)	(3,119)
Other comprehensive income/(loss), net	—	—	—	45	—	45	—	45
Common Stock issued (a)	1	(61)	—	—	—	(60)	—	(60)
Treasury stock/other	—	—	—	—	(1)	(1)	5	4
Dividends and dividend equivalents declared ($0.10 per share) (b)	—	—	(408)	—	—	(408)	—	(408)
Balance at March 31, 2022	$ 42	$ 22,550	$ 32,251	$ (8,294)	$ (1,564)	$ 44,985	$ 99	$ 45,084
Net income/(loss)	—	—	667	—	—	667	(29)	638
Other comprehensive income/(loss), net	—	—	—	(1,179)	—	(1,179)	(4)	(1,183)
Common Stock issued (a)	—	103	—	—	—	103	—	103
Treasury stock/other	—	—	—	—	—	—	2	2
Dividends and dividend equivalents declared ($0.10 per share) (b)	—	—	(407)	—	—	(407)	—	(407)
Balance at June 30, 2022	$ 42	$ 22,653	$ 32,511	$ (9,473)	$ (1,564)	$ 44,169	$ 68	$ 44,237
Balance at December 31, 2022	$ 42	$ 22,832	$ 31,754	$ (9,339)	$ (2,047)	$ 43,242	$ (75)	$ 43,167
Net income/(loss)	—	—	1,757	—	—	1,757	(94)	1,663
Other comprehensive income/(loss), net	—	—	—	551	—	551	—	551
Common Stock issued (a)	—	57	—	—	—	57	—	57
Treasury stock/other	—	—	—	—	—	—	—	—
Dividends and dividend equivalents declared ($0.80 per share) (b)	—	—	(3,241)	—	—	(3,241)	—	(3,241)
Balance at March 31, 2023	$ 42	$ 22,889	$ 30,270	$ (8,788)	$ (2,047)	$ 42,366	$ (169)	$ 42,197
Net income/(loss)	—	—	1,917	—	—	1,917	99	2,016
Other comprehensive income/(loss), net	—	—	—	(136)	—	(136)	4	(132)
Common Stock issued (a)	—	140	—	—	—	140	—	140
Treasury stock/other	—	—	—	—	—	—	(5)	(5)
Dividends and dividend equivalents declared ($0.15 per share) (b)	—	—	(610)	—	—	(610)	—	(610)
Balance at June 30, 2023	$ 42	$ 23,029	$ 31,577	$ (8,924)	$ (2,047)	$ 43,677	$ (71)	$ 43,606

(a) Includes impact of share-based compensation.
(b) Dividends and dividend equivalents declared for Common and Class B Stock. In the first quarter of 2023, in addition to a regular dividend of $0.15 per share, we declared a supplemental dividend of $0.65 per share.

FORD MOTOR COMPANY AND SUBSIDIARIES
CONSOLIDATED STATEMENTS OF CASH FLOWS
(in millions)

	For the periods ended June 30,	
	2022	2023
	First Half	
	(unaudited)	
Cash flows from operating activities		
Net income/(loss)	$ (2,481)	$ 3,679
Depreciation and tooling amortization	3,774	3,775
Other amortization	(608)	(554)
Provision for/(Benefit from) credit and insurance losses	(107)	212
Pension and other postretirement employee benefits ("OPEB") expense/(income) (Note 13)	(400)	612
Equity method investment dividends received in excess of (earnings)/losses and impairments	171	142
Foreign currency adjustments	60	(97)
Net realized and unrealized (gains)/losses on cash equivalents, marketable securities, and other investments (Note 4)	7,974	163
Net (gain)/loss on changes in investments in affiliates (Note 4)	146	(17)
Stock compensation	170	238
Provision for/(Benefit from) deferred income taxes	(1,160)	3
Decrease/(Increase) in finance receivables (wholesale and other)	(4,611)	(1,473)
Decrease/(Increase) in accounts receivable and other assets	(1,856)	(1,793)
Decrease/(Increase) in inventory	(2,507)	(3,354)
Increase/(Decrease) in accounts payable and accrued and other liabilities	3,180	6,134
Other	118	165
Net cash provided by/(used in) operating activities	1,863	7,835
Cash flows from investing activities		
Capital spending	(3,069)	(3,729)
Acquisitions of finance receivables and operating leases	(20,749)	(26,231)
Collections of finance receivables and operating leases	24,139	22,517
Purchases of marketable securities and other investments	(8,065)	(4,860)
Sales and maturities of marketable securities and other investments	11,257	7,584
Settlements of derivatives	156	(32)
Capital contributions to equity method investments	(36)	(1,047)
Other	509	(359)
Net cash provided by/(used in) investing activities	4,142	(6,157)
Cash flows from financing activities		
Cash payments for dividends and dividend equivalents	(807)	(3,794)
Purchases of common stock	—	—
Net changes in short-term debt	595	(658)
Proceeds from issuance of long-term debt	18,868	26,401
Payments of long-term debt	(24,697)	(22,213)
Other	(199)	(197)
Net cash provided by/(used in) financing activities	(6,240)	(461)
Effect of exchange rate changes on cash, cash equivalents, and restricted cash	(368)	66
Net increase/(decrease) in cash, cash equivalents, and restricted cash	$ (603)	$ 1,283
Cash, cash equivalents, and restricted cash at beginning of period (Note 7)	$ 20,737	$ 25,340
Net increase/(decrease) in cash, cash equivalents, and restricted cash	(603)	1,283
Cash, cash equivalents, and restricted cash at end of period (Note 7)	$ 20,134	$ 26,623

Goodwill was assigned to our More Personal Computing segment. The goodwill was primarily attributed to increased synergies that are expected to be achieved from the integration of ZeniMax. None of the goodwill is expected to be deductible for income tax purposes.

Following are details of the purchase price allocated to the intangible assets acquired:

(In millions, except average life)		Amount	Weighted Average Life
Technology-based	$	1,341	4 years
Marketing-related		627	11 years
Total	$	1,968	6 years

Activision Blizzard, Inc.

On January 18, 2022, we entered into a definitive agreement to acquire Activision Blizzard, Inc. ("Activision Blizzard") for $95.00 per share in an all-cash transaction valued at $68.7 billion, inclusive of Activision Blizzard's net cash. Activision Blizzard is a leader in game development and an interactive entertainment content publisher. The acquisition will accelerate the growth in our gaming business across mobile, PC, console, and cloud gaming. The acquisition has been approved by Activision Blizzard's shareholders. We continue to work toward closing the transaction subject to obtaining required regulatory approvals and satisfaction of other customary closing conditions. Microsoft and Activision Blizzard have jointly agreed to extend the merger agreement through October 18, 2023 to allow for additional time to resolve remaining regulatory concerns.

NOTE 9 — GOODWILL

Changes in the carrying amount of goodwill were as follows:

(In millions)	June 30, 2021	Acquisitions	Other	June 30, 2022	Acquisitions	Other	June 30, 2023
Productivity and Business Processes	$ 24,317	$ 599	$ (105)	$ 24,811	$ 11	$ (47)	$ 24,775
Intelligent Cloud	13,256	16,879	47	30,182	223	64	30,469
More Personal Computing	12,138	648	(255)	12,531	0	111	12,642
Total	$ 49,711	$ 18,126	$ (313)	$ 67,524	$ 234	$ 128	$ 67,886

The measurement periods for the valuation of assets acquired and liabilities assumed end as soon as information on the facts and circumstances that existed as of the acquisition dates becomes available, but do not exceed 12 months. Adjustments in purchase price allocations may require a change in the amounts allocated to goodwill during the periods in which the adjustments are determined.

Any change in the goodwill amounts resulting from foreign currency translations and purchase accounting adjustments are presented as "Other" in the table above. Also included in "Other" are business dispositions and transfers between segments due to reorganizations, as applicable.

Goodwill Impairment

We test goodwill for impairment annually on May 1 at the reporting unit level, primarily using a discounted cash flow methodology with a peer-based, risk-adjusted weighted average cost of capital. We believe use of a discounted cash flow approach is the most reliable indicator of the fair values of the businesses.

No instances of impairment were identified in our May 1, 2023, May 1, 2022, or May 1, 2021 tests. As of June 30, 2023 and 2022, accumulated goodwill impairment was $11.3 billion.

Supplemental balance sheet information related to leases was as follows:

(In millions, except lease term and discount rate)

June 30,	2023	2022
Operating Leases		
Operating lease right-of-use assets	$ 14,346	$ 13,148
Other current liabilities	$ 2,409	$ 2,228
Operating lease liabilities	12,728	11,489
Total operating lease liabilities	$ 15,137	$ 13,717
Finance Leases		
Property and equipment, at cost	$ 20,538	$ 17,388
Accumulated depreciation	(4,647)	(3,285)
Property and equipment, net	$ 15,891	$ 14,103
Other current liabilities	$ 1,197	$ 1,060
Other long-term liabilities	15,870	13,842
Total finance lease liabilities	$ 17,067	$ 14,902
Weighted Average Remaining Lease Term		
Operating leases	**8 years**	8 years
Finance leases	**11 years**	12 years
Weighted Average Discount Rate		
Operating leases	**2.9%**	2.1%
Finance leases	**3.4%**	3.1%

The following table outlines maturities of our lease liabilities as of June 30, 2023:

(In millions)

Year Ending June 30,	Operating Leases	Finance Leases
2024	$ 2,784	$ 1,747
2025	2,508	2,087
2026	2,142	1,771
2027	1,757	1,780
2028	1,582	1,787
Thereafter	6,327	11,462
Total lease payments	17,100	20,634
Less imputed interest	(1,963)	(3,567)
Total	$ 15,137	$ 17,067

As of June 30, 2023, we have additional operating and finance leases, primarily for datacenters, that have not yet commenced of $7.7 billion and $34.4 billion, respectively. These operating and finance leases will commence between fiscal year 2024 and fiscal year 2030 with lease terms of 1 year to 18 years.

NOTE 15 — CONTINGENCIES

U.S. Cell Phone Litigation

Microsoft Mobile Oy, a subsidiary of Microsoft, along with other handset manufacturers and network operators, is a defendant in 46 lawsuits, including 45 lawsuits filed in the Superior Court for the District of Columbia by individual plaintiffs who allege that radio emissions from cellular handsets caused their brain tumors and other adverse health effects. We assumed responsibility for these claims in our agreement to acquire Nokia's Devices and Services business and have been substituted for the Nokia defendants. Nine of these cases were filed in 2002 and are consolidated for certain pre-trial proceedings; the remaining cases are stayed. In a separate 2009 decision, the Court of Appeals for the District of Columbia

subject to certain limitations. We match a portion of each dollar a participant contributes into the plans. Employer-funded retirement benefits for all plans were $1.6 billion, $1.4 billion, and $1.2 billion in fiscal years 2023, 2022, and 2021, respectively, and were expensed as contributed.

<u>NOTE 19 — SEGMENT INFORMATION AND GEOGRAPHIC DATA</u>

In its operation of the business, management, including our chief operating decision maker, who is also our Chief Executive Officer, reviews certain financial information, including segmented internal profit and loss statements prepared on a basis not consistent with GAAP. During the periods presented, we reported our financial performance based on the following segments: Productivity and Business Processes, Intelligent Cloud, and More Personal Computing.

We have recast certain prior period amounts to conform to the way we internally manage and monitor our business.

Our reportable segments are described below.

Productivity and Business Processes

Our Productivity and Business Processes segment consists of products and services in our portfolio of productivity, communication, and information services, spanning a variety of devices and platforms. This segment primarily comprises:

- Office Commercial (Office 365 subscriptions, the Office 365 portion of Microsoft 365 Commercial subscriptions, and Office licensed on-premises), comprising Office, Exchange, SharePoint, Microsoft Teams, Office 365 Security and Compliance, Microsoft Viva, and Microsoft 365 Copilot.

- Office Consumer, including Microsoft 365 Consumer subscriptions, Office licensed on-premises, and other Office services.

- LinkedIn, including Talent Solutions, Marketing Solutions, Premium Subscriptions, and Sales Solutions.

- Dynamics business solutions, including Dynamics 365, comprising a set of intelligent, cloud-based applications across ERP, CRM (including Customer Insights), Power Apps, and Power Automate; and on-premises ERP and CRM applications.

Intelligent Cloud

Our Intelligent Cloud segment consists of our public, private, and hybrid server products and cloud services that can power modern business and developers. This segment primarily comprises:

- Server products and cloud services, including Azure and other cloud services; SQL Server, Windows Server, Visual Studio, System Center, and related Client Access Licenses ("CALs"); and Nuance and GitHub.

- Enterprise Services, including Enterprise Support Services, Industry Solutions (formerly Microsoft Consulting Services), and Nuance professional services.

More Personal Computing

Our More Personal Computing segment consists of products and services that put customers at the center of the experience with our technology. This segment primarily comprises:

- Windows, including Windows OEM licensing and other non-volume licensing of the Windows operating system; Windows Commercial, comprising volume licensing of the Windows operating system, Windows cloud services, and other Windows commercial offerings; patent licensing; and Windows Internet of Things.

- Devices, including Surface, HoloLens, and PC accessories.

- Gaming, including Xbox hardware and Xbox content and services, comprising first- and third-party content (including games and in-game content), Xbox Game Pass and other subscriptions, Xbox Cloud Gaming, advertising, third-party disc royalties, and other cloud services.

- Search and news advertising, comprising Bing (including Bing Chat), Microsoft News, Microsoft Edge, and third-party affiliates.

which can include allocation based on actual prices charged, prices when sold separately, or estimated costs plus a profit margin. Cost of revenue is allocated in certain cases based on a relative revenue methodology. Operating expenses that are allocated primarily include those relating to marketing of products and services from which multiple segments benefit and are generally allocated based on relative gross margin.

In addition, certain costs are incurred at a corporate level and allocated to our segments. These allocated costs generally include legal, including settlements and fines, information technology, human resources, finance, excise taxes, field selling, shared facilities services, customer service and support, and severance incurred as part of a corporate program. Each allocation is measured differently based on the specific facts and circumstances of the costs being allocated and is generally based on relative gross margin or relative headcount.

Segment revenue and operating income were as follows during the periods presented:

(In millions)

Year Ended June 30,		2023		2022		2021
Revenue						
Productivity and Business Processes	$	69,274	$	63,364	$	53,915
Intelligent Cloud		87,907		74,965		59,728
More Personal Computing		54,734		59,941		54,445
Total	$	211,915	$	198,270	$	168,088
Operating Income						
Productivity and Business Processes	$	34,189	$	29,690	$	24,351
Intelligent Cloud		37,884		33,203		26,471
More Personal Computing		16,450		20,490		19,094
Total	$	88,523	$	83,383	$	69,916

No sales to an individual customer or country other than the United States accounted for more than 10% of revenue for fiscal years 2023, 2022, or 2021. Revenue, classified by the major geographic areas in which our customers were located, was as follows:

(In millions)

Year Ended June 30,		2023		2022		2021
United States [a]	$	106,744	$	100,218	$	83,953
Other countries		105,171		98,052		84,135
Total	$	211,915	$	198,270	$	168,088

(a) *Includes billings to OEMs and certain multinational organizations because of the nature of these businesses and the impracticability of determining the geographic source of the revenue.*

Revenue, classified by significant product and service offerings, was as follows:

(In millions)

Year Ended June 30,		2023		2022		2021
Server products and cloud services	$	79,970	$	67,350	$	52,589
Office products and cloud services		48,728		44,862		39,872
Windows		21,507		24,732		22,488
Gaming		15,466		16,230		15,370
LinkedIn		15,145		13,816		10,289
Search and news advertising		12,208		11,591		9,267
Enterprise Services		7,722		7,407		6,943
Devices		5,521		7,306		7,143

(In millions)			
Dynamics	**5,437**	4,687	3,754
Other	**211**	289	373
Total	**$ 211,915**	$ 198,270	$ 168,088

Our Microsoft Cloud revenue, which includes Azure and other cloud services, Office 365 Commercial, the commercial portion of LinkedIn, Dynamics 365, and other commercial cloud properties, was $111.6 billion, $91.4 billion, and $69.1 billion in fiscal years 2023, 2022, and 2021, respectively. These amounts are primarily included in Server products and cloud services, Office products and cloud services, LinkedIn, and Dynamics in the table above.

Assets are not allocated to segments for internal reporting presentations. A portion of amortization and depreciation is included with various other costs in an overhead allocation to each segment. It is impracticable for us to separately identify the amount of amortization and depreciation by segment that is included in the measure of segment profit or loss.

Long-lived assets, excluding financial instruments and tax assets, classified by the location of the controlling statutory company and with countries over 10% of the total shown separately, were as follows:

(In millions)			
June 30,	2023	2022	2021
United States	$ **114,380**	$ 106,430	$ 76,153
Ireland	**16,359**	15,505	13,303
Other countries	**56,500**	44,433	38,858
Total	$ **187,239**	$ 166,368	$ 128,314

1st
Accounting
and
Reporting

2024년 9월 13일 초판 2쇄 발행

저 자　　 | 김용석
편집·디자인 | 유진강(아르케 디자인)
인쇄·제본 | 천광인쇄

펴낸이　 | 김용석
펴낸곳　 | (주) 이러닝코리아
출판등록| 제 2016-000021
주 소　　 | 서울시 금천구 가산동 60-5번지 갑을그레이트벨리 A동 503호
전 화　　 | 02)2106-8992
팩 스　　 | 02)2106-8990

ISBN 979-11-89168-33-9　　93320

* 잘못된 책은 바꿔 드립니다.
* 책값은 뒤표지에 있습니다.